SUFI LIGHT

THE SECRET OF MEDITATION

Ahmad Javid (Sarwari Qaderi) MD, FAAP

BALBOA.
PRESS
A DIVISION OF HAY HOUSE

ISBN: 978-1-4525-3941-6 (sc)
ISBN: 978-1-4525-3940-9 (e)
ISBN: 978-1-4525-3942-3 (hc)
Library of Congress Control Number: 2011916500

Balboa Press books may be ordered through booksellers or by contacting:

Balboa Press
A Division of Hay House
1663 Liberty Drive
Bloomington, IN 47403
www.balboapress.com
1-(877) 407-4847

Printed in the United States of America

Balboa Press rev. date: 12/07/2011

DEDICATION

This book is dedicated to my grandfather, my parents, and my wife, Sara, who has always been there for me and has made my life more meaningful in many ways.

CONTENTS

IN THE NAME OF ALLAH THE INFINITELY GOOD, THE BOUNDLESSLY MERCIFUL

INTRODUCTION

When my servants inquire from thee concerning Me,
O Prophet tell them that I am near.
I respond to the call of the caller when he calls
Me.
So should they respond to Me, and have firm faith
in Me,
That they may be rightly guided.
(Quran 2:187)

In this book I will present Sufi teachings on meditation. Before I begin, however, I would like to tell you something of myself and of the circumstances into which I was brought into this world.

I was born into a somewhat illustrious Sufi family in Bannu, a small district in the Khyber–Pukhtunkhwa province of Pakistan. Bannu is one hundred and twenty miles from Peshawar, the provincial capital, and is inhabited by Bannuchi Pashtuns, who, according to a legend, trace their ancestry to Bani-Israel (Jews). Bannuchis are Sunni Muslims; however, the area has become a breeding ground for orthodox militancy and Taliban insurgency.

Bannu strategically borders South Waziristan and Afghanistan. The whole territory is rugged terrain. Bannuchis are a proud and brave people, and fighting has been an integral part of their culture and way of life for centuries. This is why they are famous as undefeatable warriors.

When I was six years old, we went to our native village, Kulachi, with my mother and other siblings during our summer vacation. One day, I was playing outside with the other children and wandered off to the nearest well. As Kulachi is a dry, hot place with no running water, deep wells are dug to get to the underground water, which is still not drinkable due to its high mineral content and hardness. We used this water mostly for cleaning purposes, such as washing cloths and dishes. There was no electricity in our village at that time, so the well was operated by the circular motion of an ox journeying eternally to nowhere, trudging around and around to rotate the large wooden wheel over the well. The wheel was fastened to a belt made of ropes descending to the very bottom of the chasm, to which large earthen buckets were attached. As the wheel rotated, it sent down the belt, along with the buckets, into the well water, filling the containers to their brims. The water then poured into a wooden gutter leading to a large tank.

I was following the ox—which, like a bovine moon orbiting a black hole—was circling along on its journey, and just for fun was dipping a stick into the buckets. At one point I became lulled into a distracted state, perhaps by the hypnotic repetitiveness of the environment, and was standing by the very edge of the well, not knowing that the ox was coming up right behind me. Because the ox was walking in a confined space, and perhaps more than a little bored, and I was in its way, the animal gently nudged me forward with its horns. I lost my balance and fell headlong into the darkness.

With my head plunging downward and my feet in close pursuit—as if I were diving into a pool from a height—I should have hit the water soon. Miraculously, however, I stopped—with the top of my head barely an inch above the water. Somehow, my left hand had become tangled in the rope belt while my body was still hanging upside down. I could see the surface of the dark water, which was more than twenty feet deep, just below the crown of my head. I knew that if I fell into the water, the chances of my survival would be almost zero. I would have drowned, pulled deeper by the water's undercurrent, and never been found. Yet, there I hung, floating upside down in the air above the water, holding onto the rope with my left hand.

As soon as I disappeared into the well, all the children present became frightened. They began screaming and running away. At that very moment my mother's uncle, Jahangir, was ambling along. One of the children ran up to him and told him of my fate. He rushed to the rim, peered down, and beheld my topsy-turvy dangling. "Hold on," he shouted, "I'm coming down!" He was trying to reassure me so that I did not panic. On the contrary, I was quite calm and was not at all frightened. My mind was absolutely blank and my heart was unruffled and fearless.

Uncle Jahangir cautiously descended by placing one foot on the rope belt and the other on the side wall of the well, which had steps carved on the inside for workers to go down for repairs and emergencies. He slowly loomed into view, seized ahold of my foot with one hand, and hoisted me upwards as he struggled his way back to ground level.

In the meanwhile other passersby arrived to help, and soon I was out—back on terra firma. By that time the news had grapevined to my mother and family members, who were all gathered around, crying and sobbing. My mother prostrated to God and thanked Him for my safety. We all walked home with my Uncle Jahangir, and my rescue was celebrated with love and joy. The news of my fall into the well soon spread like wildfire through the rest of the village. Everybody considered it a miracle for me to be alive after a twenty-five-foot freefall into that dark place. I believe, I was saved by Divine grace. Perhaps, I thought, I was not destined to die in the well water but instead to be drowned, later, in the deep ocean of Divine Oneness.

That early experience serves as a metaphor for everything of any real significance that has happened in my life since that time. It seems that God had asked me in very physical terms, "In this life, Little Boy, are you going to plunge blindly into the dark currents of material existence or somehow float magically above them?"

The following chapters are my answer.

§

What you will find in the following pages is neither an exhaustive and scholarly history of Sufism nor a collection of Sufi thought. Today a vast trove of literature is available on these subjects, both in the East and in the West. World-renowned scholars have penned profound expositions on Sufi metaphysics. Translations of classical Sufi works are now readily available in various languages. Excellent in-depth analyses of Sufi traditions have been written.

Of course, such writings have long been available in the East. During the last few decades in the West, authorities on Islam have written extensively on Sufi teachings. In this regard the names of Annemarie Schimmel, Seyyed Hossain Nasr, William Chittick, Frithjof Schuon, Titus Burkhardt, Martin Lings, Carl Ernst, Kabir Helminski, Robert Frager, and many more stand out. These authors have presented to Western seekers the inner teachings of Sufism and its basic tenets in a contemporary and scholarly manner. However, most of these wonderful works are concerned mainly with theoretical aspects of Sufi doctrine—with metaphysics, with teachings, and with historical accounts. There is no doubt that these scholars have performed a great service to the cause and popularity of Sufism and have enlightened many hearts seeking truth. I personally congratulate these authors from the bottom of my heart on their selfless efforts and dedication.

In no way am I trying to proclaim myself an authority on spirituality or, for that matter, a Sufi master. Neither can I speak for the efficacy of Buddhist, Jewish, Christian or other methods of meditation that center on Divine Names in their respective languages and lead their followers to a Divine and luminous silence. This short treatise is not meant for experts on these subjects, but is simply an attempt to interpret the Divine Name, *Allah*, in a radically different perspective—as it was taught to me as a boy in a small town isolated from Western influences and ways of thinking. Thus, I concern myself herein mainly with the practical teachings of Sufism as my grandfather and father imparted them to me. Necessarily, then, I leave aside complex philosophical doctrines for some other time.

By *practical teachings* I mean, I have made a humble effort to shed light on the most *useful* aspects of Sufi teachings. It is my hope that this book will serve as a manual that will guide the wayfarer on the spiritual journey into the presence of the Divine Essence.

The main object of this book is to discuss and explain the simplest ways to achieve the real purpose of life—union with God.

§

The Quranic verse, "We have come from God and will return back to Him" (Quran 2:156), clearly states that we were with God in the beginning and that there was no separation between ourselves and God's Being. In other words, we were part of the Divine. We came into this world and became separated from our real source. We are here in this material world for a short period and will eventually return to our eternal abode and be united with our source once again. Thus, our lives are like raindrops that will ultimately fall back in the ocean of Divine Oneness. Every single thing returns to its source. However, here in the world of matter, our separation from our source in the spirit world is the root cause of all pain and suffering. The further we move away from our Creator, the more we suffer and endure pain.

The purpose of life is found in God's words: "I created man to know and understand Me." He created the creation so that He could be known and loved. This God realization or God consciousness is our primary goal in life, and it comes with self-realization. A *hadith* is a narrative about the words of the Prophet, Muhammad (pbuh). In the words of one *hadith*, "If you know yourself, you know your Lord." Hence it is of vital importance to know who we really are, where we came from, and where are we headed. We came from a Divine source, and traces of Divinity are present within each one of us. We are to represent Him, be like Him, and assimilate His attributes of love, forgiveness, generosity, and compassion: in the words of the Quran, God the Most High said, "I created man in the best of moulds and to be My vicegerent on earth."

God created us for a purpose; each one of us has a specific destiny in life and a unique part to play in the grand scheme of creation. Nothing in the universe is at random or by accident. Everything has been planned perfectly with great precision. As the Quran says, "The Creator creates nothing without purpose or in play or in vain." As the great twelfth-century theologian Abu Hamid AlGhazali has said, "Dear friend, know that man was not created randomly but fashioned out carefully to fulfill his destiny." That destiny is to attain union with God through complete surrender and annihilation of the self in the source with love and knowledge, and Sufism is one way to do that.

Sufis are passionate lovers of the Divine, and the Sufi way is the way of the heart and the way of unconditional love. Sufis are thus preoccupied with commemoration, concentration, and meditation on the personal Name of God, *Allah*, every moment of their lives. Through this one supreme action they have become completely absorbed in the

Divine and are in the constant presence of God. As Sultan Bahu has said,

> Love flourishes in the heart in which glows the Name of God.
>
> The love of God is the fragrance, even a thousand wrappings cannot hold it in.
>
> Or like the sun, which cannot be hidden behind one's finger.
>
> Or like a river that cannot be stopped in its course.
>
> My Friend is in me, in my Friend am I, there is no separation between us.

The quest for Absolute Truth has preoccupied Sufis for more than fourteen hundred years. Truth is the attribute and essence of God. The Divine Truth lives in the lover's heart, as the Prophet Muhammad (pbuh) has said, "The heart of the believer is the sanctuary of God, and nothing but God is allowed access there." Sultan Bahu, writing of Truth, has pronounced in his *abyats* (verses), "Those who do not attain Truth are wretched in both realms, Lovers drown in Divine unity, Bahu, see their incredible end."

Who, then are these truth seekers known as Sufis? The origin of the word *Sufism* is disputed. According to some it refers to the early mystics' preferences to wear rough clothing made of wool (*suf*). Others proclaimed that the word is derived from the Greek word *sophia* (*wisdom*). Yet the word may be linked to devout dervishes (Ashab e Suffa) at the time of Prophet Hazrat Muhammad (pbuh) who were Divine lovers and were absorbed in commemorating God, contemplating God, and meditating on God alone—thus devoted to exploring the mysteries of *fana* (annihilation of self in God), *baqa* (subsistence through God), surrender, and Divine love. Describing such a state of love, Sultan Bahu wrote,

> When the Lord revealed Himself to me, I lost myself in Him.
>
> Now there is neither nearness nor union, there is no longer a journey to undertake, no longer a destination to reach.
>
> Love attachment, my body, and soul, and even the very limits of time and space have all dropped from my consciousness.
>
> My separate self has merged in the whole;
>
> In that, O Bahu, lies the secret of the unity that is God.

Such surrender is the very essence of Sufism. In this regard, it is stated in a legend that Rabia Al Adwiyah—the first Sufi woman poet to introduce the doctrine of Divine love—prostrated one thousand times a day before the Lord, begging and seeking His pleasure without asking for any reward. On another occasion she said, "O my Beloved, if I love you out of fear of hellfire, throw me therein and let me burn, if I love you for the reward of paradise, deprive me of that, but if I love you for Who You are, then do not take away the pleasure of union with You from me." In the same vein, Sultan Bahu confessed,

Neither does my heart ask for Hell, nor is it content with fondness for paradise.

Unless you attain union with God, Bahu, this world is but a game.

Beyond this game, Sufism emphasizes the Divine unity of all life, which is realized after the attainment of a perfect knowledge of the ultimate truth concerning the Absolute. At that stage a mystic observes oneness in multiplicity and multiplicity in oneness. The unlimited attributes and beauty of God are expressed in the creation of the universe and everything that exists therein.

Humans, of course are one of God's creations. God created human beings solely as mirrors to reflect the splendors of His Divine beauty. Out of all God's creation, it is only the human heart that can know, understand, and love Him. Sufism is a name for such love interaction between human and Divine.

Regarding such love, Abdul Rahman Jami narrated a story about a student who requested a dervish to guide him to God. Complying with his request, the dervish replied, "Go away you careless soul, fall in love, once you have experienced the pain of love, then come again and talk to us."

Similarly, Sultan Bahu beautifully explained the superiority of love over faith:

Everyone asks for firmness in faith, but few for firmness in love.

They ask for faith and are ashamed of love, such arrogant hearts.

Faith has no idea of the place where love can transport you.

I swear by my faith, Bahu, keep my love firm.

Similarly rhapsodizing about love, the great poet Rumi has said to this effect,

"If in thirst you drink from a cup, you see God in it. Those who are not in love with God will see only their own faces in it."

Thus the main object of this book is to highlight the importance of adoration: of recollection, concentration, and meditation on the beautiful Names of God, and especially on what Sufis see as His supreme personal Name, *Allah*. Such adoration serves as a means to achieve oneness and to come closer to the light of God.

The original idea of meditation on His personal Name, *Allah*, was first described by Hazrat Sultan Bahu some four hundred years ago. He wrote extensively on this subject in almost one hundred and forty of his works, emphasizing the connection of the name and the named. A prolific writer in the Persian language, he discussed in great depth the Sufi way of meditation on the word *Allah*, which, in Sufism, is synonymous with the Essence of God and the root cause of all that exists.

The central theme of his spiritual teachings is meditation on that very personal Name of God, *Allah*, and only secondarily on the ninety-eight other attributive Names of God, on the formula of faith, on Quranic verses, and on the blessed name of the Prophet of Islam, Muhammad (pbuh).

The Sufi meditates on that Name before all others, because when an alert heart concentrates on something with singleness of purpose, that thing is manifested sooner or later, and thoughts turn into reality. The personal Name for God, *Allah*, is thought by Sufis to be the most powerful word in the cosmos, because Sufis believe it to be God Himself. God does not have a body, a shape, a color, or a form. He is neither matter nor created. However, "He is the first and the last, the visible and the invisible, the manifest and the concealed, and He is cognizant of everything" (Quran). For Sufis, manifesting the reality of God is through his Name, and the closest thing to the Essence of God is His personal Name, *Allah*, which indicates His Essence and signifies His totality. In order to achieve mystical union with God, we need to keep Him forever in our hearts by meditating and contemplating on His Name, *Allah*. Meditation on His supreme Name, *Allah*, is the single most effective method to concentrate the heart on nothing other than God. Such concentrated love of God is the highest station on the path. It is attained by meditating on His supreme Name, *Allah*, in the heart, thus filling it with the light of Divine love so that nothing is more lovable than Him.

How does this process of making God actual through meditation on his Name take place? Sufism teaches that the word *Allah* has to be inscribed in the heart with the power of the imagination. Yet, meditating on the Name *Allah* requires time and practice if it is to be inscribed on the tablet of the heart. Recollection of the Name *Allah* with the tongue, gazing at the written word *Allah*, and writing *Allah* at least sixty times daily on a paper, all help one significantly to be successful in this endeavor.

In practice, at times it seems impossible to fix *Allah* in the heart. For Sufis, *Allah* is the uncreated supreme Name of His Essence, and it is impossible for a created being to get ahold of His Name. Rather it is the exact opposite, His personal Name, *Allah*, will grab hold of your heart, and once it permeates your entire being, it will never let you go. As the meditative efforts take effect, His personal Name, *Allah*, will illuminate your heart, mind, soul, eyes, and all body parts.

Yet, there are other expressions that can be used to meditate on God. All the ninety-nine Names of God, the formula of faith, "*La Illaha Illallah*" (There is no deity worthy of worship save Allah), and the name of the Prophet, *Muhammad* (pbuh), can be employed for the purposes of meditation and concentration upon the heart. Each of these has a specific characteristic and spiritual effect that is transferred to those who meditate on it. In addition, when the Name of God, *Allah*, in Arabic, is broken down into its three component letters—*Lillah*, *Lahu*, and *Hu*—one by one, it still signifies His Essence only. These component Names—*Lillah*, *Lahu*, and *Hu*—are also meditated upon, along with the other beautiful Names of God. However, although meditation on other words brings merit, according to Hazrat Sultan Bahu, concentration and meditation on the personal Name of God, *Allah*, is the best form of prayer and remembrance. One should become so absorbed in meditation that one loses awareness of everything else other than *Allah*.

Meditation is God's eternal blessing unto mankind and is primarily based on Quranic teachings. In specific forms that are at the heart of Sufi teachings, the Prophet Hazrat Muhammad (pbuh) taught remembrance and imaginative contemplation (meditation) to his close companions. According to an authentic tradition, it was in the cave of Thaur, a mountain below Mecca, that the Prophet (pbuh) taught Hazrat Abu Bakr the method of silent remembrance of God (*Dhikr I khafi*) and meditation on the Divine Names. Meditation is thus a sacred and illuminative science that opens one's awareness to the source of radiant lights and ocean of direct vision. This science is a process of inner transformation that turns all attention and focus towards God. After all, God is near and not far, as Allah says: "I am near" and " . . . with you wherever you are" (Quran 57:4).

Although God is near, He cannot be seen with the eyes nor understood with the help of the intellect. God's face is hidden behind the veil of the universe and all that it contains within it. Yet, God can be found, seen only through this veil, for He is present in everything and is everywhere. As one line of Quranic verse has it, "Wherever you see, there is the face of God" (Quran 2:115). Meditation is an excellent mode of unveiling that barely hidden; One Reality that exists in everything and thereby lifts the veil from the face of God. It is used to achieve focused concentration on the Divine Beloved and provides a direct method of invoking Him.

The Quran is remembrance of God, and so are all the acts of devotion and worship. Remembrance is in fact to acknowledge what we know from pre-eternity about the covenant that we made with God on the *Day of Alast* to remember Him. Such remembrance is done by uttering and repeating the Quranic verses. Words and sentences are the means to express the Divine secrets, although in only a limited way, whereas the scope of meditation (imaginative contemplation) is infinite. What imagination can grasp, words cannot. Meditation not only brings one closer to God in this life but is a means of eternal bliss in the life of the next world. The only thing that God loves is to be remembered and glorified by human beings, and those who do so are the ones on the straight path and will be truly successful in life with God for all eternity.

For Sufis, the human soul is in fact a reflection from His Essence and separated from its Divine source for a time. Our lives here are so short that in comparison they can be called mere blips in eternity or sparks in time, and we will eventually be reunited with our source, which is the highest possible goal of human existence. The suffering and searching of the human soul for the precious moment of proximity with God can be realized through meditation on the word *Allah*.

Visualization of the word *Allah* in different parts of the body and especially the heart is the crucible of mystical experience, because in the human makeup it is only the heart that attracts Divine love. Therefore, the personal name of God, *Allah*, should be inscribed in the heart, which will invariably result in intense attraction towards God.

When you become annihilated in the Name (*Allah*) you will become merged with the source of all that exists. You will gradually assume the traits of the Divine Name as your own, and you will find all the creation including the *Throne, Chair, Heavens, and Earth* within your soul.

Meditation on the personal Name of God, *Allah*, will certainly result in Divine bliss, which is an endless outpouring of His grace that will continue for all eternity. It will lead the wayfarer to the realization of the experience of the Divine in the here and now. The special technique of meditation on the personal Name of *Allah* revealed in this book will remove the thickest layers of veils, will bring you face to face with the One Reality and is a means of an intimate conversation with God.

In the coming chapters, I have given an overview of the different meditation practices and how they differ from the meditative technique described in this book. Each chapter begins with selected verses of the Quran or with *hadith* (sayings or narratives about the Prophet Muhammad (pbuh)—the celestial beauty upon which this entire work revolves. It is my hope that this book will be both instructive and enlightening to the seekers of the Truth in their quests for the Sacred.

Chapter One

HUMBLE BEGINNINGS

Man is my secret and I am his secret. The knowledge of inner being is one of my secrets. I have put this in the heart of my servants, and no one is aware of it other than Me.

—*Hadith qudsi*, quoted by Hazrat Syed Sheikh Abdul Qadir Jilani in *Sirr-ul-Asrar*.

The main objective of this book is to explore the secrets of human and Divine love, their relationship, and their interaction through meditation on the personal Name of God, *Allah*. Such meditation is a portal to draw upon and receive the ever-shining light and a means to live in the Divine presence.

When I was a child, as far as I can remember, probably at the age of four years, I became fascinated with the questions of life and death and this amazing chain of creation—the universe. At night I would gaze up into the sky and behold the countless stars flickering and shimmering in the immense darkness. I understood that there is a God who exists neither in one exclusive place nor in one exclusive moment and yet that there is no place, nor time, where He is not present.

We lived in a small, two-story house adjacent to a large mosque. Almost every day, I climbed up to the rooftop of our home and from there would jump over to the roof of the mosque. The roof of the mosque was huge, almost equivalent to a small soccer field, with four towering minarets that looked simply majestic. The shining sun above and the birds that nested at the very top of the minarets were spellbinding. As long as I was up there, I felt myself in a different world: free, happy, and fulfilled. In fact it was my favorite heavenly retreat and it belonged to me alone. When, I would come down, my mother would ask me where I had been. I would innocently reply that I had gone to heaven.

She was surprised to hear this at first, but soon realized that the word *mosque* in our native language, Pushtu, rhymes with the word *heaven*. However, I did not understand the difference between the two terms at that age. She would then ask me jokingly, "Did you see God over there?"

To this I would always reply, "I did not see Him, but I think He was there with me all the time."

In fact, I felt His presence all over the place and within myself as well. I cannot adequately describe the experience, but to this day I still feel that He has always been with me. This has made me over-confident at times, for I thought that nothing would be wrong as long as He was with me. Perhaps I had the words of Prophet Hazrat Muhammad (pbuh) in my mind, when he said, "When you take one step toward Him, He advances ten steps towards you. But the complete truth is that God is always with you."

Similarly, God the Most High proclaimed, "We are nearer to man than his jugular vein" (Quran 50:16). Even before our physical birth, we were with God (our source), God is with us, and after death we will be with Him again, as scripture asserts, "We came from Allah and will go back to Him" (Quran 2:156). As a matter of fact, He has been with us from the beginning of creation, and after we have done our time here, we will be with Him for eternity. This forms the basis of oneness, and we ought to achieve reunion with Him through love, knowledge, and service.

I was born and raised in a traditional, religious, and spiritual household and have experienced the reality of Sufism from my early life. I have inherited my intense affection for the Divine from a long line of ancestors who were endowed with enlightenment. In fact, I am a twelfth-generation Sufi, a descendent of Syed Muhammad al Husayni Gisudiraz—he with the long tresses—the famous saint of Decan, whose mausoleum is in Gulberga, Haiderabad, India. Gisudiraz was a profound scholar and author of innumerable works. He was an authority on the sciences of the Quran, exegesis, tradition, theology, and jurisprudence. In fact, Gisudiraz is compared to the great Islamic theologian and Sufi mystic, Al Ghazalli, because both used to dictate four or five works at a time. Gisudiraz once wrote, "Everyone who traverses on the path of God is bestowed with a particular thing; God has bestowed me with the gift of explaining His secrets."

Among his works, which number over one hundred, are many commentaries on the Quran, commentaries on tradition, and a biography of the Prophet Hazrat Muhammad (pbuh). His most important work is *Asmar Al Asrar*, which deals comprehensively with all aspects of Sufism.

He himself was proud of this work, which he divided into 114 chapters, according to the number of *suras* (verses) in the Quran. Chapters 74 and 75 deal with the interpretation of the fourteen mystical letters (*muqattaat*) of the Quran. This work also shows the importance of mystical visions in the thought of Gisudiraz.

Gisudiraz, though, was immensely influenced by the doctrine of *unity of being (Wahdat al Wujud)* as elaborated by Ibn Arabi, but had a critical attitude towards it. In his opinion such a doctrine crosses the boundries of orthodox Islam and goes against the Islamic concept of unity (*tawhid*) of God. The doctrine of *unity of being* (All is He) is complicated. Unless one is drowned in the ocean of oneness and experiences its reality, it is difficult to understand even its theoretical meaning. It is so often misunderstood and confused with pantheism. That is why there are extensive works of theoretical gnosis written on this subject, and still it can be interpreted in several ways. In this regard Gisudiraz concurred with Ahmad Sirhindi and Simnani by propounding another doctrine, referred to as *unity of witnessing* (*wahdat al shuhud*). This doctrine of *All is from Him* asserts that God is present everywhere and in everything, but everything is not God. Frithjof Schuon explained this beautifully, "Existence is a manifestation of Being, and all existence issues from and belongs to Being in the same way that the rays of the sun are finally nothing but the sun."

Whether *unity of witnessing* (*wahdat al shuhud*) and *unity of being* (*wahdat al wujud*) are the two sides of the same coin is another question. In the broadest sense of the word *All is He* or *All is from Him* are the same, and the difference in the two doctrines is merely a matter of semantics. Nevertheless, Gisudiraz boldly stated, "If he (Ibn Arabi) were alive during my age, I would have made him conscious of *beyond the beyond* by taking him up into the spiritual realm and would have revived his belief (Iman)."

My great grandfather, Haji Gul Muhammad Khan, was also a pious and learned man of God. He was a scholar in Arabic and Persian. Walking on foot he undertook four pilgrimages to the house of God, the Kaaba, in Mecca, all the way from our tiny village of Kulachi, Pakistan. Along the way, he visited the shrines of Sufi saints and Imams in Afghanistan,

Iran, Iraq, and Saudi Arabia, receiving abundant spiritual blessings from them.

My grandfather, Hazrat Faqir Nur Muhammad Sarwari Qaderi, was—in his time—a mystic scholar and luminary in Islamic spiritual sciences. He authored many volumes on this subject, spending his entire lifetime in the pursuit of Sufi mysticism and research of Sufi literature. He, for the first time, presented Islamic mysticism in a simple, engaging, and understandable manner to Urdu-speaking readers in the sub-continent. His famous book, *Irfan*, first published in the 1930s, took the spiritual world in Indo-Pakistan by storm and was considered a monumental event in the history of Islamic Urdu literature. *Irfan*, which, has been translated into English as well, is a valuable compendium on spiritual wisdom and Divine secrets. Reading this book inspired unparalleled enthusiasm within Sufi circles and among seekers on the path.

Faqir Nur Muhammad Sarwari Qaderi was a great portal of Divine light, which he emanated and spread by his teachings and writings. After surrendering his soul to the creator of the universe, his successor, my father, Faqir Abdul Hamid Sarwari Qaderi, began spreading his mission and blessings of God to those around him. His very presence brings peace, harmony, and healing. His followers in Pakistan and other countries, especially South Africa, will testify to this fact. Although old, now ninety-five years of age, he is blooming like a rose emanating spiritual fragrance. He is gracious, kind, and very humble by nature. He is full of love and Divine glory. There is a special charm about him. He is a wonderful conversationalist. He always welcomes his vistors with an enchanting smile that never fails to win their hearts.

Inspired by my family lineage, I can say that writing this book has been my earnest desire for a long time. Yet, I have to admit that I am not a writer. Moreover, English is not my native tongue. However, I do want to share the secrets of Divine meditation and my personal spiritual experiences with all those who are interested in Sufism, seekers of the path, and most importantly lovers of God the Most High.

In the coming chapters, I will be describing in a simple manner the science of meditation on the very personal Name of God, *Allah*, which is the infinite source of His light, grace, and favors. I have learnt and practiced this method of meditation on the Divine Names, as described in Hazrat Sultan Bahu's and my grandfather's books. Now it is my duty to disseminate this knowledge, which has been hidden from seekers in the West.

How much Divine light you can draw on or how much closer you can come to God depends entirely upon yourself. It certainly depends on the firmness of your faith, your sincerity of intention, your purity of heart, and above all your love of God.

§

I was fortunate to have been brought up by living examples embodying all the qualities of a Sufi seeker. I had a strong affection for my grandfather, though I remember few occasions when I saw him. These were when I was only four or five years old. Those memories are so vivid that I can still feel them until this day. I first read his writings and teachings when I was in the sixth grade—and fully understood them.

My father used to practice concentration and meditation on the personal Name of God, *Allah*. I remember that early in the morning, long before dawn, he would offer his prayers, glorifying, praising, and thanking God constantly. After performing his daily *dhikr* (meditation), he would then place in front of him a frame in which the word *Allah* was carved in a mirror in beautiful Arabic letters, on a black background. The word *Allah* would shine and reflect brilliant light, and he would gaze and concentrate on it. He then would go into a meditative state. I would imitate him and would do so in my heart. He would later on narrate some of his spiritual visions and experiences to inspire us to follow the path of light.

Following my father's example, in those days, I used to recite the Name of God, *Allah*, constantly. As a matter of fact, it became my favorite pastime, and the Divine Name would keep on resonating within my memory and heart every moment of the day. This practice led to the opening of my esoteric eye at quite an early age, and I enjoyed some wonderful spiritual experiences at that time. In my visions and dreams, I was able to see events that would happen in the future. I was able to see things behind walls and closed doors. While meditating, I was able to travel long distances in an instant to see what was happening.

I have been very close to my father, who is also my spiritual guide (*murshid*). Although I was born in Bannu, in the Khyber-Pukhtunkhwa province of Pakistan, and grew up there, I attended medical school in Peshawar. My father was practicing medicine in Bannu at that time. He is also a writer and a poet, both in Urdu and Pushtu, and was involved in many literary and spiritual societies in Bannu. He won a Writer's Guild award for his collection of Pushtu poetry, *Inspirations*. He was also awarded a gold medal by the Sultan Bahu Academy for translating *Abyat e Bahu* (*Spiritual Verses*) in Pushtu. The book is considered a masterpiece of Pushtu literature and compared to the *Masnavi* of Rumi.

After school, I used to join my father in the small clinic he ran and would stay in his company for the rest of the day. He used to coach me in literature, poetry, and spiritual sciences. We used to discuss a wide variety of subjects. I learned a great deal of esoteric knowledge from him as a result. I also witnessed some of his extraordinary charismatic talents and spiritual experiences. The following is a glimpse of such penetrating accounts.

It was a dull summer afternoon around 5 p.m. I was with my father in his clinic. After my school hours, I used to go there and would stay with him till the end of the day. He used to close his office around the time of evening prayers. I would do my homework, and he would offer his help with literature, poetry, and essay writing. The following incident happened when I was in the eighth grade.

One of my father's acquaintances came to see him. He was a respectable man who was also the chief of his tribe in Bannu. Out of respect, he was called Malik Sahib (chief). He was a middle-aged fellow and had just returned from *Hajj* (pilgrimage) to Mecca. He was accompanied by two other men, who were his tribesmen and subordinates. My father greeted him, and they embraced each other as a sign of mutual respect. He congratulated my father on his wonderful pilgrimage (*Hajj*) and showed signs of amazement that he had managed to visit the tomb of the Prophet

Muhammad (pbuh) from the inside, because the inside of the tomb of the Prophet (pbuh) is locked, and no one is allowed to visit the actual grave of the Holy Prophet. Only the members of the Royal Saudi family are allowed to go inside the tomb and visit the Holy grave of the Prophet of Islam.

On hearing this, my father told him that he had not gone for *Hajj* at all and that he may have mistaken somebody else for him. Malik Sahib was astonished at first to hear this, but thought that my father must be pulling his leg. Malik Sahib insisted that he personally met my father inside the Prophet's mosque and prayed together with him. He added, "After the evening prayer you left to visit the Prophet's (pbuh) tomb. Upon seeing you, the guard opened the locked door for you, and you entered inside the tomb. This is a great honor because only high-ranking officials and members of the Royal Saudi household have the privilege to enter inside the mausoleum."

My father reiterated that he had not physically gone on *Hajj* (pilgrimage) this year, but spiritually he had an intense longing to go on pilgrimage and, in his mind, that is what happened—exactly.

Another incident concerns one of my father's disciples, Ahmad Saeed, who is an elderly Indian Muslim from South Africa affectionately called Uncle Bob. He is a disciple of my father, Faqir Abdul Hamid. He stated, "One night I was praying all night and continued doing so until the time of early morning prayers. I was absolutely absorbed in devotion and overpowered by Divine presence. With tears in my eyes, I was ceaselessly performing my *dhikr* (remembrance). I suddenly heard the door bell, around 3 a.m., but was taken aback that anyone might be ringing it at that time. I therefore ignored the bell and continued with my prayers. The bell rang again. This time I was worried and hesitated to open the door. However, when the bell rang for the third time, I reluctantly got up to see who it was. As soon as I opened the door, I was pleasantly surprised to see my spiritual master (Faqir Abdul Hamid) at the door. I immediately fell at his feet and kissed his hands. My Sheikh smilingly told me that he had come to see me and enquired about my well-being." This happened although my father had been in Kulachi, Pakistan, at that time and Ahmad Saeed knew that for a fact. Ahmad Saeed further added, "We both talked for a while, and then my master disappeared as mysteriously as he had come. The experience is difficult to describe, but my heart was thrilled and it intensified my love for my master."

Another South African disciple of my father, named Moses, who converted to Islam, narrated the following: "I was traveling with my teenage daughter in a car outside Johannesburg. After a while we were passing through a thick forest. The road was deserted, with almost no traffic either way. Suddenly my car lost power. The radiator was overheated and it needed cold water. I had no water with me to pour into the radiator. I was very worried being alone in a deserted area along with my young daughter. I was afraid of robbers and evil men. It was getting dark, and I had to do something about it. Finally, I took a container and set out to find some water. I told my daughter to stay inside car all the time and never to get out.

I started running in search of water. I had hardly gone for half a mile when I saw Faqir Abdul Hamid, along with Khalifa Ali coming towards me on foot. I was stunned to see my spiritual master in the middle of that jungle. I was dumbfounded and could not speak a word. Faqir Abdul Hamid looked at me and asked what the matter was. I told him that my car had broken down and that my teenage daughter was sitting in the car alone. He told me to return to the car immediately and said that a white man has just arrived there and is waiting to help me. I paid my tribute to my Sheikh, kissed his hands, and returned to my car in quite a hurry. As I approached my car, I saw a white Englishman waiting for me. He helped me fix the car. I was soon on my way towards my destination and thanked God for this miracle in the middle of nowhere. It was real, and later I found out that my Sheikh was in Pakistan at that time." He was amazed to see his spiritual guide appearing in physical form, helping him in a dangerous situation and was convinced that his Sheikh was fully aware of the needs of his disciples at all times—even if they were thousands of miles away.

His whole life is marked by many strange manifestations and extraordinary events. In Sufi literature, the phenomenon of being present in two locations has been exhibited in the lives of many saints. There is a legend about Hazrat Syed Sheikh Abdul Qadir Jilani that once he met at the same time with seventy of his disciples, although each was in a different geographical location.

In addition to the above experiences, since my early childhood, I have been blessed with close encounters with subtle beings such as spirits, angels, *jinn*, and ghosts—not by my own merit—but because of my family circumstances. My grandfather was a great saint and had hundreds of *jinn* as his disciples. They would come to him to learn religious and spiritual matters. Many of them were with him for months in the form of ordinary adepts, but their mannerisms and extraordinary powers used to raise suspicions. These adepts would not eat with other people and would rather be absent at meal times.

When we lived in Bannu, a family of *jinn* used to live in our house as good neighbors. The group consisted of a woman, short in stature, who was the head of the family, and four small children. All the children were surprisingly of the same size. They looked exactly like human beings except that they had long ears. They were quite friendly and peaceful and never created any problem for us. Once, I was sleeping on my bed at night and saw four children running around playing hide and seek. Suddenly they dashed under my bed and were quite loud. They seemed excited and were having a lot of fun. At first I enjoyed their game, but later on was becoming nervous. In a flash, I saw their mother come after them and take them out. All of them ran quickly and disappeared into the wall of the compound. Out of curiosity, I went and touched the wall. It was hot at the point where they apparently had disappeared.

On another occasion, during one summer noon, I was playing in the compound alone. My parents and sibling were napping in the room to avoid the merciless heat. I saw four small children (*jinn*) come out of nowhere and start running after one another in hot pursuit. They were laughing and screaming aloud. I tried to calm them down and started chasing them. They ran into the storage room. I followed suit, but three of them just vanished in thin air. The fourth one rolled over the ground and turned into a large snake, moving violently across the room. At this unexpected outcome I was frightened and started screaming, "Snake! Snake!" My parents came out running, and I told them that I had just seen a large snake in the storage room. However, I did not tell them the whole story. When my parents went into the room, there was no snake to be found.

During summer nights we all used to sleep on the roof of the house. Bannu has hot summers—with no wind blowing at all—making it even more intolerable. The rooftop was much cooler during the night compared to the ground level. My bed on the roof was the nearest to the stairs, then my father's bed, and then the beds of the rest of the family. Once, after midnight, I heard somebody knocking at the door. I was awake, but I kept quiet because I did not want to go down and see who it was. My father was awake and he did not move as well. He thought it might be somebody who wanted some medicine at midnight or wanted to take him to see a sick person at those late hours. My father would not go out at night and do home visits because it was not safe to do so. I heard the knock one more time. After some time, I heard three to four people coming up the stairs. I was quite frightened and remained motionless. My father was surprised too; he sensed something extraordinary and leaned down to see what was going on. I saw three men advance up the stairs and sit near the foot end of my father's bed. My father asked who they were and for what purpose they had come. At this one of them said, "I am Abu Saeed, and we are *jinn* from the mountains of Karakoram. I have come to become your disciple. Please initiate me into your spiritual order." My father was amazed to hear this. Karakoram is a large mountain range spanning the borders between Pakistan, India, and China. I saw Abu Saeed taking *bayah* (an oath of allegiance) at the hands of my father. They talked for a while. Abu Saeed also made some future predictions, and later on the three of them disappeared. My father has written about this incident in his autobiography. Since then Abu Saeed has been of great assistance to my father in various tasks.

Thus my father and my grandfather have exercised a deep impact and impression on my soul and spirituality. Both of them have been my mentors—directly or indirectly. Later on in my life, and until now, I have enjoyed hundreds of esoteric visions and experiences with them on the path of truth and oneness, which is the ultimate goal of Sufis. Here it is not my intention to describe all these events and spiritual visions, though, some of them will be narrated for the interest and inspiration of the readers.

Many spiritual events took place when I was in Iran. After I graduated from medical school in Peshawar, I traveled to Iran and practiced medicine there for the next seventeen years. My sojourn in Iran was a golden period of my life. I had the chance to extensively study Sufi literature and mystic poetry, which were abundantly available in the Persian language. I studied masters such as Jalal ud Din Rumi, Farid ud Din Attar, Khayam, Hafiz Shirazi, Saadi, Firdousi, Baba Tahir Uryan, Abu Saeed Abul Khair, Jami, AlGhazali, and many more. I had the chance to visit the shrines of the famous Sufi masters. These were great souls, portals of heavenly light, and channels of God's blessings. I certainly received abundant spiritual blessings and light through them.

My ability to receive the blessings I did in Iran, however, is the result of my birth and family. I have been blessed and touched by the Divine since I was born. God has been with me all the time and He has miraculously saved me time and again. For example, when I was one year old, I contracted typhoid (enteric fever) and became seriously ill for three months with fever, chronic diarrhea, and malnutrition. I had a very poor appetite and as a result was emaciated and reduced to skin and bones. I suffered from sores all over my body, including the corneas of my eyes. My parents had no hope of my recovery, feeling I was destined to die at any moment. Then, one day my grandfather, Faqir Nur Muhammad Sarwari Qaderi, visited us unexpectedly. I was sitting with him on a *charpai* (cot). He looked at me and was deeply moved by my deteriorating health. He took me in his hands and prayed for me. My father was practicing medicine at that time and had been treating me in consultation with one of his physician friends who was working in the missionary hospital in Bannu. So far, I had shown no signs of recovery. Rather, my condition was becoming more and more complicated. The next morning, through his friend in the missionary hospital, my father obtained a new antibiotic called *chloramphenicol*, which was the latest medicine for treating typhoid fever. Within forty-eight hours of taking the new medication, I started recovering and was completely cured in ten days.

Another incident happened, when I was seven years old. I was in the second grade, and we were still living in Bannu. Our home was close to the school, and I used to walk to school every day. At noon I would come home for lunch and go back to school after I had eaten. One day at lunch time, instead of going home I went to my father's clinic, which was also near home. My father had gone home for lunch, and I was alone in the small office. There was a small fridge in the clinic. The clinic was in an old, rat-infested, three-storey building. In order to get rid of the rats, my father had bought rat poison. He mixed it with dough and made small, rounded pellets for the rats. He left it in the fridge in a closed container. He was certainly not expecting me to be there at noon time. Out of curiosity, I opened the fridge and discovered the rounded, sweet pellets in a container. I thought they were some kind of candy or sweets and presumed that my father had bought them for me. I was hungry and gobbled down all of them. When I was finished, I closed the fridge door and was just about to leave for home. By then, my father arrived unexpectedly and saw me licking my fingers. He immediately became suspicious and asked me what I had eaten. I told him I had wolfed down the sweets in the fridge. His face turned pale. He immediately rushed me to the missionary hospital—five minutes away—on his bicycle, all the way reciting Quranic verses, praying, and invoking God's mercy. For the first time in my life I saw tears rolling down my father's cheeks.

We were soon in the emergency department of the hospital. I was taken to the procedure room by the staff. The doctor there—a retired physician from England doing missionary work in Bannu, along with other British volunteer nurses—administered a stomach lavage by inserting a wide-bore red tube via my mouth into my esophagus and stomach. He thoroughly washed out my stomach contents and also gave me a laxative. For a period of forty-eight hours, I was admitted into a private room for close observation and for further testing. I retain only vague memories of my stay in the hospital, of nurses constantly monitoring my vital signs, hovering above me like a host of angels, robed in white, floating comfortingly near me all through the night.

My death would have been certain had I not received medical help in time. If my father had been late by a minute, I would have gone home or to school and would have succumbed to the effects of the deadly poison. However, it so happened that I survived that poisonous ingestion, by the grace of God. As God says, "Nothing shall ever happen to us except what Allah has ordained for us" (Quran, 9:51).

For the last fifty years, every day I have been meditating on His personal Name, *Allah*, as well as on other attributive Divine Names, on the formula of faith, and on Quranic verses. In fact, *dhikr* (commemoration) has been my favorite preoccupation for as long a time as I can remember.

In the beginning of this practice, I was in a state of intoxication, by the grace of Divine love. I was overpowered by the intense attraction of His affection. I loved to perform my *dhikr* audibly and loudly. I used to chant and shout the *dhikr* repeatedly, and it used to send me into ecstasy and sometimes into extreme spiritual rapture. I would do so for hours, unaware of the surroundings—and most of the times all night long. I would go out to the wilderness during the day—if that was possible—and chant the Divine Names loudly, in a melodious voice, becoming ecstatically absorbed in His remembrance. The majority of the time I would do so until past midnight— with the pretext of studying—when everybody else was sleeping.

When I was in the eleventh grade, I occupied a room on the second floor, quite separate from the rest of the house. I would study until midnight and then would begin my repetitive recitations (*dhikr*) loudly. I would pace across the room so that I would not fall asleep and continued that until the *Adhan* (call for Morning Prayer time). My method of *dhikr* was fast and loud, and so mumbled that anyone listening would not be able to understand it. It would sound like unintelligible shouts of a drunkard, except for the sound of *Hu* (His Essence).

Once, my father had a guest who was sleeping overnight at our house in the room situated exactly below my room. In the morning my father had breakfast with him. He asked the guest how he had slept. The guest replied that whenever he had awakened during the night, he had heard a dervish constantly chanting *dhikr*. My father smiled knowingly.

During that period of time I received numerous spiritual experiences and visions, most of them related to the Divine. Then one night I was overwhelmed by Divine presence and was blessed with the vision of God the Most High, the account of which will be coming in a later chapter of this book. Since that time, I have been blessed with sobriety. I have been doing quiet *dhikr* ever since, and have been remembering Him in the silence of my heart. As a matter of fact, I am in a state of inward drunkenness and outward sobriety.

Most recently, I was blessed with a vision of Prophet Moses (pbuh) and Prophet Jesus (pbuh). The account of which is as follows: I saw in a clear vision that my father and I were traveling in a small caravan of six people towards Jerusalem in the Holy Land. Our group was headed by Prophet Moses (pbuh) along with Prophet Jesus (pbuh). Prophet Moses (pbuh) was walking one step ahead of Prophet Jesus (pbuh), but it appeared as if they were walking side by side. There were two other men in our group, who seemed to be the disciples of Prophet Jesus (pbuh), and they were right behind the two Prophets. Our party of six men was passing through a desert. The land we were travelling upon was dry, sandy, and deserted—with a few low, thorny bushes scattered here and there. It seemed as if we had been on the way for a while. Our destination was the Dome of the Rock in Jerusalem (Al Aqsa Mosque). My father and I walked side by side, behind the four of them, following in their footsteps.

Off and on Prophet Jesus (pbuh) would turn around and gaze upon us affectionately. He glowed, with a glorious face, with a white complexion, prominent cheeks, large black eyes, and beautiful eyelashes. He wore medium-size tresses, an average-size beard, and had a slightly pointed nose and thin lips. His face was resplendent with God's light and was emanating His glory. His beauty overshadowed the grandeur of Prophet Moses (pbuh), who was walking most graciously along with him. I could not recognize, who the other two men were. We had been travelling the whole night and now were in the last part of the night. The entire place was lit by moonlight, and I could quite clearly see the surroundings and the people in our group.

The dawn was at hand, and early morning hours were approaching. I could see the city walls in the far distance and behind them the Dome of the Rock. Our destination was near, and we were moving at a constant pace, very quietly, without talking or whispering. There was sweet serenity in the atmosphere, and Divine presence was felt everywhere. I was in a state of awe and extreme spiritual bliss. I felt so fortunate to be in the company of two great Prophets of God the Most High, a saint (my father), and two men of the unseen. We were coming close to the city and could see its gate in front of us.

Outside the gate was an average-size raised pool filled with clear water. As soon as we reached the pool of water, I saw Prophet Moses (pbuh) and Prophet Jesus (pbuh) entering the water with bare feet. The water was up to their knees. I noticed that Prophet Moses (pbuh) and Prophet Jesus (pbuh) started to make their ablutions with water by washing their hands and faces. I then saw Prophet Jesus (pbuh) take water in both of his hands and pour it over his own head. After that, he took some water in his hands again and this time poured water over my head. The cool liquid then ran down my face onto my body. A blaze of illumination came over me. I felt as if he had poured light on my head, illuminating my entire being. I had never felt like that before. I was totally immersed in Divine light. At that very moment I heard the *Adhan* (call for Morning Prayer). The sound of *Adhan* (God is Great) resonated in the air. It permeated my heart and shook my whole body violently. I woke up from my vision. It was actually the time for Morning Prayer; the sound of *Adhan* was being announced from the speakers on my computer. This was a unique and blissful spiritual experience for me.

Most recently I was blessed with the vision of Prophet Jesus (pbuh) once again. He had already showered me with his blessings and favors. This time, however, he bestowed upon me a unique gift of his healing power. I saw in the vision that Prophet Jesus (pbuh) was standing in a large gathering of people. Among them were people who were sick, blind, lepers, and lame and who had come to see him to become cured and healed. People had come from faraway places to receive blessings and healing. Jesus (pbuh) was healing them one by one, holding both of his hands over them. It seemed that as soon as he did that the sick, the blind, the lepers, and the lame were cured.

I was standing beside Prophet Jesus (pbuh) and was witnessing all these miracles happening right before my eyes. I was in a state of awe while witnessing these people being cured. Then, suddenly, Prophet Jesus (pbuh) looked at me intently with piercing eyes and said, "I am giving you my healing powers. From now onwards you should heal people." A wave of heavenly bliss overwhelmed my heart. He then held both of his hands over me and transferred his miraculous healing powers to me. It seemed as if he had sent waves of light towards me that permeated my entire body and being. Each part of my body was illuminated and glowing with the Divine light. I was feeling his miraculous healing powers inside myself and was overjoyed with this unexpected great gift and favor from Prophet Jesus (pbuh). I was humbled and immeasureably grateful from the bottom of my heart.

However, I dared to ask His Holiness, "How, am I going to heal people and how will it work?" He smilingly replied, "Do as I did, but remember: only those who have faith will be healed." I then came out of my vision into wakefulness, with my heart still filled with light and joy.

I had yet another spiritual experience recently. I saw in a vision of a dream that I was still residing in Iran. One day I went to the village of Kharaqan, near Nishapur, in the province of Khurassan, where the famous Sufi saint Abul Hassan Kharaqani is buried. Sheikh Abul Hassan Kharaqani was an *Uwaysi* Sufi master. That means he was directly guided by the Divine and thus did not have a human master (*murshid*). The *Uwaysi* Sufis are sometimes led by the Prophet Khidr and guided by the unseen men of the invisible spiritual hierarchy. The *Uwaysi* strand of Sufism was founded by Uways Al Qarani, from Yemen, who personally never met the Prophet of Islam but accepted Islam. About him the Prophet Hazrat Muhammad (pbuh) has said, "I smell the breath of the Merciful from Yemen."

As I was wandering outside the village of Kharaqan and intended to proceed inside the village to meet the Sheikh, I saw that a supremely dignified sheikh whose face was radiant with Divine light and who was dressed in traditional Sufi attire was approaching towards me. When he came closer, he smiled and greeted me with a warm handshake and an affectionate embrace. He was deeply pleased with my presence, as if he had been waiting for me. He then conversed with me for a while, which resulted in the transmission of Divine knowledge. As I was reverently biding farewell to the illumined Sheikh, he bestowed upon me a black robe of honor (*khirqa*), investing me with his esoteric power. After receiving the *khirqa* at the hand of Sheikh Abul Hassan Kharaqani and all the *baraka* (blessings) along with it, I woke up and was amazed by the vision I had just experienced.

Death is the end of our journey through this material world, yet it is the beginning of the new, infinite life and soul's journey towards its real source of origin. The unseen and invisible afterlife is of course mysterious and vague and has generated intense intrigue and interest. At the same time, different schools of thought have come forward throughout the ages to answer the endless stream of questions about life, death, and eternity. All these schools have hypothesized extensively to solve this enigma. Almost all Divine religions have discussed the purpose of life, human and Divine relationship, and the achievement of oneness.

In the next chapters, I will discuss and explain the secrets of life and light as seen by mystics: What is the shortest and surest way to God? How does one receive divine light? How does one achieve union with the Lord of the universe?

CHAPTER TWO

THE MYSTERY OF CREATION

Know they not how Allah creates (life) in the first instance, and then repeats it? That indeed is easy for Allah.

Tell them: travel in the earth and behold how He has created (man) in the first instance and thus, too, will God bring into being your second life.

Surely Allah has the power to will anything.

(Quran 29:20-21)

§

The process of creation is continuous; He originates the creation and then repeats it. (Quran 10:5)

§

But the process is gradual and proceeds by stages.
All perfect praise belongs to Allah,
Who nourishes, sustains, and leads stage by
stage towards perfection all the worlds. (Quran 1:2)

When we look at the amazing, ever-expanding, and infinite universe—with billions of galaxies and trillions of stars set in an orderly fashion—our intellects become lost in utter astonishment. There are more than 170 billion galaxies spanning across space, each one comprising somewhere betweem 100 million to a trillion stars (averaging 200 billion stars). We humans inhabit a tiny speck in this vast universe, on planet earth, orbiting an average-sized sun, which is but one of 200 billion other stars in our Milky Way galaxy. Never before have we so unraveled the mysteries of the physical cosmos, which is much larger than we can truly comprehend.

The distances in the outer space are measured in light years. A light year is the distance light travels in one year, which is about 5.87 trillion miles. Our galaxy is part of the small group of galaxies known as the *local group*. This group spans a volume of space about 6 to 8 million light years across and has a combined mass of 2 trillion suns. Some of the nearest galaxies are 90 million light years away from our Milky Way, whereas proto-galaxies are 10 trillion light years distant.

According to a more recent astronomical estimate, the diameter of the known universe is at least 93 billion light years. At this time, whether the universe is finite or infinite, is beyond our comprehension.

Our sun, which is a million times larger in volume than the earth, has been burning since its birth, 4.6 billion years ago. It has been generating and consuming more than half a billion tons of hydrogen each second since its inception, yet, still there is more than enough in the core of the sun to keep on burning for another 6 billion years.

Our universe is continually expanding at a more accelerated rate than ever before. As a matter of fact, it is running away from itself in all directions, like the raisins in a rising loaf of raisin bread. Being aware of such an explosive expansion makes us wonder how this same universe could have been much smaller at one point in time. The whole cosmos came into existence in what is known as the Big Bang, originating probably from a dime-size drop of matter—some 13.7 billion years ago.

According to the multi-universe theory, our universe is a part of a set of disconnected and independent "universes"—although that is partly semantics, because all these different "universes" can also be thought of as different aspects of one. However, in the multi-universe concept, each "universe" has its own space and time and is subject to its own physical laws. These universes are other than non-physical, esoteric realms or hierarchies and are not related to the spiritual, metaphysical, and alternate planes of consciousness.

Though we may never fully understand the reasons behind the universe, we find this wonderful chain of creation subject to laws of physics and working perfectly in harmony. Not a single sign of negligence or disorder is evident throughout its creation or functioning. From giant stars to the smallest of atoms, each one is working according to an established principle and formula based on wisdom and knowledge.

This splendid, mysterious, incomprehensible, and infinite universe—with all that it contains—did not come into existence from nothingness, as an accident, or randomly. It certainly did not spring out of senseless ether or from an unintelligent source of energy by itself. The majority of scientists, physicists, philosophers, theologians, and learned people have agreed that the universe was created in an instant in the Big Bang, simultaneously with the time and space.

Common sense dictates that the Creator of such a vast, grand, and complicated universe should possess attributes of life, knowledge, wisdom, power, intention, hearing, sight, speech, and so on. As the Quran says, "Verily the knowledge of God surrounds everything." (Quran 65:12).

Knowledge and wisdom—which are attributes of the Absolute Being—are the causal agents and sustaining reasons of this cosmos, along with everything that exists. In the words of scripture, "And the sun goes on a set course. This is the measure set by the most powerful and learned God. And for the moon We have determined stages, until it diminishes like an old date palm branch. Neither can the sun overtake the moon nor the night forestall the day. All are moving in set circles" (Quran 36:38-40).

The Creator of the universe is infinitely good. He is the God of mercy, the bestower of all bounties, and the most beautiful. He is one, the only, and the unique. He has no partner, nor is anything like Him. He is constant and free from all defects. His essence is only His. He is before the before and after the after—eternal. He always was and He always will be, forever. He is everlasting, all knowing, all seeing, and all hearing. He possesses neither shape nor form, and He is other than all we know or can imagine. As a Persian Sufi poet has said,

O thou! Who's art above conjecture, imagination, fancy, and whim.
And all that has been said, heard, and read about.
The book of thy praise will be finished and life will come to an end.
But as yet we shall be left in the first step of thy praise.

God created each and every thing from nothingness and can turn everything into nothingness. If he spread out this universe with a Big Bang, He can wrap it up in an instant with a Big Crunch. In the words of scripture, "On that day We shall roll up skies as written scrolls are rolled up; and as We brought into being the first creation, so we shall bring it anew, a promise which We have willed upon Ourselves; behold, We are able to do all things." (Quran 21:104).

COSMIC DREAM

I have always pondered over the story of the creation of the cosmos, the Big Bang, primary matter, primordial light, and so on. Often, I have contemplated the wonders of the birth and rebirth of stars, of constellations, of galaxies, and of the entire universe. One day, after a long and deep meditation on the words of God, "To be" (*Kun Faya Koon*), I was graced by an extraordinary vision, which suddenly burst on my consciousness.

I beheld a column of amazingly bright, living light descending from above, bursting into flames, and transforming the whole scene into a strange phenomenon. It was an explosion of lights and colors of different intensities and hues, as if I were witnessing the Big Bang. Circles of lights and whirlpools of flames were all around me. There were splashes of lights reflecting red, yellow, orange, and gold, blending all together perfectly with the freshness of life. Everything was shining. The beauty of the scene was awesome beyond compare. It seemed as if The Great Artist (*Al Musawwir*) has splashed a blend of bright colors and glittering lights on the canvas.

There was an array of explosions. One explosion would result in sending billions of sparks filling the entire space. Each spark in turn would explode into a billion more sparks. There were constant explosions, one after the other.

Oceanic clouds glittering with lights and changing colors were to be seen all over the cosmos. It was as if fountains of light were pouring out brilliant colors. I had a panoramic view, and the whole universe lay bare before my eyes. Everything was foaming, vibrating, and milling before my vision. I was in the center of all this, awestruck, astonished beyond measure, and motionless. It seemed as if the entire drama of existence was replayed only for me to behold. It was simply a manifestation of His imagination or merely a reflection of His Essence. I felt that the entire universe was being created in my consciousness. The dazzling lights, like fireworks, were spreading beyond the farthest boundaries of the cosmos. It was an indescribable experience. Stars, constellations, and galaxies were coming one after the other and were circling around me in a Divine dance. Sparks of light emanated everywhere, as a pouring rain, every spark transforming into a star, galaxy, or universe, and all of this floating and foaming in a fathomless ocean of oneness. It was the most breathtaking display of God's infinite beauty and creative power.

I was intoxicated with rapturous ecstasy. My entire being was whirling along with the revolution of the planets. All the created entities were singing His praises and extolling His glory. I could hear His voice throughout the cosmos. The humming sound of the words of God "To be" (*Kun Faya Koon*) was ceaselessly reverberating in the cosmos with the constant birth and rebirth of the celestial bodies. Each moment there was a renewal of creation of all things in the universe. This creative activity is never-ending because, "He is the Creator at all times." Vision after vision of blinding lights and intense colors were being unfolded before my eyes. I was awestruck in my dream by this amazingly brilliant display. This spellbinding cosmic experience transformed my human consciousness in line with the Divine consciousness. I could clearly see through His eyes the drama of creation as it unfolded step by step before me. I was awestruck at this strange and amazing vision. It was without doubt one of my most incredible spiritual experiences.

§

God's will is eternal as He is. He does what He wills.

Everything in the universe exists because He willed it to be. He said "Be" and everything became, and all will be gone when He says "Be gone." This creative power of God is firmly asserted in the Quran, "He is Allah the Creator, the shaper out of naught, the fashioner, the designer. His are the attributes of perfection. All that is in Heavens and on earth extolls His glory; for He alone is Almighty and Wise." (Quran 59:24). He needs no one and all are in need of Him. He neither eats nor drinks, and sleep does not overcome Him. He begets not, nor is He begotten. He is the Creator and owner of everything that exists. He created our bodies and breathed his spirit into it, in the words of scripture, "And breathed into him of My spirit." (Quran 38:72).

§

He is the one Who created our eyes, ears, hands, feet, color of the skin, features, and intelligence. All good and evil are from Him. According to the scripture, "Evil and good are both from God the Almighty." (Quran)

§

No one has the right to question Him. All power belongs to Him and He governs all and everything. There is divine wisdom in His plans, and what He does we cannot comprehend. He does not become, He always was. He is alive, self-existent, and does not depend on anything or anyone. We all need Him and depend on Him. His Divine Essence is unknown to anyone but Himself, as scripture proclaims, "There is nothing like unto Him and He alone is All Hearing, All Seeing." (Quran 42:11)

§

He has no form or shape. He cannot be seen by visible eyes, touched, or tasted. Yet, He can be known by His attributes. For, He is the Light, the Truth, the Guide, and the Source of all goodness. He is the most Merciful of Merciful, the Forgiver, the Generous, the Rewarder of thankfulness, the Giver, the Loving one, the Glorious, the Beautiful, the Bestower of all bounties, the Just, the Responder to prayers, and the All Comprenending.

According to Sufi metaphysics, the creation of the cosmos is explained in light of the famous *hadith qudsi* which states, "I was a hidden treasure; I loved to be known; therefore I created the creation so that I might be known."

The whole universe came into being through the interplay of the Divine Names and attributes. The Names of God are not just words, but actual realities corresponding with particular aspects of the Essence. Everything in the cosmos is a mirror in which God's face (determinations of the Essence) can be seen. This is why those who have esoteric vision can see God everywhere and in everything.

By creating the universe, God causes multiplicity to appear from the chamber of unity. The universe of multiplicity is thus a magnificent display of His Names and attributes exhibiting the infiniteness of God's creative capabilities and perfection. According to the above-mentioned *hadith*, God's mercy and love are the causes of all creation. In fact the existence of the universe in itself is an act of kindness and infinite mercy that flows from God.

The universe reflects the stunning beauty of its supreme Creator and displays His qualities constantly in every moment: "Every day He appears with a new glory" (Quran 55:29). Ibn Al Arabi therefore said, "The whole cosmos is the locus of manifestations for Divine Names."

Not only all things come from God but in a way they also manifest God. Divine Names are the creative forces and latent possibilities inherent in God. God created Adam in His Own image or upon His Own form that is upon the form of the Name *Allah* because this Name contains and embraces all the ninety-nine most beautiful Names. Thus Human beings contain all the meanings as well as the potential to attain perfection by meditating on the Name *Allah* and can therefore assume the character traits of God. God has three books—the Quran, the universe, and the Human Being—all displaying and announcing His signs and pointing to His limitless glory. Out of all of these, the Human Being is the greatest of all the books of God. Humans are the only means for God to manifest His Essence, or hidden treasure to its full extent so as to achieve the purpose of creation. The Quran and the universe both manifest His glory, but neither can know it fully. In order to be known and loved, God needs human beings who can fully comprehend the knowledge of His Essence. Other creatures in the universe display some of God's Names and qualities, but not all of them. Only Human beings can manifest this hidden treasure in its totality.

Human beings are the most perfect creations of God the Most High because they have the ability to manifest every existent thing in the universe within themselves. The Divine sees His Essence in the mirror of the perfect human beings. That is why they were selected—for trust and not just for sport.

Divine Essence is beyond human comprehension and therefore cannot be determined and defined. The Name *Allah* stands for Divine Essence. *Allah* also refers to all the Names and qualities of God and is the root cause of all creation and manifestations. *Allah* denotes both the personal and impersonal aspects of the Divinity. It signifies the one Reality, which is absolute and infinite.

It is through the sacred Names revealed by God in the Quran that men and women can return to Him by contemplating and meditating on them. It is through the practice of remembrance and meditation that we can realize who we really are and draw closer to the light of God.

The Quran refers to its own verses as *signs* (*ayat*), which serve as reminders for people to turn unto God. The Quran also refers to the creatures and the cosmos as the *signs* of the Almighty. Everything in the universe displays God's *signs* and glory. So is everything in ourseleves a manifestation of His Names and attributes (signs): "We shall show them Our signs upon the horizon and in themselves" (Quran 41:53).

The first thing God created was the light of Prophet Muhammad (pbuh)—his spirit—from the light of His beauty. As He has said, "I created the spirit of Muhammad (pbuh) from the light of My countenance" (*hadith*).

Then, after that, God created the heavenly Throne from the light of Muhammad's (pbuh) eyes and from the heavenly Throne; He created all the rest of existing entities.

Sheikh Abdul Qadir Jilani (may God be pleased with him), in his book *Sirr al Asrar*, and quoting Prophet Muhammad (pbuh) said, "The first thing God created was my spirit and light. God also created pen and intellect as the first objects." This means that they are all the same. They are all the Muhammadan Reality, which is collectively called the *light* because it is pure and pristine. As God says, "There has now come to you from God a light and a clear Book" (Quran 5:15). This light is also called *intellect* because it comprehends universal truths. It is called *pen* as well because it is the instrument of transmission of God's knowledge in the realms of letters.

The light of Muhammad (pbuh) is thus the origin of all the entities that exist, the first of all beings, and the highest manifestation of God's attributes. The Prophet (pbuh) has said, "I am from God, and the believers are from me" (*hadith*). Sheikh Abdul Qadir Jilani further explained that "God created all spirits from him (Prophet Muhammad, pbuh), in the realm of Divinity in the best of molds. As a matter of fact *Muhammad* is the name of all perfect human beings in that realm, and he is the original home."

Prophet Hazrat Muhammad (pbuh) is the best of God's creation, the seal of the prophets, the mercy unto the worlds and all humanity until the end of time. The essence of prophethood has always been present in his first created soul, even before the creation of Adam, the first man, for Prophet Muhammad (pbuh) himself has said, "I was a prophet when Adam was between water and clay" (*hadith*).

Though he declared prophethood in the body at the age of forty, he was the first prophet in creation and the last in resurrection. Muhammad (pbuh) is the perfect human being, the living Quran, and the role model for all Muslims. He was sent to complete excellence of character. All the seekers of the truth follow his footsteps in order to come closer to the light of God and to achieve union with Him.

Prophet Muhammad (pbuh) is the greatest portal of God's light. In Islamic mysticism it is through him that all Divine blessings, favors, light, wisdom, and knowledge flow to the seekers. His love and reality is the love and reality of God: "If you love God, follow me, and God will love you" (Quran 3:31).

Prophet Muhammad (pbuh) further stressed this fact in a *hadith*,

"None of you have real faith unless I am dearer unto him than his father, his child, and all mankind" (*Bukhari*).

To fully understand the spiritual aspects of the prophet's life—to whom God revealed the ultimate truths of His creation—is impossible. However, for all of his lovers, his *faqr (poverty of spirit)* and mysticism is a living example to be followed.

Chapter Three

REMEMBRANCE OF GOD, THE LOVING ONE

I am as My servant thinks of Me, and I am with him when he remembers Me. If he remembers Me in private, I remember him with in Myself. If he remembers Me in company, I remember him in better company.

(*Hadith* qouted by Hazrat Sheikh Syed Abdul Qadir Jilani in *Sirr Al Asrar*)

Individual Sufi masters and organized Sufi orders have both described different paths leading to union with God. When one Sufi teacher was asked about the way to God, he replied, "There are as many ways to God as the number of created beings." However, although there may be countless paths, commemorating the Names of God (Allah) is the surest way to achieve the knowledge of reality—that being the knowledge of oneness. The more you remember God through His Names, the closer you come to the Divine light. God Himself says, "Remember Me, and I will in return remember you" (Quran 2:152).

For mystic lovers the ultimate destination is God Himself. How Sufis reach this goal is by adhering strictly to the laws of *shariah*, the basic tenets of which are the five pillars of Islam. These in turn are but to remember, to contemplate, to concentrate, and to meditate on God.

Meditation on the word *Allah*, the unique and supreme personal Name of God, is the secret code to unravel the mysteries of the Essence and the Named. This enigma has been discussed and elaborated on by all Sufi masters, and they have all agreed that the name and the named are the same.

REMEMBRANCE

Remembrance of God is the main occupation of all Muslims, and especially for those who love God dearly. Mentioning His personal Name, *Allah*, or His other attributive names is done by performing daily prayers, reciting the Quran, and partaking in all other spiritual practices. Remembering God by constantly reciting the word *Allah* (*kalimat ullah*), is the same as glorifying God, thanking Him, and keeping Him above everything. We should speak of Him as if we see Him. Commemorating His name is the best way to keep Him in our minds and hearts. As the saying goes, "When you love somebody you talk about them." This is achieved by constant *dhikr*, which is the practice of reciting His Name.

Thus the first step towards achieving union and Divine knowledge is the remembrance of God by tongue. This practice leads us to assimilate the name and the named in our minds and hearts. As the Quran admonishes, "Allah's are the most beautiful names, so call on Him thereby" (7:180). God Almighty says as well, "Remember God while standing, sitting, and sleeping" (Quran 4:103).

The word *Allah* is the easiest of His Names to recite. By perpetual commemoration we can imprint the word of his Essence in our minds and carve it in our hearts. The Prophet Muhammad (pbuh) said, "God has ninety-nine Names, one less than a hundred; whoever, counts them will achieve eternal bliss" (*hadith*).

As already mentioned, out of His ninety-nine Names mentioned in the Quran, the greatest and the most supreme one is His personal Name, *Allah*. All the other attributive Names are contained and hidden in this one. The whole Quran—which is the uncreated, pure, and living word of God—is summarized in the *Al Fatiha* or "Opening Chapter" of the Quran. This "Opening Chapter" itself is contained in the Quranic phrase, "*Bismillah Ar Rahman Al Rahim*" ("In the Name of Allah, the infinitely Good and the boundlessly Merciful"). The *Bismillah* phrase, in turn, is condensed in the word *Allah*. Therefore, *Allah* is the most powerful and the greatest name for *dhikr* (meditation) and commemoration, for all Sufis.

Allah, the Name of God, is thus a great gift to all seekers, because God does not have form, shape, body, or likeness. Nobody knows His Essence, which is beyond comprehension and imagination. Therefore, all that we know about Him is His supreme personal Name, *Allah*, which denotes His Essence only. By commemorating the Name, we can reach the Divine presence and come closer to His light. As, God has revealed His Names in the scripture, Himself, therefore, His Essence is present mysteriously in His Names.

Thus, the goal of all Islamic practices is the remembrance of Allah, through His Name, but it must be in a manner worthy of His sacred Reality. The invocation, remembrance, and commemoration of the Divine

Names should be done with full presence of mind and heart: "No prayer except with presence of mind is acceptable" (*hadith*).

Sufi metaphysics is primarily based on the Divine Names and Divine attributes revealed in the Quran. Over time, Sufis developed the important science of the Divine Names, which are not only reflected in the cosmos as God's "Self knowledge through Self-Manifestation and Self-Discloser," but, His Names also act, for Sufis, as a means of unveiling His Essence and methods by which the commemorator can gain access to Him.

Although in the Islamic era, *Allah* is the supreme and all—comprehensive Name of God, in the pre-Islamic era the word *Allah* was used to denote the supreme deity or the Creator, God. All Arab-speaking followers of the Abrahamic faith—both Jews and Christians—used the Name *Allah* in reference to God.

The word *Allah* is derived from *Al-Ilah*, meaning "the One God," Who is Unique, Omnipotent, the Creator of the cosmos, and the All Powerful. The word *Allah* can be found in Syriac, Aramaic, and Hebrew languages in the forms of *Aloho, Elaha, Allaha,* or *Elohim*.

The word *Allah* is reserved only for Him. It is not derived from any other name or root. God has truly said, "Do you know anyone worthy of the same name as He." (Quran 19:65). When the word *Allah* is broken down in Arabic into its component letters, it still indicates His incomparable Essence. Any combination of the component letters of *Allah* and each constituent part is His Name only. This is a unique quality inherent in His personal Name.

Removing one letter at a time yields the following Divine Names:

ALLAH—LILLAH—LAHU—HU

The entire creation, according to Sufi philosophy, is produced from these letters and other names of Allah, which express the unlimited attributes of Allah. The ninety-eight attributive Names of Allah and the one proper Name, *Allah*, are thus reflected in the universe and fully manifested in the perfect human being. The beauty, grandeur, sublimity, strength, power, knowledge, wisdom, and love of Divinity are manifest in all objects to the extent with which God has entrusted them with it. His love and magnificence emanate all around us without an end. All the existing manifestations and the endless chains of creation exist by the virtue of His Names. Ibn e Abbas (May God be pleased with him) said, "In everything there is a name from amongst His Names, and the name of everything comes from His Name."

Thus, Divine reality is a spoken reality and so necessitates speaking beings to perceive it. The entire universe could not exhibit all His attributes and Beauty, so He created the human being, who is capable of holding and expressing His Eternal Beauty through the process of commemorating his Names. Both God and humans are speaking realities. Thus, in the mirror of the human being, the Divine can see and hear Himself: "The heart is a mirror in which the Beauty of God is reflected" (*hadith*). On the day of creation all the souls were created by Almighty Allah from His own spirit, in the words of scripture, "And I blew my spirit into Adam'" (Quran 38:72).

In short, human beings have linguistic traces of the Divine in them. God has placed linguistic traces of Divinity in each one of us, especially in our hearts, in the form of His personal Name, *Allah*. The seed of His Name is embedded in the soil of our hearts as a gift of Divine grace.

When we descended from the realm of spirits into the realm of this material world, into an elemental body, we lost our contact with the Divine. We became involved and preoccupied with worldly matters to the extent that we totally forgot our real abode and source. The only way we can come closer to our source and the light of God is by remembering God, commemorating and reciting His personal Name, *Allah*, so that the seed of His personal Name, which has been placed in our hearts by the Divine, is nourished and blossoms into a firmly rooted tree of faith. Prophet Hazrat Muhammad (pbuh) has said in this respect, "There is polish for everything that takes away the rust, and the polish of the heart is the remembrance, the invocation of God" (*hadith*).

The Prophet (pbuh) also said, "God created man in His own image," or in another way, "Allah created Adam upon His own form." Here the word *Allah* is specifically mentioned, which is to say, "upon the form of the word

Allah." Because all the other attributive Names of God are contained in the word *Allah*, therefore, Adam in himself reflects all the Names of God. That is why God said, "He taught Adam all the Names" (Quran 2:31).

According to a Persian Sufi poet,

The earth, the heaven, the throne, and the chair,

All are within you O man,

You need not seek them outside,

And whom are you asking for that.

Therefore, all that we seek is within us. We only need to look inward. God the Most High proclaimed, "And We have kept all things in a perfect human being" (Quran 36:12). And scripture further proclaimed, "And His signs are within yourselves but you do not perceive" (Quran 51:20).

Ibne Al Arabi wrote in Fusus Al Hikam, "Man is the spirit of the cosmos, and the cosmos without man is like a proportioned and well—balanced body: ready and waiting for God to breathe His spirit into it, but lifeless as long as man has not appeared." It is for this reason that Ibne Al Arabi calls the perfect man the "pillar of the cosmos; without him the cosmos would collapse and die, which is precisely what will happen at the end of time when the perfect man departs from this world for the hereafter."

To become a perfect man or woman, one needs to commemorate and constantly recite the Names of God. The process of constant repetition in fact will result in your assuming the traits of the Names of Allah, as is commanded in the following *hadith*: "Clothe yourself with the excellent qualities of God the Most High. God has ninety-nine virtues. Whosoever puts one of them on will surely enter the Garden" (Prophet Muhammad, pbuh).

It follows, then that a person is not perfect by the mere fact that he or she is born as a human being, but by following the spiritual path—remembering God, contemplating, concentrating, and meditating on His Divine Names, and especially by meditating on His supreme Name, *Allah*.

One cannot achieve perfection without knowledge, because it is the means by which one arrives at the realization and affirmation of the

Oneness of the Lord of all the worlds. In Islamic mysticism, knowledge of the self is of vital importance, as the Prophet (pbuh) has said, "He who knows himself knows his Lord and his Creator and complies with His command" (*hadith*).

Comprehensive wisdom and knowledge is the direct experience of the Truth and should be pursued without hypocrisy and desire for fame. Illuminative knowledge, meaning the realization of oneness, can be attained by remembrance, reflection, contemplation, and meditation on the Name of God, *Allah*, the real source of Truth.

The practice of reflection is of vital importance in this respect.

Prophet Hazrat Muhammad (pbuh) has said the following, highlighting the value of reflection:

1. "A moment of reflection is worth more than a year of worship." If someone truly reflects on the details and importance of the branches of religious knowledge and in reality comprehends its significance, then a moment of reflection is worth more than a year of worship. It is not enough to profess the formula of faith and follow the Divine law, but one should have a deeper understanding of the inner dimensions of the religion.

2. "A moment of reflection is worth more than seventy years of worship."
   If someone reflects for a moment on the true significance of worship incumbent upon him or her and not only realizes worship as a time with God but also a means for knowing and loving Him, that kind of reflection is worth more than seventy years of worship. Once we have acquired faith, surrendered to the will of God, and understood the basic teachings of Islam, then we can focus our efforts on worshiping God as if we are able to see Him. That is why Hazrat Ali (may God be pleased with him) said, "I would not worship a Lord whom I do not see."

3. "A moment of reflection is worth more than a thousand years of worship."

If someone reflects for a moment on the illuminative knowledge of Allah and has inner experience of His Divine presence, that is worth more than a thousand years of worship.

God has said, "I did not creat *Jinn* and Mankind except to worship Me." (Quran 51:56). That is to say, "To know and understand Me." If someone does not know and understand Him, how can he worship Him? Sufis in this regard prefer to say, "To know and love Me." What matters to them is knowing and loving God through meditation.

Inner knowledge is attained by removing the veils, especially of the lower self, from the mirror of the heart, and cleaning and polishing it by the remembrance of God. It will then reflect the treasure (the Beauty of Allah) hidden in the heart's core. Those who seek to keep God in their hearts forever must do so by commemorating His beautiful Names or by meditating on these Names.

Illuminative knowledge that comes from the direct personal experience of God is of two types:

1. Knowledge of the attributes (*sifat*) of Allah.
2. Knowledge of His Essence (*dhat*).

Knowledge of the attributes can be attained by counting and reciting the ninety-eight attributive Names of Allah over and over again, and can be experienced by the physical body in both domains. However, knowledge of the Essence can best be attained by reciting the Name *Allah*, the proper Name of God, constantly and can be experienced by the spirit fully in the hereafter. These experiences are attainable by the exoteric (the sacred law, *shariah*) and esoteric (direct understanding, *marifah*) knowledge as mentioned above.

The Prophet Hazrat Muhammad (pbuh) said, "Knowledge is twofold: knowledge conveyed by tongue and the knowledge conveyed by the heart." Regarding the remembrance of Allah, Sheikh Hazrat Syed Abdul Qadir

Jilani (may God be pleased with him) said, "There are different levels of remembrance and each has different ways. Some are expressed outwardly with audible voice. Some are felt inwardly and silently from the center of the heart. It then rises to the soul; then reaches the realm of the secret, further to the hidden; and to the most hidden of the hidden. How far the remembrance permeates, the level it reaches, depends solely on the extent to which Allah in His bounty has guided us."

Traditionally it is said that the spirit entered Adam, and hence every man, by the personal Name of God, *Allah*. As God says, "And We blew our spirit therein" (Quran 38:72).

The spirit of God is the word *Allah*, which is the beginning and the end of all the cosmos and creation and which is directly related to the Everlasting, All powerful, unparalleled Creator and His Magnificent Essence.

When someone recites and commemorates the Name *Allah*, he or she directly establishes a link and a relationship with the Named, because the Name and the Named are essentially the same. He or she therefore, invokes all the attributes contained in the Name *Allah*. Constant recitation and commemoration releases God's favors, blessings, and love.

The more one remembers God, the more one comes closer to Him (His light). In the words of scripture: "Whosoever strongly clutched the Name of God, found guidance towards the right path" (Quran 3:101). The word of God, His beautiful Names, and especially His Supreme Name, *Allah*, are synonymous with the light of God, pure and pristine. All the attributes of Allah are encompassed by His light, which is the closest to the Essence of God. This fact is frequently mentioned in the Quran: "Allah is the light of the Heavens and of the earth" (Quran 24:35). Another verse stated, "O Muhammad, We have sent down to you a manifest light" (Quran 4:174). In yet another place God commanded man, "O faithful, follow the light that We have sent down with our Prophet" (Quran 7:157). Therefore, it is abundantly clear that commemorating the Name of Allah constantly with presence of heart and mind unfolds the light of God, which connects the commemorator with the commemorated: "To Him ascend (the light of) pure words and to Him mount (the light of) righteous deeds" (Quran 35:10).

Because all spiritual progress and esoteric advancement depend on the remembrance of Allah (reciting the Name of God), one must do so correctly. At first one should recite the word *Allah* by tongue, then recite it within one's heart and mind, paying full attention to the Essence of the Lord and His Name. One should pay undivided attention and approach Him with love and sincerity, as if one is seeing the Divine and is in His presence.

The worshiper should close his or her thoughts to anything else, close his or her eyes to any other object, and close his or her ears to any other sound. One should concentrate only on the Name of the Divine and open one's heart to the light of Allah to receive. In this regard, a Sufi poet has written, "Close the eyes, ears, and lips. If you miss the Divine truth then ridicule me."

Islamic mysticism lays profound stress on the intention of the heart and presence of mind. The intention of the seeker, by commemorating the Name of Allah, should be to accept and surrender to the will of God: "Man's actions are counted with his intentions" (*hadith*). As one traditional saying has it, "In the eyes of God, no prayer, except with the presence of mind is acceptable." (hadith).

The central theme of Islamic mysticism and all the devotion performed including the five pillars of Islam is to concentrate on the name of *Allah*. The object and goal of these spiritual and religious endeavors is to come closer to the light of *Allah* and achieve oneness with that unparalleled and imperishable Essence.

FORMULA OF FAITH

The most essential and fundamental pillar of Islam is the acceptance and recitation of the formula of faith (*kalima*), without which one can neither become a Muslim nor follow the path of truth (Sufism). The formula of faith (*La Illaha Illallah, Muhammad ur Rasul Allah*) means *None is worthy of worship except Allah, and Muhammad (pbuh) is the Prophet of Allah*. One has to negate everything else in the cosmos and affirm the reality of *Allah*. Moreover, one has to set one's eyes, mind, and heart on the remembrance of *Allah* and concentrate and meditate on His Essence only. By declaring the formula of faith, we negate all other gods—that is everything else save Him. Thus the formula of faith (*La Ilaha Illallah*) is regarded as the greatest commemoration of all, the foundation of faith, and the epitome of all spirituality. The Prophet of Islam has said, "He who recited the formula of faith, *La Illaha Illallah, Muhammad ur Rasul Allah*, entered paradise without reckoning and undergoing chastisement." In this regard, in a *hadith*, Prophet Muhammad (pbuh) has said, "If the seven heavens and seven earths were put in one scale, they would be outweighed by *La Ilaha Ill Allah* in the other."

As we accept and surrender ourselves to the Omnipotent and Omniscient Creator of the universe, we are under His loving care and should have firm faith without any doubt in Him. "Surely, He is the best disposer of all affairs." (Quran 3:173).

For Him everything impossible is possible, whether small or big. He is infinitely good and boundlessly merciful. His mercy encompasses everything in the universe. He is merciful, kind, and loving to us even if we are unbelievers and sinners, because mercy, kindness, love, forgiveness, and all other attributes are in His Essence, and He cannot be other than His attributes: "My mercy encompasses everything" (Quran 7:156).

PRAYER

Similarly daily prayer is performed only to remember, glorify, and thank *Allah* for everything that He has given us: our lives, our bodies, our minds, our health, our eyes, our ears, and our intelligence are gifts from Him, as tradition asserts: "I have created the universe for you, and you for Myself" (*hadith qudsi*). He thus mandated, "Perform the prayers for commemorating Me" (Quran 20:14). Elsewhere, He said, "He certainly achieved salvation who purified himself and performed the prayers by commemorating the Name of his Lord" (Quran 87:14-15).

It is clearly evident that the first two pillars of Islam are manifestations of this single act—commemoration of *Allah*. God, therefore, tells us to remember Him and draw near to Him by reciting His beautiful Names.

All the Divine attributes are hidden dormant in our hearts, and it is our task to bring them into our consciousness and live by them.

God the Most High wanted to be known, remembered, and loved. He created the universe with everything that exists out of His yearning love. The whole cosmos with all its beauty, grandeur, and magnificence in reality is a manifestation of His attributes.

Prayer is a direct, one-on-one opportunity to talk to the loving, kind, and merciful Lord of the universe without any intermediary. It is a time with God for conversation and mutual fulfillment.

In prayer, you are standing right in front of *Allah*, face to face, you are in His very presence and you talk directly to Him. Prayer is but to glorify Him and thank Him for all His goodness, blessings, and gifts that He has poured on us unconditionally, as scripture asserts: "Glorify the Name of thy Lord, the Most High" (Quran 87:1). In prayer we repeatedly chant, "God is Great, and Glory be to my Lord, the Most High. Only He may be glorified and praised for He is the Lord of Glory, Eternal, Self-Existent, All Perfection, All knowing, All Hearing, and All Seeing." Prayer is remembering, glorifying, and thanking God the Most High. Prayer should not be performed merely as a religious duty or obligation, but should be performed with extreme devotion, sincerity, and for the love of Allah. It should be done with complete presence of mind and attention of the heart. In every act and performance the heart should be inclined towards God and the mind should concentrate and meditate on Him only. You should think and imagine that you are in His Divine presence as though His beautiful light is shining on you like a pouring rain.

Recite the prayers, commemorate His Name with a joyful heart, and pay undivided attention to His Essence, because, God looks at the heart of the commemorator and worshiper only, not to his words and actions of his body, as tradition has advised us: "God does not behold your figure nor actions but peers through your heart and intention" (*hadith*).

Thus, the real secret of remembering God lies in the mind and heart and not in external performance and verbal commemoration. Many people engage themselves in verbal utterances all night long while their minds and hearts are totally absent from their ceremonial prayers. These are just acts of hard labor, in vain.

My grandfather, Faqir Nur Muhammad Sarwari Qaderi, narrated such an incidence in his book *Irfan*, as follows: "Once I was retiring in a mosque to perform *etikaf* during the last ten days of the Holy month of Ramadan. There was another man also in the mosque to sit for the performance of *etikaf*. He kept awake all the night and uttered '*Allah, Allah*' till morning and did not sleep for a moment. When I saw this, I went and said to him, 'O man of Allah! What are you doing and reciting all night long?' He said his spiritual guide had commanded him to repeat and utter the Name of *Allah* twelve thousand times every night and that he had been doing this since the last ten years, regularly. I asked him if he had received any sort of light, observation, or any other benefit in the long course of ten years. He replied, 'No, nothing have I felt or received of that kind, but I am performing and obeying the word of my spiritual guide and master, and the day this order is fulfilled, my heart feels happy within and I am satisfied.' I said to the poor fellow, 'Your labor is very hard, but it is fruitless and valueless.'"

Thousands of people such as him practice ceremonial prayers and devotion without any use or benefit. As Almighty God says, "They gain nothing except toil and tiresomeness" (Quran).

Allah is Everlasting, Eternal, All Knowing, All Seeing, and All Hearing. He is also Omnipotent, near, and responsive, as scripture tells us: "And when my servants ask thee concerning Me, surely, I am near. I answer the prayer of the supplicant when he calls upon Me. So should they hear My call and believe in Me, that they may walk in the right way" (Quran 2:186).

He sees everything that is visible or invisible. He hears what is audible and inaudible. Neither does distance prevent Him from hearing, nor does darkness prevent Him from seeing. He is aware of the tiny ant on a black rock in pitch darkness. He knows the vibrations of protons and neutrons inside an atom and fully knows the secrets and intentions of the hearts of which even you are not aware. He has the knowledge of everything before it exists and He is aware of it after it is gone. Hence, there is no reason that a man may worship and call upon Him sincerely with devotion and love and He should not respond by saying, "Here I am, O My obedient servant."

It is of vital importance to know that presence of mind and heart is mandatory in devotion, submission, invocation, commemoration, and meditation.

All the fundamentals and pillars of Islam are based on the commemoration of His personal Name, *Allah*. This is the key to the gnosis and union with the Essence of the Creator. All the good deeds and praiseworthy virtues, especially the five pillars of Islam, are various manifestations of His personal Name, *Allah*. God the Most High has repeatedly stressed the importance of prayers in order to be rememebered.

If we want to come closer to our Creator and draw nearer to His light, we have to cleanse and purify our hearts from the love of worldly occupations and begin the inner transformation by getting rid of our lower selves. As we know, God's attributes are reflected in His creation and found to a greater degree in human beings. These Divine attributes are innately hidden in each one of us, and we have to strive to bring them out to the utmost degree. As God has said, "And those who strive towards us will be shown our path." (Quran 29:69). This can be achieved by remembering God, by reciting His beautiful Names, and especially His supreme and comprehensive Name, *Allah*. When the heart of a devoted commemorator recites His Name, *Allah*, it produces pure light, waves and vibrations in the invisible world above that invariably reach to the Essence of God. God has indicated this by saying, "I am very near to man, closer than his jugular vein and self. If anyone desires to meet Me, he can do so by commemorating Me" (Quran 50:16). It is also evident from the following Quranic verse, "Remember Me; I will remember thee". (Quran 2:152).

Thus, reciting the Name of Allah is the sole method of connecting the commemorator with the commemorated and the worshiper with the worshiped. This esoteric connection is established via thoughts of the devotee in the act of commemoration with the incomparable and peerless Essence of God the Most high. Through constant and perpetual commemoration of God the Most high, the inferior qualities of the lower self gradually disappear and one acquires the praiseworthy and pure attributes of the Creator. This eventually brings nearness and union with the Lord, and finally Almighty God absorbs him in His Divine Light, as He said, "God is pleased with them and they are pleased with God" (Quran 8:98). Then, as scripture asserts, "They love Him, He loves them" (Quran 5:54).

THE LAST REVELATION

The glorious Quran is the true living word of God. It is His final word and revelation. The Holy Quran is the last of the Divine scriptures; its meaning is infinite and forever. It contains Allah's commands, judgments, and laws that pertain to all His creation. His word is the most powerful and the root cause of all that exists.

We have already seen that the entire Quran and all its chapters begin with the Name of God, "In the Name of Allah, the most Compassionate, the most Merciful." We have learned that the whole Quran is condensed in the opening chapter, which is considered a summary and mission statement of the Quran. We have also learned that the opening chapter in itself is contained in the *Bismillah*: "In the Name of Allah, the most Compassionate, the most Merciful." Similarly, we have been taught that the gist and cream of the *Bismillah* is the sacred Name of God, *Allah*. Therefore, we have learned that we can say confidently that the magnificent Quran is contained in the personal Name of God, *Allah*, like a tree in the seed. In short the word *Allah* is the DNA of the entire cosmos and everything contained in it. The Quran is a detailed commentary and commemoration of the Name *Allah* and His attributes. Therefore, when someone remembers God by His personal Name, *Allah*, it is as if he is remembering and honoring Him with all His attributes and the Quranic verses. By the grace of His personal Name, *Allah*, all the realities and hidden secrets of the Divine are revealed to the commemorator. The entire Quran is the praise, eulogy, magnification, sanctification, and glorification of the Exalted One.

THE GIFT OF QURAN

During the course of writing this book, I collected more than ten different English translations of the Holy Quran. I have in my possession the most famous, timeless, and wonderful translations, such as those by Ala-Hazrat Ahmed Raza Khan, Muhammad Asad, Muhammad Zafar Ali Khan, A. J Arberry, Muhammad Muhsin Khan, Majid Fakhry, M. Abdul Haleem, M Pickthal, N.J. Dawood, and Laleh Bakhtiar. Every verse that I intended to quote therein, I would look up all the different translations in order to fully understand its deeper and inner meaning. I would then contemplate and meditate upon them and ask Almighty God to bestow me with the insight and reveal to me what He really wanted to reveal.

One day, a pharmaceutical representatives came to see me. He has been visiting me for the last couple of years. When I met him, he said to me, "I have come to say goodbye today. I will not be working for my company anymore." At first, I was worried for him, for I thought that he must have been laid off due to downsizing of the company. But he told me otherwise and said, "I am joining a seminary school in my hometown to become a preacher. It has been my wish and heart's desire to do so for a long time. Finally, I am ready to pursue my calling." I was thrilled to hear that, and we started discussing religion.

He had quite an open mind about different religions. I told him that all monotheistic religions, especially Judaism, Christianity, and Islam are derived from the Abrahamic faith. All of these religions believe in the Oneness of God and share the same fundamental tenets. In the broadest sense of the word, it is the One Reality that is the goal and destination of the followers of these faiths.

As he was departing, I told him, "I would like to give you a copy of the Holy Quran as a gift. I would like you to read it impartially with an open heart and see for yourself the truth revealed in its verses." He was quite delighted to hear that. I told him to come by next week and pick it up. He dropped by the following week according to our mutual arrangement, and I presented him with a copy of the Holy Quran translated by Muhammad Zafar Ali Khan.

After a few days, I needed to see some Quranic verses and compare the different translations. I was curious to see how Muhammad Zafar Ali Khan had translated them. I had also heard about the beautiful translation *The Message of Quran*, done by Muhammad Asad. However, I was unable to obtain that so far. Asad's translation is considered to be the most accurate and very close to the original meaning, even though the Quran can not be translated, because the living word of God is embodied in the Arabic language. However, in order to understand the Quran in depth, Asad's version is the most helpful.

Muhammad Asad was born in a Jewish family in Austria. After graduation he worked for a telegraph company and later became a correspondent and traveled to the Middle East, where he studied Arabic at Al Azhar University in Egypt. He was also well versed in the Jewish scripture. He converted to Islam in 1926, after long and thoughtful contemplation. He traveled all over the Arabian Peninsula with the Bedouin tribes for more than six years to learn the language of the Quran. The Bedouin tribes still speak the same language that had been spoken in the time of the Prophet.

One week later, on a Friday, my receptionist came into my office. She had a package in her hand and said that a lady had left this at the front window for you. I asked who she was. She said, "She did not say anything. She just dropped this package and left." I asked the receptionist again, "Was she one of our patients?" She said, "No, I have not seen her before."

As soon as I opened the package, I was delightfully surprised to see a beautiful translation of the Quran by Muhammad Zafar Ali Khan. In fact, it was a larger version of the Quran than the one I had given to the pharmaceutical representative who became a seminary student. My heart was overjoyed at this unexpected gift of the Word of God that had been delivered to me mysteriously.

A few days later, to my astonishment, one of my patient's father, who is an Iraqi refugee and a cleric, presented to me something unique. It was exactly what my heart had longed for some while. He gave me the most beautiful Quran as a gift translated by Muhammad Asad. He said, "I received this from the department of CAIR today. I just had this feeling in my heart that I should give this Quran to you."

This was truly a blissful moment for me that filled my heart with boundless joy. Time and again during the course of writing this book, I would come across books, references, and spiritual material that would help and inspire me. Most of the time thoughts and ideas would come to my mind as an inspiration while I was working—and sometimes even in my dreams.

PILGRIMAGE

Pilgrimage to the Holy House of Allah (*Kaaba*) is the fifth pillar of Islam. It is obligatory on those who have the financial means to visit the House of the Lord. Pilgrimage inculcates the spirit of sacrifice and devotion. One has to leave his family, friends, business, and all other worldly affairs behind to worship and commemorate *Allah* with solitude and peace of mind. All the rituals and ceremonies during the pilgrimage consist of praising *Allah*, remembering Him, and chanting His glory. The Kaaba (The House of the Lord) is a physical place of rendezvous of the self with the source, and pilgrimage is a rite of thanking the Lord for all His bounties and goodness. It is emphasized in the Quran that, "when you reach Arafat commemorate Allah near Muzdalifa". In another place it said, "and when you have performed the rites of pilgrimage, commemorate Allah as you commemorate your forefathers" (Quran 2:200).

FASTING: PURIFICATION OF THE SOUL

The third pillar of Islam is fasting in the month of Ramadan. During this month, Muslims fast from dawn until sunset and avoid eating, drinking, and sexual activity. This strenuous practice and ritual is done to cleanse the body and soul from all sorts of impurities. Muslims who observe the fast are encouraged and ordained to commemorate Allah, recite the Quran, perform supererogatory prayers, and give charity generously to achieve spiritual transformation and advancement.

The prescribed charity (*Zakat*) has to be given in the month of Ramadan. It is equal to 2.5 % of one's extra wealth and has a formula for calculation. It has to be given to the poor, needy, orphans, and widows, and can also be used for public welfare, propagation of religion, and other virtuous deeds.

Ramadan is a month of revelation, during which the Holy Quran was revealed, which laid the foundation of a new heavenly code of life that contains every commandment, full of wisdom and knowledge for all humanity.

Ramadan is the month of mercy and compassion, during which God showers His blessings on mankind and multiplies the rewards of good deeds.

God in a prophetic tradition said, "The fast is for Me, and I am the reward that comes with it." Fasting illuminates the heart, purifies the soul, and leads the spirit into the presence of God. Therefore, the Prophet Hazrat Muhammad (pbuh) said, "Make your bellies hungry, livers thirsty, and leave the world alone, then perhaps you may see God with your hearts."

It is also said, "For one who fasts, there is a double delight, delight in the breaking of the fast, and the delight in seeing the Everlasting One."

Sheikh Nizam Ud Din Awliya commenting on this said, "The delight of the faster in the breaking of the fast is not due to food or drink but that he experiences delight because he has completed the fast and now he is hopeful of the blessing of seeing God." He further explained, "Every act of obedience has a specific reward since the specific reward for the one who fasts is the blessing of a vision of the Lord, every time that he completes the fast he is overfilled with the joy of that blessing."

Fasting is a reminder of one's dependency on God. The great Sufi master Abu Madyan wrote, "I have examined the writings of the Prophets, the pious, the companions, the successors and the scholars of the past generations, yet I have not found anything that causes attainement of God the Most High without (the addition) of hunger. This is because, one who is hungry becomes humble, one who is humble begs, and the one who begs attains. So hold fast to hunger my brother and practice it constantly, for by means of it you will attain what you desire and will arrive at that for which you hope."

There are many stories of fasting in Muslim tradition. The fasting of Rabia Al Adwiya is one source of inspiration for mystics. It is narrated in Tazkirat Al Auliya that once Rabia fasted for a full week without drinking, eating, or sleeping. She prayed constantly to the One Being day and night. After a week she was extremely hungry and weak. In the meantime a visitor came to her door and brought some food as a gift. Rabia accepted it, and because it was in the dark of the night, she went to get a lamp. When she came back with the light, she found that the cat had overturned the bowl and spilled the food on the ground. "I will go and fetch a pitcher of water and break my fast with the water," she murmured to herself. When she had brought the water pitcher, the lamp had gone out. She tried to drink the water in the dark, but the pitcher fell out of her hands and broke. She sighed and lamented, "O Lord, what is this that you are doing to this helpless slave of yours?" She heard a Divine voice, "Have a care, if you want Me to bestow on thee all worldly blessings, but take away from thy heart the desire of Me. Love for Me and worldly blessings can never be brought together in a single heart. Rabia you desire one thing and I desire another. The two of them can never be joined in one heart." Rabia stated, "When I heard the Divine, I cut off my heart from worldly desires and after that whenever, I have prayed for the last thirty years, I have presumed it to be my last prayer."

All the religious acts, virtues, and fundamentals including the formula of faith, daily prayers, pilgrimage, fasting, and charity are but to remember, praise, glorify, and thank *Allah*. He is far and above everything in the universe and takes precedence over all.

One can come closer to the light of god by constant remembrance, performance of extra prayers and other spiritual acts of devotion and be completely absorbed in it. As God has said in a *hadith qudsi*, "An obedient servant of God approaches God Almighty through good deeds until He becomes his eyes, ears, hands, and tongue and he sees, hears, catches, and talks through Him."

Commemoration of *Allah* is the best of acts concerning devotion. It is narrated in a tradition that Prophet Moses (pbuh) said, "O my Lord, if Thou art nigh (near), I will address Thee softly and if afar I will do so loudly. I can hear Thy sweet voice but can't see Thee. Tell me where art Thou."

God replied, "I am to thy front and rear, right and left. O Moses! I sit with My slave when he commemorates Me and I am with him when he calls Me."

In another tradition God spoke to Moses (pbuh) and said, "Do you wish Me, O Moses, to stay with you in your house?" Moses (pbuh) fell prostrate and said, "O Lord! How can you stay with me in my house?" God replied, "I sit with one who remembers Me and whenever My slave seeks Me, he invariably finds Me."

The common factor in all these acts of faith is the commemoration of God, the Most High. The basic requirement in performing such acts of devotion to be acceptable to the Lord is the sincerity of the devotee and the passionate love of the seeker. Without love and humility no worship, prayer, or offering is fruitful.

Remembrance of God is the essence of religion. It has been mentioned in the Quran more than one hundred times. Believers have been advised to remember God abundantly. Allah has placed His remembrance above ritual prayer in value by making prayer a means of remembrance.

The Prophet Hazrat Muhammad (pbuh) in this regard said that the people of paradise will regret only the time when they were not engaged in the remembrance of Allah. The Prophet (pbuh) has also called the assemblies of remembrance (*dhikr*) as the gardens of paradise.

During the night of ascension, the Holy Prophet Hazrat Muhammad (pbuh) was taken to a place where he saw a man who entered the light of *Allah*'s Throne. The Prophet (pbuh) asked, "Who is this person? Is he an angel?" He was told, "No." He asked again, "Is he a prophet?" It was said to him, "No." The Prophet enquired, "Who is it then?" The answer was, "This is a man who ceaselessly remembered God while he was in the world, and his heart was attached to the prayers, and he never disobeyed his parents."

Another *hadith*, narrated by Abu Huraira, the Prophet (pbuh), said that God the Most High has angels who seek the people of remembrance (*dhikr*). When they find such assemblies of remembrance they encompass them until they reach the first heaven. Then Allah asks his angels, "What are My servants doing?" The angels reply, "O Lord of the universe, they are praising and glorifying You by constantly remembering You." Allah *said*, "Have they seen Me?" The angels would reply, "O Lord, they have not seen You." Allah would say, "They are praising Me without seeing Me, what if they were to see Me?" The angels would answer, "If they were to see You, they are going to do more and more praise and remembrance." Allah would ask the angels again, "What are they asking for?" The angels would say, "They are asking for Your paradise." Allah would ask, "Did they see My paradise?" The angels would say, "O our Lord no, they have not seen it." God would say, "How would it be if they saw My paradise?" The angels would answer, "They would become more eager to reach it." Then Allah would ask them, "What are they afraid of?" The angels would reply, "They are afraid of Hellfire." God would ask, "Have they seen My fire?" The angels would say, "O Lord, they have not seen the Hellfire." Allah would again ask, "How it would be if they saw Hellfire?" The angels will reply, "If they see Your fire, they would be running away from it and be more afraid of it." At this Allah would say, "I am making you all witness that I have forgiven them of all their sins." One of the angels would say, "O our Lord, someone was there who did not belong to that group but came for some other business." Allah would say, "Those are My beloved ones who are remembering Me and anyone who sits with them no matter for what reason that person will also have his sins forgiven."

SUMMARY AND EXERCISES

If you have fondness for Islamic mysticism and spirituality and intend to follow the path to the truth of the Absolute Being, then you should start performing *dhikr*. *Dhikr* is the commemoration and remembrance of God the Most High.

For the purpose of commemoration, the following are prescribed most frequently:

1. The formula of faith (*La Illaha Illallah, Muhammad ur Rasool Allah*).
2. The ninety-nine beautiful Names of Allah.
3. Various Quranic verses.
4. Other Divinely inspired prayers.

At the end of this chapter, I have included a table consisting of all the beautiful Names of Allah, their meanings, and method of recitation.

The formula of faith, *La Illaha Illallah, Muhammad ur Rasool Allah*, is the greatest of all commemorations (*dhikr*).

Commemorating the supreme Name of God, *Allah*, is one of the best forms of prayer concerning religious devotion and spiritual advancement. In His personal Name, *Allah*, all the other ninety-eight attributive Names are fully reflected. Therefore, reciting Allah alone is the most comprehensive form of invoking God's blessings, favors, and bounties.

His beautiful Names and the sacred verses of the Quran are the real sources of healing and mercy. Says the Most High, "And that which We reveal in the Quran is a source of (inward and outward) healing and mercy for the faithful" (Quran 36:12).

The Names of God can be commemorated singly or in any possible combination of the Names. There are different ways of reading these attributive Names and every Name and combination has unique qualities.

The different combinations of God's beautiful Names in the Quran are as follows: *Huwallaa hullazi Laa Ilaha Illa Hu: Al Malik ul Quddus us Salam ul Mumin ul Muhay Minul Aziz ul Jabbar ul Mutakabbir* (Quran 59:23). And further, *Allah ur Rahman ur Rahim ul Quddus us salaam*.

Some mystics will combine His personal Name, *Allah*, with every attributive Name as a supplement, by doing so it produces powerful spititual effects: The Names are such as *Ya Allahu ya Rahman, Ya Allahu ya Rahim*, and *Ya Allahu ya malik*. God the Most High said, "Say: it is the same whether you call on Allah or on Rahman (the Most Gracious), to Him belong the most beautiful Names" (Quran 18:110).

PRACTICE

I have been reciting the following great Names of God and Quranic verses since my early life and have gained and experienced abundant Divine blessings and inspirations in my life. I strongly urge all of you and especially those who are Divine lovers and seekers of the truth to do so. Recite the following on a daily basis:

Recite the formula of faith, *La Ilaha Ill Allah, Muhammad ur Rasool Allah*, one hundred times.

Recite *Ya Allah*, one hundred times.

Recite *Allah Hu*, one hundred times.

Recite *Ya Hayyu, Ya Qayyumu, Ya Wahab*, one hundred times.

Recite the verse of chair (*Ayat ul Kursi*), eleven times.

Recite *Sura Muzzamil*, eleven times.

Recite the benediction and salutation on the Holy Prophet Muhammad (pbuh), one hundred times.

The above-mentioned *dhikr* (commemoration) makes up my daily routine. I also recite the Four *Quls* (*Al Ikhlas, Al Kafirun, Al falaq, Al Nas*), the "Opening Chapter" (*Al Fatiha*), and other formulas (*kalimas*) frequently. Most of the time, I am so engaged and absorbed in commemoration that my recitation exceeds the numbers I have mentioned.

The most common combination of the Divine Names used for commemoration is the five Great Names of Allah, as follows:

Ya Allah, Ya Rahman, Ya Rahim, Ya Hayye, Ya Qayyum.

BREATH CONTROL (*PAS INFAS*)

Pas infas or watchfulness over breath has been practiced by many Sufis as an adjunct to the commemoration practice. It helps to achieve spiritual blessings in a shorter period of time by enhancing concentration. This should be done as described below: During inhalation (breathing in) you should say *La Ilaha Illallah.* And during exhalation (breathing out) you should say, *Muhammad ur Rasool Allah.* You should continue reciting the formula of faith while watching over your breath for at least one hundred times daily.

Similarly you should say *Allah* while inhaling, and during exhalation you should say, *Hu.*

Commemoration combined with breath control successfully leads a seeker into the living presence of the Divine.

I would also strongly advise all of you who wish to follow the path of illumination to give charity as much as you can to fulfill the needs of the helpless and to feed the hungry. A small act of kindness and a little charity along with remembrance of God may result in spiritual blessings beyond expectations and sooner than you can imagine. I personally have experienced these blessings. In fact this is the sole cause of my good fortune and spiritual progress time and again. Therefore, expressing kindness and love even in small ways would definitely make the world a more blissful place to live.

هُوَ اللهُ الَّذِى لَا اِلهَ اِلَّا هُوَ

Ar-Rahmân	اَلرَّحْمنُ		Allah	اَللهُ
The All-Compassionate			God	
Al-Malik	اَلْمَلِكُ		Ar-Rahîm	اَلرَّحِيْمُ
The Absolute Ruler			The All-Merciful	
As-Salâm	اَلسَّلَامُ		Al-Quddûs	اَلْقُدُّوْسُ
The Peace			The Holy	
Al-Muhaymin	اَلْمُهَيْمِنُ		Al-Mu'min	اَلْمُؤْمِنُ
The Guardian			The Faithful	
Al-Jabbar	اَلْجَبَّارُ		Al'-Aziz	اَلْعَزِيْزُ
The Compeller			The Mighty	
Al-Khâliq	اَلْخَالِقُ		Al-Mutakabbir	اَلْمُتَكَبِّرُ
The Creator			The Greatest	
Al-Musawwir	اَلْمُصَوِّرُ		Al-Bâri'	اَلْبَارِئُ
The Shaper of Beauty			The Maker of Order	

Al-Qahhâr	اَلْقَهَّارُ	Al-Ghaffar	اَلْغَفَّارُ
The Subduer		The Forgiving	
Ar-Razzâq	اَلرَّزَّاقُ	Al-Wahhab	اَلْوَهَّابُ
The Sustainer		The Bestower	
Al'-Alîm	اَلْعَلِيمُ	Al-Fattâh	اَلْفَتَّاحُ
The Omniscient		The Opener	
Al-Bâsit	اَلْبَاسِطُ	Al-Qâbidh	اَلْقَابِضُ
The Reliever		The Restrainer	
Ar-Râfi'	اَلرَّافِعُ	Al-Khâfîd	اَلْخَافِضُ
The Exalter		The Abaser	
Al-Muzill	اَلْمُزِلُّ	Al-Mu'izz	اَلْمُعِزُّ
The Humiliator		The Bestower of Honours	
Al-Basîr	اَلْبَصِيرُ	As-Sami'	اَلسَّمِيعُ
The Seer		The Hearer	
Al-Adl	اَلْعَدْلُ	Al-Hakam	اَلْحَكَمُ
The Just		The Judge	
Al-Khabir	اَلْخَبِيرُ	Al-Latîf	اَللَّطِيفُ
The All-Aware		The Subtle One	
Al-Azîm	اَلْعَظِيمُ	Al-Halîm	اَلْحَلِيمُ
The Magnificent		The Forebearing	

Ash-Shakûr	اَلشَّكُورُ	Al-Ghafûr	اَلْغَفُورُ
The Most Grateful		The Forgiver	
Al-Kabîr	اَلْكَبِيرُ	Al'-Alî	اَلْعَلِيُّ
The Greatest		The Highest	
Al-Muqît	اَلْمُقِيتُ	Al-Hafîz	اَلْحَفِيظُ
The Nourisher		The Preserver	
Al-Jalîl	اَلْجَلِيلُ	Al-Hasîb	اَلْحَسِيبُ
The Sublime		The Accounter	
Ar-Raqîb	اَلرَّقِيبُ	Al-Karîm	اَلْكَرِيمُ
The Watchful One		The Generous	
Al-Wâsi'	اَلْوَاسِعُ	Al-Mujîb	اَلْمُجِيبُ
The All-Comprehensive		The Responder to Prayer	
Al-Wadûd	اَلْوَدُودُ	Al-Hakîm	اَلْحَكِيمُ
The Loving One		The Perfectly Wise	
Al-Ba'ith	اَلْبَاعِثُ	Al-Majîd	اَلْمَجِيدُ
The Resurrector		The Glorious	
Al-Haqq	اَلْحَقُّ	Ash-Shahîd	اَلشَّهِيدُ
The Truth		The Witness	
Al-Qawî	اَلْقَوِيُّ	Al-Wakîl	اَلْوَكِيلُ
The Possesor of All Strength		The Trustee	

Al-Wâlî	اَلْوَلِيُّ	Al-Matîn	اَلْمَتِينُ
The Governor		The Forceful One	

Al-Muhshi	اَلْمُحْصِى	Al-Hamîd	اَلْحَمِيدُ
The Appraiser		The Praised One	

Al-Muʿîd	اَلْمُعِيدُ	Al-Mubdi'	اَلْمُبْدِئُ
The Restorer		The Originator	

Al-Mumît	اَلْمُمِيتُ	Al-Muhyî	اَلْمُحْيِىُ
The Taker of Life		The Giver of Life	

Al-Qâyyum	اَلْقَيُّومُ	Al-Hayy	اَلْحَيُّ
The Self-Existing One		The Ever-Living One	

Al-Mâjid	اَلْمَاجِدُ	Al-Wâjid	اَلْوَاجِدُ
The Glorious		The Finder	

Al-Ahad	اَلْأَحَدُ	Al-Wâhid	اَلْوَاحِدُ
The One		The Only One	

Al-Qâdir	اَلْقَادِرُ	As-Samad	اَلصَّمَدُ
The All Powerful		The Satisfier of All Needs	

Al-Muqaddim	اَلْمُقَدِّمُ	Al-Muqtadir	اَلْمُقْتَدِرُ
The Foremost		The Creator of All Power	

Al-Awwâl	اَلْأَوَّلُ	Al-Muakhkhir	اَلْمُؤَخِّرُ
The First		The Delayer	

Azh-Zâhir	اَلظَّاهِرُ	Al-Âakhir	اَلْآخِرُ
The Manifest One		The Last	
Al-Wâlî	اَلْوَالِىُ	Al-Bâtin	اَلْبَاطِنُ
The Protecting Friend		The Hidden One	
Al-Barr	اَلْبَرُّ	Al-Muta'âlî	اَلْمُتَعَالُ
The Doer of Good		The Supreme One	
Al-Muntaqim	اَلْمُنْتَقِمُ	At-Tawwâb	اَلتَّوَّابُ
The Avenger		The Guide to Repentance	
Ar-Raùf	اَلرَّؤُوفُ	Al'-Afu	اَلْعَفُوُ
The Clement		The Forgiver	
Zul Jalâli Wal Ikrâm	ذُوالْجَلَالِ وَالْاِكْرَام	Al-Mâlikul Mulk	مَالِكُ الْمُلْكِ
The Lord of Majesty and Bounty		The King of Supreme Dominion	
Al-Jâmi'	اَلْجَامِعُ	Al-Muqsit	اَلْمُقْسِطُ
The Gatherer		The Equitable One	
Al-Mughnî	اَلْمُغْنِىُ	Al-Ghanî	اَلْغَنِىُ
The Enricher		The Rich One	
Ad-Daar	اَلضَّآرُ	Al-Mâni'	اَلْمَانِعُ
The Creator fo Harm		The Preventer of Harm	
An-Nûr	اَلنُّورُ	An-Nâfi'	اَلنَّافِعُ
The Light		The Creator of Good	

71

Al-Badi'	اَلْبَدِيعُ	Al-Hâdi	اَلْهَادِى
The First Cause		The Guide	

Al-Warîth	اَلْوَارِثُ	Al-Bâqi'	اَلْبَاقِى
The Inheritor of All		The Everlasting One	

As-Sabûr	اَلصَّبُوُرُ	Al-Rashîd	اَلرَّشِيدُ
The Patient One		The Unerring	

Saadiq-ul-W'ad	صَادِقُ الْوَعْدِ
True to His Word	

CHAPTER FOUR

MEDITATION ON THE NAME OF ALLAH

Contemplate the Name of your Lord and be
completely absorbed in it. (Quran 78:9)

§

And meditate deeply about the creation of the Heavens
and the earth. (Quran 3:191)

§

Has not the time arrived for believers that
their hearts in all humility should engage in the
contemplation of God. (Quran 57:16)

In the beginning was the Word, and the Word was with God, and God was the Word (Tradition)

This ancient tradition, according to mystics, means (a) that God's personal Name, *Allah*, is the word that was with God the Most High since the beginning, before the creation of the cosmos, and (b) that the word *Allah* was God the Most High Himself.

Very few people actually realize that the Name *Allah* in reality is the named, that it is the very Essence and the very self of God. The name and the named are synonymous and interchangeable. In the Quran the word *Allah* is used in the sense of the Name and denotes His Essence, which is the ultimate Reality. All other attributive Names of God designate His activity in relationship to the cosmos, or everything other than God.

Allah has no form, shape, or color, and no one knows His Essence, for the Essence cannot be known by any human faculties. Only Allah knows Allah. The only thing we know about Him is His Name, *Allah*, which is the sign of His Essence.

Esoteric treasures, inner knowledge, and Divine secrets are attained by meditating on the personal Name of God, *Allah*. All the lights of the Essence, attributes, acts, and Names and all the hierarchies of man, angels, power, and God are reached through meditation on His Name only. Various stages of sacred law (*shariah*), the path (*tariqah*), truth (*haqiqah*), and gnosis (*marifah*) are traversed by meditating on the Divine. Similarly all the esoteric personalities of the self (*nafs*), heart (*qalb*), spirit (*ruh*), secret (*sir*), hidden (*khafi*), most hidden (*akhfi*), and ego (*ana*) are surmounted by the Name of Allah. All the ranks of Islam—faith (*iman*), certainty (*aikan*), gnosis (*marifah*), proximity (*qurb*), affection (*muhabat*), observation (*mushahida*), and union (*wasl*)—can be reached by meditating on the Name of God the most High.

Meditation and prayer have been integral and important components of many world religions. Their practice outside religious contexts has been universally used both for spiritual and for non-spiritual goals. People have used them for achieving enlightenment, loving kindness, higher consciousness, God realization, self-awareness, healing, relaxation, and peace of mind.

There are different types of meditative techniques. Every religion, faith, and school of thought has its own methods and ways of performing meditation.

The basic elements of meditation are as follows:

1. Sit in a quite place, preferably your own safe haven at home. Meditate at least for fifteen to thirty minutes, at the same time daily. During the early morning hours before sunrise is probably the best time for contemplation and meditation.
2. Sit in a comfortable position, either cross-legged on a cushion, with the back in an erect posture or in a chair, with the feet touching the floor. Whatever position is comfortable for you, assume that position. The goal is to be peaceful, comfortable, and relaxed.
3. Minimize all distractions and interruptions if possible, such as noises, bright lights, doorbells, and phones. Otherwise keep all sources of distraction to a minimum level.
4. Close your eyes; this will help you to relax and concentrate more easily.
5. Take a few deep breaths and exhale completely, do this at least ten to fifteen times, while paying close attention to your breath only. This practice will help in achieving focus on the desired object.
6. Relax your body and muscles from head to toes and avoid any tension and stress.
7. Choose a word or phrase that you strongly believe in. For Muslim mystics that word is *Allah*, *Allah Hu*, or their favorite phrase is the formula of faith, *La Ilaha Illallah* ("There is no deity worthy of worship except Allah"). For others it could very well be *Allelujah*,

Amen, Holy or simply the sacred sound *Ahhhh*, which is the seed sound of Divine Names. Both religious and non-religious people can meditate on this inter-spiritual sound *Ahhhh*. Alternatively, any other word that has a deeper spiritual meaning or has an inner connection with one's soul can be used.

8. Begin your meditation with infinite leisure, listening *mentally* to the sound of your object of meditation with adoring intent as it arises in your mind. Do not mind any thoughts that may arise. Bathe deeply in the ocean of that sound, adoring it mentally as it wells up in your mind in resonant pulses or waves. As it resonates softly, attend to where it wells up as sweet sounds, as subtle feelings, as pulses of honeyed light, and attend to the silence each wave of sound dissolves into when it fades away—and expand into formless, silent spirit. Simply be.

9. Open your heart and mind by being in a receptive mode and keep a positive attitude. Do not worry about your progress. The primary goal is to focus your thoughts, attention, feelings and inner energy on your selected object of adoration.

10. When you are done with this practice, sit quietly for a while without thinking about anything, and simply be.

11. With continued practice you find your inner potential and energies unfolding.

Various other techniques are also used for meditation. Some of them are quite simple; others may be complex, requiring formal training and guidance from a master or sheikh. Different techniques may suit people differently. Some people are good at one or another technique. There is also a considerable overlap between these techniques.

Movement meditation is a popular form of devotional practice. It consists of a gentle flowing of the whole body to produce a meditative state. During this activity the body sways rhythmically in a dance-like fashion. It is like dancing with the Divine. The whirling dervishes of the Mevlavi order practice dancing as a part of their devotional worship, in order to achieve spiritual bliss and ecstasy. This is like the dance of a flower in a gentle breeze. Slowly you are lost in the bodily movements and go beyond the threshold of time and space.

Vibrational meditation, also known as *sound meditation*, is a unique and inspirational way of praying. Some people make deliberate noises, chanting, or singing loudly in order to release stress and find inner peace and tranquility. The meditator utters a chosen word or words and repeats that over and over again, as described above. He or she focuses on nothing, but continues on muttering the words. Let the words resonate and vibrate throughout your body—from your brain to your extremities. Feel it and let it pass out. This act promotes relaxation and induces a pleasant, trance-like state. Sufi *sama* (audition) is a kind of vibrational meditation. It is most powerful when combined with movement meditation (dancing) and is practiced by some Sufi orders.

The important thing is to actually *do* meditation rather than just think about it. Prophet Muhammad (pbuh) has said, "A moment of meditation is better than worship of the two worlds" (*hadith*).

Unlike some forms of prayer or meditation that seek material gain, Sufis are interested neither in material goods, objects, and wealth, nor do they worry about their physical health and ailments. They know and believe that when they come close to the light of Allah, the Most High, and attain union with Him, all their ailments, impurities, pain, and suffering will vanish: "He who has the Lord has everything" (tradition).

Muslim mystics do not ask for any recompense or worldly gains, rather their eyes are on the highest prize—the Lord Himself.

As Rabia Al Adwiyah, the first Sufi women poet, who used to prostrate and pray a thousand times a day has been quoted, "I ask for no gains but only to seek Your pleasure." In this respect Khaquani, a Persian poet has said, "After thirty years of meditation Khaquani learnt the point that a moment with God is far better than the kingdom of Solomon, the Prophet." To this effect God said in a Divine tradition, "There are some who ask this world from Me in their prayers, and I give them this world, but they have no portion of the hereafter. And some ask Me for the hereafter, and I give them the hereafter, but they have no portion of this world. And some love only Me and ask for Me alone and I give them Myself and this world and the hereafter."

This spiritual orientation of prayer in Sufism stems from the Quran, which is the true word of God, a manifest light, and a complete and perfect guide for all humanity till the end of time. The Quran is full of verses in which God the Most High stresses the importance of contemplation and meditation on His Name, for instance, "Commemorate the Name of your Lord and be perfectly absorbed in that" (Quran 78:9).

§

God has bidden that His Name be raised and commemorated in houses. (Quran)

§

Remember Me and I will remember thee. (Quran 2:152)

§

Perform the prayers in order to commemorate Me, verily the prayers stop one from detestable and commemorating God is a great thing.
(Quran 29:45)

§

God the Most High called those who remember Him, commemorate His Name, and praise and glorify Him as His friends and said, "God is pleased with them and they are pleased with God" (Quran 98:8), and, "They love Him, He loves them" (Quran 5:54).

Islamic prayer (*salat*) is a unique form of meditation combining aspects of movement, sound, and vibration—all in a beautiful manner. If performed with presence of mind and heartfelt sincerity, it is a direct communication with Allah, without any intermediary or veil. It takes the form of a dance between the lover and the Beloved. There is constant chanting of "*God is great, praise and glory be to Allah,*" and a continuous expression of sincere gratitude. It is a love song from the heart to appreciate the beauty of the Beloved. It is all about Him. We should really know the reason and the real importance of why we should pray to Him. In other words, if we know Him and love Him, the simplest performance of prayer will take us beyond our human consciousness into Divine consciousness and into the presence of His Essence. That is the reason Sufi saints used to pray excessively—in order to be present with God the Most High and achieve oneness. God has said in a *hadith qudsi,* "Nothing is more pleasing to Me, as a means for My slave to draw near unto Me, than worship which I have made binding upon him, and My slave ceaseth not to draw near unto Me with added devotions of his free will until I love him, and when I love him I am the Hearing wherewith he heareth and the Sight wherewith he seeth and the Hand whereby he graspeth and the Foot whereon he walketh."

Hence in prayer and commemoration, the heart and mind should be fully engaged with Allah, and every word spoken should be a message of love towards Him. This in return brings back the light of God and his blessings to the commemorator. In short, prayer is nothing else but the singing of His praise and glory and offering gratitude. As it is said in the Quran, "Everything in the Heaven or on the earth praises Allah" (Quran 64:1). In another verse the Quran says, "The seven Heavens and the earth and all beings therein extol His limitless glory. And there is not a single thing that does not glorify Him with His praise, but you do not understand how they declare His glory. Verily He is oft forbearing, most forgiving" (17:44). God the Most High commanded men and women in another verse, "O faithful! Commemorate Allah abundantly and praise Him morning and evening" (Quran 33:41-42).

In prayer we focus and meditate on God, which leads to the blissful state of inner peace. It is the journey of the soul to the ultimate Truth, which is the reality of God. Thus the last advice of the Holy Prophet Hazrat Muhammad (pbuh) to us was, "Do not ever abandon prayer, do not ever abandon prayer, and do not ever abandon prayer. And fear Allah in your treatment of those under your control" (*hadith*).

The secret of His pleasure while praying is that we should know Him, love Him, and pray with sincerity and not out of fear and obedience only. We should not remember Him with our tongues but within our hearts. We should not be preoccupied with worldly thoughts, but our hearts and minds should be with Him only. We should not be prisoners of our desires and egos but should hold onto Allah Himself. We should look upon the creation and people with love and compassion as the Creator Himself does.

If we are able to cleanse ourselves from worldly cares, pray, and yearn for the truth, we will most certainly find the truth. For God said, "I am with the one who calls on Me."

The one with the inner (esoteric) eyes should be able to see Him. If we do not see Him, but feel His presence during the prayers, we should know that "God hears those who praise and thank Him." That is the reason the Holy Prophet Muhammad (pbuh) said, "Worship Allah as if you see Him, and if you do not see Him, certainly He sees you" (*Bukhari*).

DHIKR MEDITATION:

Has not the time arrived for believers that
their hearts in all humility,
should engage in the contemplation of God? (Quran 57:16)

§

Dhikr involves the repetition of the ninety-nine beautiful Names of God in the Quran, the formula of faith, and various Quranic verses. It is a form of prayer and meditation and has been practiced by the majority of Muslims.

Dhikr may be done individually or by a group of devotees. Some Sufi orders perform it as a ceremonial activity. It may be simple recitation of the Names of Allah in the form of singing and chanting or remembering God in one's heart.

In the beginning, when all the spirits were created by God the most High, He addressed them saying, *Alastu birabbikum* (Am I not your Lord, the Creator?) Quran 7:172. To this all the created spirits replied in unison, "Yes indeed, You are our Lord." The spirits heard for the first time the Name of their Lord, *Allah*, and it was implanted deeply in their hearts as a gift of Divine Grace. This was the first *dhikr* given to the spirits directly by the God the Most High. This was the first conversation and covenant between God and men. The men of God since then started pondering over His Name and recognized its wonderful qualities and powerful effects in their spirits.

Thus, the remembrance of Allah goes back to pre-eternity, when the Lord of the universe spoke to spirits directly. Ever since, men responded by recollecting Allah with words of adoration and glorification in order to pronounce their submission and surrender as they did at the moment of the initial Divine address.

Remembrance of Allah is therefore the true nourishment of the restless souls and the means of proximity and union. The light of the personal Name of Allah has been placed in the human heart and soul by the Creator of the universe Himself, and man is connected directly through this light with His Essence. We need to rekindle the flame of His love in our hearts by constantly commemorating His Name, *Allah*.

The glorious Quran in itself is the *dhikr* and praise of Allah and of his beloved Prophet Hazrat Muhammad (pbuh), hence the recitation of the Quran in any form is the praise and remembrance of God the Most High and the Prophet Muhammad (pbuh). The Quran is all about God, it came from Him, and it will take the reader on a straight path to His presence alone. Recitation of the Quran and all remembrance (*dhikr*) is a means of concentration upon God, which is the mainstay of all spirituality.

Several Quranic verses emphasize the importance of commemoration:
Be aware that commemoration of Allah and his remembrance gives contentment and satisfaction to hearts. (Quran 13:28)

§

And if thou shouldst forget, call thy sustainer to mind. (Quran 18:24)

§

O Believers remember God often. (Quran 13:28)

§

Dhikr can be performed loudly (lyrical chanting) or slowly and silently in the heart. Whatever method you choose, the main purpose is to become completely absorbed in it and enter a meditative state of consciouness.

"Call upon Him as *Allah* or call upon Him as *Al Rahman* (the Most Gracious) by whatever Name you call upon Him, His are all the attributes of perfection" (Quran 17:110).

MEDITATION ON THE PERSONAL NAME OF GOD, *ALLAH*

The term *Tasawr e Isme Allah Dhat* or concentration on the personal Name of God, *Allah*, was first coined and described by Sultan ul Arifin Hazrat Sultan Bahu (may God be pleased with him) some 400 years ago. Sultan Bahu was a great Sufi saint, poet, and a prolific writer in both the Persian and Punjabi languages. He has written extensively in the Persian language—somewhere around one hundred and forty books on Islamic mysticism.

Meditation on the personal Name of God, *Allah*, is the central idea of his spiritual teachings and the basis of his Divine wisdom. All his works are essentially detailed explanations and commentaries on the science of meditation on God's personal Name. He considers meditation on the personal Name of God, *Allah*, to be synonymous with meditation on the Essence of God Himself. He considers this method of meditation to be the shortest and surest way that leads to God's presence and to the attainment of oneness with Him. He thinks that meditation on *Allah* is like a lift that exalts the practitioner instantly to the higher levels of experience, states of ecstasy, and perfect union. In meditation, "Who begins with Him also ends in Him."

Through meditation on His personal Name, *Allah*, a two-way channel is opened between the seeker and God. As it flows from God it will take you back to God.

Hazrat Sultan Bahu described meditation as a continuation of commemoration and concentration on the personal Name of Allah, culminating in a deep, meditative state. According to his teachings, commemoration and concentration are prerequisites to successful meditation. All these three methods of praying can be combined into

One—or each one can be performed in different combinations, depending upon the seeker's personal way of praying and meditative technique.

Commemoration of the personal Name of Allah has been discussed earlier. It is also called *dhikr* and can be done silently by a single individual or can be performed in a group. Some devotees form a group or a circle and engage themselves in *dhikr* by doing lyrical chanting and moving in wave—like fashion—resulting in ecstasy and trance.

In some Arab countries, remembrance is performed in communal gatherings called *hadra*, which consists of song recitals, music, and whirling dance. To these participants prayer (*dhikr*) is a gift of Divine Grace, and chanting His Name is an integral part of their spiritual life. Singing His Name—*Allah Hu, Allah Hu*—is the nourishment of their intoxicated souls. The climax is reached with the cries of His Name—*Allah, Allah*—thus losing their selves as consciousness transports them to the presence of His Essence.

For the purpose of remembrance (*dhikr*), the following are recited most commonly: *Ya Allah, Allah Hu, Ya Hayye Ya Quyyum, La Ilaha Ill Allah*, and *Muhammad ur Rasool Allah*.

Everything created in the universe performs *dhikr* (remembrance) by uttering praise and thanking its Creator in its own way. The sun, moon, stars, earth, oceans, rivers, trees, flowers, and birds sing to the glory of God by glittering, moving, humming, fragrance, color, and beauty. Those who are in love with God will not only hear the voices of the creation but also His voice in every voice. Whenever, I see a beautiful thing—whether flower, plant, tree, bird, brook, or rainbow in the sky—my heart admires His beauty and sings His praise along with the rest of the created things.

There is an inspiring story about a sheikh in Istanbul, Turkey narrated by Annemarie Schimmel. Before his death, he wanted to choose a successor for his spiritual order. He asked all of his disciples to bring flowers to decorate the *khanqah* (place of spiritual worship). All his disciples brought beautiful bouquets of flowers to please their Sheikh. One of them came late, with a single withered flower. The other disciples laughed and ridiculed him for bringing just one withered plant. The Sheikh asked him, "Why did you bring the withered flower?" He answered, "All the beautiful flowers in bloom were busy in the remembrance of God and praising His Lordship. I did not dare to interrupt their prayers. I saw this one had just finished its recollection. Therefore, I brought this one."

On hearing this, the Sheikh made him his successor, for he could see and hear through his heart the real nature of things.

Not only are objects in the physical world constantly performing *dhikr*, there are billions of spiritual and subtle beings such as angels, spirits, and *jinn* that are engaged in the remembrance of God every moment of their existence. I had quite a thrilling experience of witnessing such an episode. It was during one of my vacations when I was visiting my parents in my native village Kulachi, in Pakistan. Kulachi is a remote, small village, forty miles away from Dera Ismail Khan, which is the nearest town of any size with a small airport. The airport is no longer used for civil aviation. It is currently utilized by the military in collaboration with the United States in their fight against the Taliban insurgency in South Waziristan.

Dera Ismail Khan is situated on the banks of the Indus River and through a series of broken bridges connected to Punjab. Kulachi itself has remained undeveloped for decades, with the majority of roads still dirt paved. There is no sewage system in the village, and all the garbage is dumped in the streets. Fortunately the village has electricity now and some running water for the last ten years. The lifestyle is still pretty much the same centuries-old tribal one.

My vacation time in my village is basically time spent with my parents. During that time, I also visit my relatives and old friends, which strengthens my spiritual bond with them.

It is a time for reflection, meditation, and prayer for me. I spend a lot of time visiting the mausoleum of my grandfather, Faqir Nur Muhammad, who is the patron saint of Kulachi. I am so closely related to my father and grandfather in the realm of spirituality that at times I strongly feel we are the same, three in one, or one in three. It seems as if we are connected through the same divine light, which radiates through my grandfather to my father and then comes down to me, with the only difference being that it shines ever more brightly.

Once, I was praying and meditating at the mausoleum of my grandfather for hours. I went there at 8 p.m. and stayed there until late. It was past midnight. I was totally immersed in a state of meditative trance. Knowing, I was going to stay late during the night, I had closed the door to the mausoleum from inside so that I would not get interrupted in my devotional prayers. Around 1 a.m. I was suddenly aroused from my meditative state by a humming sound. At first, I thought that it was probably due to the blowing of the wind. However, the sound approached nearer and became louder. At the same instant the inside of the room was lit by a dazzling opaque light. I saw thirty to forty figures coming in through the closed door. They were like bright shadows floating in the air and going around the grave of my grandfather. They were performing *dhikr* (remembrance) of Allah, loudly.

These subtle beings belonged to a Muslim *jinn* tribe who live in the mountains of Sulaiman (*Koh e Sulaiman*) outside Kulachi. *Koh e Suleman* is a wide mountain range extending from our village to Balochistan and some parts of Punjab. According to a legend, the mountains of Sulaiman are heavily inhabited by different tribes of *jinn*. There is a famous, huge, and deep cave, where it is said that some of the evil *jinn* are imprisoned until this day by Solomon (pbuh) the Prophet.

The mountains of Sulaiman have special significance for our village and tribe. Our great ancestor Syed Muhammad Gisudiraz settled here while he was visiting the area spreading the message of Islam. He stayed among the three tribes of Pashtuns. He took three wives at the behest of the local tribal chiefs, who became his followers. This was the custom of the land to honor one another by strengthening the bond of friendship through marriage. He had four sons, named Stoori, Mashwani, Wurdak, and Hani. We are the progeny of Hani's son Tari, who was famously called Gandapur. Today Gandapurs are a big tribe numbering several hundred thousands over a large area at the foothills of *Koh e Sulaiman*.

This group of pilgrim *jinn* was enthusiastically chanting the formula of faith, *La Illaha Illallah* (There is no deity worthy of worship save Allah) and *Allah Hu*. They were so absorbed in their ceremonial *dhikr* and were in some sort of mystical trance that they did not pay any attention to me sitting quietly in the corner of the room. Their robes were flowing, and their faces were glowing in the darkness.

I was awestruck by this strange and mysterious spectacle, but at the same time the hair stood up on my whole body. I had never seen so many *jinn* simultaneously in such a ritualistic activity. According to scripture, *jinn* are subtle and unique beings created from fire by Almighty Allah. They are greater in power than ordinary human beings. They performed their *dhikr* for more than half an hour, and then all of a sudden, all of them vanished through the closed door. Once again the mausoleum was quiet and peaceful. I was spellbound.

All the beautiful Names of God can be recited individually or in any combination. Selected verses of the Quran can be recited as well. There is no restriction on the number of times you should do the recitation. The minimum number for recitation is one hundred times per day. Actually, to be effective, you should recite the Name of Allah a thousand times a day. It may seem a lot initially, but with time it would seem like the easiest thing to do. Once you get into the habit of recitation, recitation takes its effect and starts to illuminate one's heart and soul. Constant remembrance eventually leads to total absorption in Allah.

The word of God, and especially His Divine Names, are pure light, and after a while they descend as powerful inspirations to the heart. Personally I am so much engaged in the remembrance of Allah consciously or unconsciously that the sound of His Name keeps on resonating in my mind and heart all the time. Sometimes, I am overwhelmed by the experience of waking up in the middle of the night or in the early morning hours performing the *dhikr*.

When a person commemorates whichever Name or attributes of God the Most high, the Divine light of the same Name or attribute descends on that person to the extent that he or she becomes completely immersed in the light of God. For example, when a person constantly remembers God with the Name of *Ya Arhamal Rahimin* (the most Merciful of Merciful), God Almighty shines the light of the same attribute on Him, so that he becomes the instrument and channel of all-encompassing Divine mercy. The mercy of God pervades the whole universe, through which compassion, affection, and love exist between human beings and all the creation. He pours His infinite mercy on all of his creation without any distinction between good and bad.

The commemorators of the Divine Name *Rahman* (Merciful) therefore find the light of *Rahman* within themselves and use this bounty as He wills them, caring for His creation. Those who find the qualities of *Allah's* attributes in their beings through constant remembrance come so close to the Creator that they look upon the rest of creation through the eyes of the Creator.

Similarly, when a person remembers God with the name Hearer (*Al Sami*) or Seer (*Al Basir*), he or she is invested with the attributes of God, the All Hearing and the All Seeing, according to his or her sincerity and spiritual capacity. The commemorator acquires esoteric hearing and seeing through the bounty and gift of God the Most High. Such a person hears the Divine inspiration and sees the divine plan of things.

All the other attributes should be conjectured in the same way. Therefore, remembrance of the Divine Names is extremely important for mystical awareness. God has been described in the Quran as possessing the most beautiful Names; these are, however, not the proper Names but derivatives, yet He is mysteriously present within all of them. Jawad Nur bakhsh has said something to this effect, "Continuous attention (remembrance) to God produces the general transformation of the attributes of the lower self into the attributes of God."

One night while Hassan Basri was engaged in the remembrance of God, he heard a Divine voice say, "O Abul Hassan, do you wish Me to tell people what I know about you? They may kill you by stoning." "O Lord," he replied, "do you wish me to tell people what I know of Thy Mercy and what I perceive of Thy Grace, that none of them need ever again to worship Thee?" The voice answered, "Keep your secret, and I will keep Mine."

God is a treasure of inexhaustible Mercy, just as He is a treasure of Love and beauty.

Ayub Ansari, a prominent companion of the Prophet Muhammad (pbuh), when he was on his death bed said that he had hidden until then something he had heard the Prophet (pbuh) say, fearing that it might be misunderstood, and he recited the following prophetic tradition: "If humankind had not sinned, God would have taken them away and replaced them with sinners so that he could forgive them" (Muslim).

Sufis have written extensively about the qualities of the Divine Names. These writings can be grouped into two broad categories:

1. Divine Names connected with God's Beauty and Loving kindness.
2. Divine Names associated with His Wisdom and Majesty.

These Divine Names and attributes are permeating the entire universe and interact with all the creation, especially human beings, who are intimately connected to them due to their capability to express them fully.

Mystics have developed different ways of performing *dhikr*: (a) remembrance with the tongue, which consists of reciting the Names of God audibly; (b) remembrance of the self (*nafs*), which is the inner feelings of the Divine Names; (c) remembrance of the heart, when the heart meditates in its inner core or center on the Divine qualities; (d) remembrance of the spirit, when the commemorator perceives the light of the attributes; (e) remembrance of *sirr*, when God's mysteries are revealed; (f) remembrance of the secret, which is obviously the light of Oneness; and (g) remembrance of the most secret of secrets, which is the direct experience and vision of the Reality of Absolute Truth.

However, the remembrance of God the Most High should be learned with patience and perseverance. There is a legend about Sahl at Tustari, who said to one of his disciples, "For one day you should constantly say, *Ya Allah, Ya Allah. Ya Allah* and do the same the next day and the day after that, until you become used to saying those words." Then he told him to repeat them at night also, until he became so used to them that he uttered them even in his sleep. Then he said to him, "Do not recite them anymore, but let your entire being be engaged in remembering God." One day when he was in his house a piece of wood fell on his head and broke it. The drops of blood that trickled to the ground recited, *Allah, Allah, Allah.*

Remembrance is the first step in the way of love, for when someone loves God, he constantly thinks, contemplates, and recollects His Name. As a result, the love of God becomes deeply implanted within his or her heart, and it is then that it becomes a permanent sanctuary of God.

Remembrance should penetrate the mystic's whole being so that he or she forgets the recollection of everything else except God. The goal of remembrance is to reach a stage when the subject is lost in the object, in which the commemorator and the commemorated become one again, as they were before on the day of creation. Excessive commemoration eventually leads to annihilation of the subject in the object, and the two become so intertwined that they are no longer distinguishable.

True meditation is beyond words and thoughts; it is a state of complete silence and stillness, for it is in the stillness of the heart that God can be found.

Thoughts and breath are deeply connected with remembrance of and meditation on the Divine, because it is through the faculty of thinking and breathing that we are aware of the Lord. Sahl At Tustari said, "Human breaths are counted, every breath that goes out without remembering Him is dead, but every breath that goes out in remembering the Lord is alive and is connected with Him."

. Concentration and meditation on a single idea, thought, or object is essential for spiritual growth and advancement as we join forces with the

Source of everything. Concentration hence is instrumental for increasing our esoteric capabilities in order to know God intimately and attain union with Him. In this regard, Faqir Nur Muhammad wrote the following: "There is a deep connection between the breath, thoughts, heart, and mind of the seeker and the Divine Essence. The heart of a Gnostic is a garden, and when the breath passes over it like a morning breeze, it comes out laden with the sweet fragrance of remembrance of Allah. The angels then take it to the presence of the Absolute Being as a precious gift from the commemorator and it is stored for him as a priceless jewel in the treasury of the next world. When the breath comes back it is accompanied by the Divine favors, blessings, and loving kindness." (Irfan).

MEDITATION ON *ALLAH*

Meditation means thinking with concentration so as to understand the true nature of things and to distinguish truth from falsehood. Mystics have been contemplating and meditating on the mysteries of the universe and the root cause of all that exists for thousands of years. There are literally hundreds of ways to meditate, each depending upon the spiritual capability of the practitioner to succeed.

Dhikr meditation (remembrance) is done by chanting and repeating words. Words and sentences are limited means of expressing the Divine secrets, whereas the scope of meditation (imaginative contemplation) is infinite. What imaginations can grasp, the words cannot.

Contemplative imagination is the most powerful force in the cosmos, which creates impossible things and turns imaginations into realities. It is the source energy that brings into existence all the entities from non-existence. Ibn Al Arabi referred to the cosmos as, "imagination" or "The dream of the Real" because it is a never ending birth and rebirth of forms. It is the unbounded "imagination" of God that is constantly manifested every moment in the universe and is undergoing persistent change from one state to another. God created the cosmos by first imagining it and therefore has the complete knowledge of everything. He then brought everything from His storehouses of non-existence by simply speaking His words, "To be" that translated imaginations (information and knowledge) into all beings and entities.

We can do the same through contemplative meditation (imaginative thinking) on the supreme Name of God, *Allah*, and tap into the infinite source of God's storehouses and create unimaginable possibilities for ourselves and those around us. We live in an imaginative world. The world of imagination is the greatest and strongest of all creations because it embraces all things. The world of imagination is the world of non-manifest where every possibility exists and all manifest things spring out of this world. Only humans have the power of imagination (meditation), so they are capable of doing anything impossible.

The Holy Prophet Hazrat Muhammad (pbuh) used to contemplate and meditate in the cave of Hira, outside Mecca, for sustained periods, sometimes for weeks at a stretch. It was during one of these intensive meditative states that he received the first revelation of the Quran brought down by the archangel Gabriel from God the Most High. This was the historic moment in human history when the miracle of the Quran, the true and living word of God, came from the blessed lips of the Holy Prophet (pbuh). No one has ever before and none will until the end of time be able to write such beautiful and meaningful verses.

The story of Islam began with the Name of the Lord, *Allah*, when the archangel Gabriel appeared before Prophet Hazrat Muhammad (pbuh) and instructed him to,

Recite with the Name of your Lord

Who created humans from a clinging substance.

Read, for your Lord is Most Gracious.

He taught people through the use of pen

That which they did not know before. (Quran 96:1-5)

To this, Prophet Hazrat Muhammad (pbuh) honestly replied, I can't read." The archangel Gabriel embraced Prophet Hazrat Muhammad (pbuh) and squeezed him so hard that it took the breath out of him. "Read," Gabriel repeated. Prophet Hazrat Muhammad (pbuh) replied again, "But I can't read." Again Gabriel embraced him, this time so tightly that the Prophet (pbuh) felt as if his lungs were going to burst. "Read," the archangel instructed for the third time. This time the Holy prophet (pbuh) said, "What should I read?" The archangel Gabriel recited in a melodious voice, "Read in the Name of your Lord, *Allah.*" The Holy Prophet of Islam repeated those non-created words of God several times until he memorized them.

What was meant by the Name of the Lord was the personal Name of God, *Allah.* The prophethood of Hazrat Muhammad (pbuh) started with the Name of Allah and forever changed the history of human civilization, bringing a revolution that spread like wildfire throughout the world—with almost a billion followers.

This was the Name *Allah,* with which God addressed all the spirits on the dawn of creation: *Alast u Birabikum* (Am I not your Lord, *Allah*?). This was the Name *Allah,* which God the Most High taught Adam after He blew His breath unto it.

The Name *Allah* is synonymous with the Named, which is the Essence of God Himself. Very few people know the real importance of the Name *Allah.* Hazrat Sultan Bahu said, "If the heart says *Allah* once its reward is equal to finishing the whole Quran with the external tongue seventy thousand times."

Hazrat Sultan Bahu was the first to describe in detail the method and importance of concentration and meditation on the personal Name of God, *Allah.*

METHOD OF MEDITATION

Once you have made up your mind, take a clean shower and perform ritual ablution for the external purification of the body. You should wear clean clothing and sit in a peaceful place of your choice, either cross-legged or in any other comfortable position. Empty your heart and mind of worldly distractions and sensual thoughts.

You should recite the following *suras* of Quran three times, so as to make the meditation more effective:

1.   The opening chapter, *Al Fatiha*
2.   The Verse of the Chair, *Ayat ul Kursi*

3. *Sura Al Ikhlas*
4. *Sura Al Kafirun*
5. *Sura Al Falak*
6. *Sura Al Nas*
7. The formula of faith, *La Ilaha Ill allah, Muhammad ur Rasul Allah* one hundred times.
8. Invoke blessings on the Holy Prophet Hazrat Muhammad (pbuh) one hundred times.

The first step in this devotion is the remembrance of Allah (*dhikr Allah*) by reciting His personal Name. This can be done by either reciting *Ya Allah, Ya Allah* or by reciting *Allah Hu, Allah Hu*. Whichever of the two of His Names attracts and absorbs you the most or comes naturally to you should be commemorated. Recite the Name *Allah* with all your heart and with complete presence of mind. You should recite the Name of Allah (*Ya Allah*) at least one hundred times a day initially and increase the number gradually to a thousand times a day. Reciting the Name *Allah* a thousand times per day is not that difficult. With time and practice the Name will slowly become absorbed into your heart, mind, soul, and entire being. There will come a time when you will be unconsciously commemorating the Name of Allah even in your sleep.

The second step is to write the Name *Allah* on a paper in beautiful Arabic calligraphy. For the sake of your convenience, the Name *Allah* in Arabic can be found at the end of this chapter. You can frame the Name *Allah* and mount it on a wall in front of your eyes or place it on a table. You should sit down quietly after reciting the already mentioned Quranic verses and after reciting *Allah, Allah* as many times as possible.

You should now gaze at the inscription of *Allah* and concentrate on the written Name of God, *Allah*, in Arabic for at least ten to fifteen minutes every day. The best time to do these spiritual practices and worship is before sunrise, the early hours of the dawn. One hour before the call for morning prayers (*adhan*) is probably the best time to do so after you have performed the *Tahajud* prayers, which are the ten cycles of voluntary prayers.

If you cannot comply with this regimen, you can do the meditation any time of the day or night, as your schedule permits. You should continue the practice of reciting the Name *Allah* and fixing the gaze on the written Name *Allah* for a reasonable period of time, until you become accustomed to these two spiritual exercises.

The third step is the actual practice of meditation on the Supreme Name, *Allah*. When you are ready for this step of devotional worship, you should sit down after performing your prayers, as mentioned earlier. Choose a place where you can sit quietly and peacefully all the time while engaging in the practice of meditation. Complete solitude and silence are of vital importance, but not mandatory.

Next, you should practice breath control by taking deep breaths and relaxing. When you inhale you should say *All* and prolong that to *alla* until the end of inhalation. When you exhale you should say *ah*. Together this should pronounce the word *Allah*.

You should concentrate on the word *Allah*: during inhalation recite *All* and while exhaling say *ah*. This should produce the sound of the actual Name, *Allah*.

You can also use the word *Allah Hu* for the purpose of breath guarding or control. That is to say *Allah* during the active process of inhalation and to utter *Hu* during the passive act of exhalation. The underlying doctrine is the same, which is to meditate on the Essence of Allah.

During cycles of inhalation and exhalation, I find the sound of *Allah* more natural, easy to say, and effective in transporting my awareness to the presence of Allah.

Pas anfas, or breath control, is an important and extremely helpful tool in Sufi meditation. Each breath that comes in is a precious gift from God, and it should be returned with the remembrance of Allah. Nobody can reach God without constantly thinking about Him. As one Sufi has said, "Life without the thought of Him is altogether meaningless." Breath control, or watching over your breath, while uttering *All-ah* during the process of inhaling and exhaling leads to concentrated recollection, which generates tremendous spiritual power that accelerates progress on the path of illumination.

The next step is the most important aspect of meditation on the personal Name of God, *Allah*. This involves intense contemplation on the Name *Allah*, written in the mystic's heart, until it is inscribed in brilliant letters emanating the light of God.

Now you should try to write the Name *Allah* on the heart, in your chest, with the help of an imaginary pen, or with the help of an imaginary finger tracing the letters of the word *Allah* in Arabic calligraphy, as shown in the diagram at the end of this chapter.

You should imagine that your body is like a dress that you are wearing and that you are inside the dress. Now with the help of your forefinger or a pen, write the word *Allah* from inside the dress, where the heart is situated. You should continue to concentrate on His personal Name, *Allah*, by repeatedly writing it on the heart—even though, it may not become fixed in the heart initially. It is a misconception that after a while His personal Name, *Allah*, will be fixed on the heart permanently and will remain there ever-illuminated, so that whenever, you look towards your heart you would see the Name *Allah* printed on the heart.

Another way to inscribe the Name *Allah* on the heart is from outside. It should be done as described in the following way. While you are sitting down in a quite place, concentrate on the Name *Allah* on your heart. You should slightly flex your neck as if you are actually looking at your heart. Remember that you are doing this with your eyes closed and imagining the whole process of meditatation. Imagine that you are holding your heart in your left hand and then gently lift it up upward towards your face. The heart normally is hanging in the chest, to the left side, with its apex pointing downward. Its base, which is the broader part of the heart, is upwards, as if it is hanging upside down. Now imagine, your left hand lifting the heart so that the pointed part comes up and the heart is lying horizontally, so that when you look at it, it is right in front of your eyes. Now, write the Name of God, *Allah,* on it with an imaginary pen or finger and trace the Arabic word of *Allah* repeatedly. By practicing this way you can inscribe *Allah's* Name on your heart from the outside.

This is a powerful and interactive way of meditation. Visual imagination of *Allah* on body parts, especially the heart, is of central importance in attaining the light of God as well as proximity and mystical reunion with Him. In your imagination, as you hold your heart in your hand, you will feel it pulsating with His Name and becoming filled with the light of His Essence.

The heart is the center of human consciousness, the seat of the Divine spark and the bed where the seed of His personal Name lies dormant since pre-eternity (the day of *alast*). By constant meditation and remembrance, human consciousness transcends all reality, the Divine spark turns into a blazing fire of His love, and the seed of His Name grows into a tree of faith (*iman*). It is through the way of heart that one can find one's way to the presence of God and reach the goal of creation.

No one can bring His personal name, *Allah*, under his or her control, but it is the other way round. Through repeated concentration and meditation, the heart, mind, soul, and the whole being come under the intense influence of the personal Name, *Allah*, which not only receives and assimilates but also overtakes and penetrates. This phenomena is an act of love, as is said in a holy tradition, "When I love him (My servant), I am the Hearing with which he hears and the Sight with which he sees." In another tradition it is said, "Verify yourself with the attributes of Allah".

When a seeker immerses himself or herself in the meditation of the Name *Allah*, his or her entire being is lost in the Name. Through constant meditation he or she reaches a stage when God the Most High, through His Grace and Mercy, absorbs the seeker in the ocean of light of His personal Name, *Allah*. The meditator becomes a perfect mirror to God the Most High, and all His Names and attributes become manifest in Him. Therefore, he or she reflects the lights of the Essence, attributes, and the Names of Allah and attains purity of the soul, cleansing of the heart and illumination of the spirit.

He or she becomes the symbol of a perfect man, Adam or Eve, who was taught all the Names by the Lord.

Without meditation on His personal Name, *Allah*, the heart cannot be revived, the esoteric path cannot be traversed, and the direct presence of God cannot be experienced. It cannot be achieved by fasting all day, keeping vigil all night, renouncing, or performing back-breaking ascetic exercises. Meditation is the only key to the knowledge of and proximity and union with God. To attain this, His personal Name, *Allah*, is the most comprehensive and best tool. Similarly, total-body meditation should be performed and practiced by writing the personal Name, *Allah*, on the forehead, eyes, ears, nose, tongue, throat, heart, chest, naval area, either side of flanks, and the palm of hands, and legs.

You should imagine that you are sitting inside your forehead, and with your imaginary forefinger, or with the help of an imaginary marker, you are drawing the Name *Allah*, from within, on the forehead, in brilliant letters. To write His personal Name, *Allah*, on the place of the eyes, you should imagine you are wearing glasses, and then try to inscribe the Name *Allah* on the inside of the glasses. His Name should be written on the ears, nose, tongue, throat, heart, chest, and all body areas as mentioned earlier.

With continuous practice, His personal Name, *Allah*, will become inscribed in your heart in the form of light, which is also called the *light of faith*. God the Most high shines towards the meditator with the Name and attribute on which he meditates: "Allah has the power to appear with the attribute with which you remember Him" (Quran 12:18).

Hence during meditation on His personal Name, *Allah*, all the body parts should be inscribed with the bright letters of *Allah*. The body parts on which His personal Name becomes written through meditation become revived and illuminated with the light of His Essence.

All the beautiful and attributive Names of Allah can be meditated upon. In the spiritual world, His Essence appears as a sun, Names appear in the form of Stars, and His attributes appear as moons.

The heart of the believer is like a polished mirror upon which—when the sun of His Personal Name, *Allah*, Shines—it reflects the light, glory, and majesty of His Name, which not only illuminates the entire being of the meditator but also emanates the light of God near and far. God has no form, shape, figure, or resemblance. It is the heart of the perfect man that acts as a mirror capable of totally reflecting His attributes. God the most High manifests Himself in a perfect man by the way of reflection.

Jesus Christ (pbuh) used to concentrate and meditate on God's attributive Name *Holy* (*Quddus*), to the extent that he would become totally absorbed in it and would become filled with the light of His attributive Name. The light of His attributive Name *Holy* would descend on Jesus Christ (salutations be upon him) in the form of brightness and sometimes physically manifested as a white dove flying around him. During such a state of illumination, when Jesus Christ (pbuh) would touch a leper, a blind man, a lame person, or a lunatic, they would become cured by the power of the light of *Holy* (*Quddus*). The accounts of Jesus Christ (salutations be upon him) looking towards heaven, meditating on God's Holiness, becoming filled with the Holy Ghost (Light), and curing the sick are amply recorded in the testaments.

God's personal Name, *Allah*, was the manifest light that the archangel Gabriel placed as a bright seed in the chest of Prophet Hazrat Muhammad (pbuh) in the cave of Mount Hira by commanding the words, "Read in the Name of your Lord, *Allah*." This later on developed into the blessed tree of the Glorious Quran.

It was the staff of the Prophet Moses (pbuh) that he used to lay down with the Name *Allah*, whereby he delivered Israelites from the yoke of Pharoah. It was the inscription of His Name on the ring of Solomon (pbuh). In reference to this the Quran says, "This is from Solomon, and this is in the Name of God the Infinitely Good and Boundlessly Merciful." (Quran 27:30).

To become qualified with the attributes and virtues of the Lord, it is important to purify the soul, cleanse the spirit, and polish the heart with the innate light of the personal Name of God by meditating on it. It is through the special favor of God the Most High that the sun of His Essence, the moons of His attributes, and the stars of His Names shine on the heart of a meditator and reflect and emanate the Divine light.

It is through meditation that the esoteric senses are opened; all the veils between God and man are lifted so that the heart becomes the temple of the Most High Lord. Meditation is turning away of one's thoughts from all that is not God. Hence it is the foundation of all blessings in this world and the hereafter. It is in meditation that you find a way to God and obtain presence with Him. All forms of devotion and prayer's pleasure will last for a time, but meditation on Him is a delight forever.

You should remember that Sufi meditation is not just a cat nap or idle thinking but is the result of a rapturous love for the Divine. It is through love that one can attain to such a degree that his whole being is absorbed in the thought of his Beloved and he sees nothing else. That is why Muhammad bin Wasi said, "I never saw anything without seeing God there in." When you turn your eyes from the worldly things you will invariably see God with your heart. This is why God says, "Tell the believers to close their eyes." (Quran 24:30).

Contemplative meditation is deeply connected to the vision of God. Meditation on His personal Name *Allah* is like time spent in seeing Him with the spiritual eyes and not the bodily eyes, for God cannot be seen with the physical eyes.

Chapter Five

THE WAY OF THE HEART

Where's the mind to grasp your sovereignty?
Where's the soul to mirror your majesty?
Beauty's face, I know, you could unveil,
But where are eyes to behold your beauty?
(Qazi Hamid ud Din)

The Ultimate Truth that is the destination of all cannot be understood by normal human faculties and perceptions. The world's most renowned Sufi poet, Jalal ud Din Rumi, composed more than seventy-thousand couplets over a period of twenty-five years and yet was unable to fully explain the mysteries of Divine love. The great master, Ibne Al Arabi, wrote hundreds of volumes on the Essence of God, but could not provide a proper definition of God, in his entire lifetime. Similarly, the philosopher Al Ghazali could not figure out whether he was on the right path or not, and once he did, he wrote over four hundred works merely to point to the way. Not the least, Hazrat Sultan Bahu extemporaneously dictated his famous *Abyats* (*Verses*) of celestial beauty as well as more than one hundred and forty works to emphasize the importance of the personal Name of God, *Allah*, but did not find enough words to explain his experiences with the Divine and left countless unanswered questions.

To delineate the path is a task that is something impossible. The amount of literature on the subject is so broad and mysterious that nobody can even attempt to fully explain it.

The basic tenet of all religions is the consciousness of one Reality. Some call it *wisdom*, *light*, *love*—or *nothing*. That is why Dara Shikoh, an Indian prince said, "In the Name of Him, Who has no Name, Who appears by whatever Name you will call Him."

Some mystics are so overwhelmed and are in a state of such awe and intoxication that they see nothing but God in everything. For instance, Jami expressed this feeling of God inherent in everything as follows:

Sometimes we call Thee wine, sometimes goblet,

Sometimes we call Thee corn and sometimes snare,

There is no letter save Thy Name on the tablet of the world,

Now, by which Name shall we call Thee.

Reason and philosophy cannot point to the way leading to God. The wisdom of the heart and the inner light illuminate the path to reality. Love of the Absolute can carry the mystic's heart to the Divine presence.

Because of the inability of reason to grasp Divine love, traditionally Sufis are divided into two groups: the sober ones and the intoxicated ones. The first group is associated and linked with the sober school of Baghdad, lead by Junaid Baghdadi. The intoxicated group began with the emergence of Abu Yazid Bastami in Khorassan, Iran. He was the founder of the ecstatic (drunken) school of Sufism. During one of his ecstatic states he proclaimed, "Glory be to me." The legend of his ascension to heaven has been described in detail in Tazkarat ul Awliya by Farid ud Din Attar as the "flight of the alone to alone." The synopsis of this journey is included for the interest of the readers. In this regard, Abu Yazid Bastami stated, "I looked upon God's light with the inner eye; He freed me from all creation, made me independent, and blessed me with His glory. In comparison to the light of His Essence, I was all darkness. I found Him pure and pristine but saw myself foul. When I looked again, I saw myself by His light. I perceived my glory to be the reflection of His grandeur and glory. Whatsoever, I did, I did it through His power. All my worship was the result of His grace only. I asked, 'O God what is this?' He said, 'All that I am and none other than I.' He opened my eyes to the mysteries of the creation. As soon as He revealed Himself to me, I was completely annihilated in Him and became everlasting with Him. He granted me inner knowledge and illuminated my eyes with His light. He then said, 'Ask Me, whatever you wish.' I replied, 'I wish Your presence only, for me You are better than any treasure and greater than any future. I am happy and content with You and beg of You not to keep me away from You, for everything else is far inferior to You.' He crowned me with His glory and opened the door of oneness for me. When my being was fully annihilated in His attributes, He named and addressed me with His Essence. At that very moment duality vanished completely and only Oneness prevailed. He said, 'I am pleased with you and you are pleased with Me.' He then spoke, 'My creatures wish to see you.' I said, 'I have no wish to mingle with them. But if it is Your command, I will do so. People may see Your Art through me.' He ordered, 'Come before My creatures.' No sooner I stepped out of His presence, I fell down. I heard Him say, 'Bring him back to Me, for he cannot live without Me, he knows not anyone else except Me.'"

The above account of Abu Yazid Bastami clearly highlights what Sufis are aspiring for. They want the Beloved every moment of their lives and would take nothing else for it.

Sufi spiritual experiences are categorized in a double approach towards the Beloved. In *kash ul Mahjoob* Hazrat Ali Usman Hajwiri discussed this phenomenon as follows: "There is a difference between one who is burned by His Majesty in the fire of love and one who is illuminated by His Beauty in the light of contemplation." In another place Hajwiri wrote, "There is a difference between one who meditates upon the Divine acts and one who is amazed at the Divine Majesty. The one is a follower of friendship; the other is a companion of love."

The phenomenon of Sufism is like a multifaceted diamond: any description would be just touching upon a single facet. Each individual will have a different kind of experience with the Divine, each one unique, awesome, and indescribable. As the Quran says, "Every day He appears with a new glory." (Quran 55:29).

Hazrat Junaid Baghdadi wrote that one cannot become a Sufi by strictly adhering to the laws of *shariah*, but that one should have an open heart and a generous soul. He also enumerated the qualities of a Sufi, which he compared with the qualities described in the revelation regarding the Divine messengers. A wayfarer should possess and aspire for the following virtues:

1. The Generosity of Prophet Abraham (pbuh), who offered his son for the sake of God's pleasure and did not hesitate for a single moment.
2. The obedience of Prophet Ishmael (pbuh), who sacrificed his life gladly by submitting to the will of God.
3. The patience of Prophet Job (pbuh), who chose affliction and suffering to comply with the command of His Lord.

4. The symbolism of Prophet Zachariah (pbuh), to whom God said, "The commandments for thee are that thou shall not communicate with people except by signs."

5. The strangeness of Prophet John (pbuh), who remained aloof and lonely among his own tribe for the sake of God the Most High.

6. The pilgrimhood of Prophet Jesus (pbuh), who possessed only a cup, and a comb which he abandoned when he saw a man drinking in his hands and another one combing his hair with his fingers.

7. The woolen dress of Prophet Moses (pbuh), who wore only rough woolen garments all his life.

8. The poverty of Prophet Hazrat Muhammad (pbuh), who took pride in his poverty and implored God to keep him fed one day and hungry for another.

Sufis have added their wise sayings to fashion a framework for defining Sufism. Some of them emphasized complete dissociation from the world and avoidance of the ego. Sufis do not care about worldly possessions and are free as a result. Therefore, they are generous, kind hearted, and loving in their dealings with others. According to Nuri, "Sufis are tireless in their search and know no disappointment when denied." Dhun-Nun Almisri said, "Sufis are the favorite people of God and they keep God ahead of everything else." Sahl-at-Tustari defined a Sufi as one, "Whose blood and whose possessions can be confiscated by his brethren in faith, for what he receives, he sees it from God and believes in God's all embracing lovingkindness."

Junaid and Nuri also stressed the social and practical aspects of Sufism. Nuri in particular said, "Sufism does not consist of ceremonial prayers and rituals but is composed of good morals." He also added, "A better Sufi is the one who has a good moral character and who obeys the sacred law with loving devotion and spiritual zeal."

Hujwiri *wrote* in Kash al Mahjoob, "A Sufi keeps his heart clean from all sorts of discord. Love itself is a concord and the lover is the one who strives to keep the commandments of the Beloved. So if the object of desire is one, how can discord arise?"

While writing the above beautiful quote from Ali Ibn Uthman Al Hujwiri, I am delighted to acknowledge his great spiritual powers and *baraka* (blessings), which emanate from his shrine until this day. Thousands of seekers of Truth—both Sunnis and Shiites—visit his shrine daily to pray and receive waves of Divine light and eternal blessings. I have experienced two spiritual episodes with this great Sufi master, who was not only a treasure of illuminative knowledge and gnosis, but God's agent of love and compassion as well, as described below.

After I had taken my twelfth-grade examination, I was free and had two months of summer vacation. I went to see my elder sister and brother in law, in Gujranwala, Punjab. My brother in law, Abdul karim Khan Kundi, is a retired chief justice now. At that time, he was posted as a district judge. One Friday he decided to go to Lahore and visit the shrine of Al Hujwiri. He asked me whether I would like to join him on the spiritual trip. I was excited at the proposal, and we both went to Lahore. It was a lazy summer day. We reached our destination in the afternoon, probably between 4 and 5 p.m. We made our way among the throngs of worshipers passing to and fro and paid our respects by reciting verses of the Holy Quran, for his blessed soul. After paying our tribute to the great Sufi master, we proceeded towards the mosque to perform ritual prayers. There we saw a dignified old man with a completely white head and beard. He was heavily built. He gracefully approached us and greeted my brother in law in Pushtu, with an Afghani accent. He had an illustrious face radiant with divine light, displaying a gentle smile. He embraced my brother in law affectionately, and later the two of them shook hands warmly. He looked at me with a soul-awakening gaze that has captivated my heart to this day. He gave me a fatherly hug and held my hands.

The three of us sat down on the ground, and he started conversing with my brother in law. Out of respect, I remained silent all this time, only occasionally looking at his face, which was emanating God's love. We departed after an hour. As we were reverently bidding farewell to the illumined master, he showered us with abundant blessings.

As soon as we came out of the shrine area, my brother in law asked me, "Do you know who that elderly man of God that we just met is?" I had no idea, and honestly said, "I don't know." He told me that he was Hazrat Ali Ibn Uthman Al Hujwiri, himself. He then narrated, "I recently visited my spiritual guide. During conversation, he asked me whether I visit the shrine of Al Hujwiri in Lahore. I said, "Yes." He then asked me whether Hazrat Hujwiri had blessed me with his presence. I replied, "No." At this my spiritual guide told me that whenever next I visit his shrine he would meet me in person.

It was all due to the blessings and attention of my brother in law's spiritual guide. Perchance due to my good fortune I was with him and had the honor to meet one of the great Sufi masters of all time.

In yet in another vision—while writing this book—I saw Ali Ibn Uthman Al Hujwiri. I saw him sitting in an ordinary room, which looked like his library. There were some old wooden shelves on the far end of the room loaded with volumes of books. He was sitting on a mat on the ground. A small, low table was on one side, with some writing papers on it. On the back wall was a small window, probably to permit light to enter the room. I entered the room and greeted him with peace and blessings of God. He got up and welcomed me like an old friend and embraced me in a hug. We sat down on the mat, and he started imparting his illuminative knowledge and Divine wisdom to me. He specifically stressed the importance of rapturous love for and of reverential fear of God. We talked for a while, and I enjoyed and benefited from his heavenly advice.

At the end, he asked me, "What do you wish?" I was humbled and answered, "I do not desire anything for myself. The only thing I wish for is His pleasure." He was well pleased with me, and as soon as I bid farewell, my heart was filled with the delight of meeting one of God's friends.

True inner knowledge, namely the gnosis of the Lord, is not attained through reading books. As the Prophet of Islam has said, "I take refuge with Thee from the knowledge that profiteth naught." In fact, some would agree that the first step on the path (*tariqah*) is "to break the inkpot and tear up the books." The following story is noteworthy in this regard: In his young age, the founder of the Suharwardi Sufi order, Hazrat Ummar

Suharwardi, was extremely fond of scholastic theology. He had studied a great deal of books on the subject and had memorized them by heart. His uncle was not happy with his scholarship. So one day he brought him to Syed Sheikh Abdul Qadir Jilani (may God be pleased with him) and requested him to advise the young man regarding spiritual matters. Sheikh Abdul Qadir Jilani put his hands on the boy's chest and made him forget all he had studied. At this, the young Ummar was nervous and astonished, fell at the feet of the Sheikh, and broke into tears. Sheikh Abdul Qadir Jilani put his hands on his chest again and filled his breast with *Ilme Ludani,* the illuminative knowledge derived from God. This was the miracle of Sheikh Abdul Qadir Jilani by suddenly washing away the knowledge he thought was of no avail to his student.

Sufis deliberately avoid engaging in philosophical discussions about the cosmos and consider it a distraction, as Farid ud Din Attar has rightly alluded to it, "From words such as *Primary matter* and *Primary cause* you will not find the way into the presence of the Lord." Abu Yazid bastami said to this effect, "The thickest veils between man and Allah are the wise man's wisdom, the worshiper's worship, and the devotion of the devotee."

LOVE:

Divine love is considered superior to gnosis and is regarded as a universal religion by some mystics, whereas its depth and beauty cannot be expressed in words.

I have separated my heart from this world
My heart and Thou art are not separate
And when slumber closes my eyes
I find Thee between the eye and the lid.
Sumnun

Without mentioning the name of martyr mystic Mansur Al Hallaj, any discussion about Divine love will be incomplete. Hallaj's life, love, and death have deeply influenced the development of Islamic mysticism. In the course of time he became a symbol of both "suffering love and unitive experience," for he, with incredible courage, lifted the veil of oneness.

When in prison Hallaj was asked, "What is love?" He answered, "You will see it today, tomorrow, and the day after tomorrow." And that day they cut off his hands and feet, the next day put him on the gallows, and the third day burned him and gave his ashes to the wind.

In his book *Kitab at Tawasin*, Hallaj's poems give utterance to the transcendence of God and his immanence in the human heart, along with the mystery of loving union. Once Hallaj went to Junaid's house and knocked at the door. Junaid asked, "Who is there?" Hallaj answered, *"Anal Haq,"* "I am the Truth."

In *Kitab at Tawasin* he discussed his own claim with that of Pharaoh and Satan. Pharaoh proclaimed, "I am your Great Lord," whereas Satan announced, "I am superior to Adam." Hallaj, however, declared, "I am the Absolute Truth."

Later on, the Sufis asserted that *"I"* of the Pharaoh was a demonstration of infidelity, whereas that of Hallaj was an expression of Divine Grace. A Divine revelation puts this into perspective in the following way: "Hussain annihilated himself and found Me, while Pharaoh saw himself and lost Me."

Hallaj's poems are tender expressions of mystical yearning. His verses convey deep theological ideas and Divine meaning and are so beautiful that they can be enjoyed even by those without religious and spiritual understanding. According to Hallaj, God is hidden in every atom of the universe—visible only to those who love Him in their hearts. In one of his verses he described God as the one who permeates a broken heart as do tears in a sore eye. His book also contains beautiful poems in praise of and honoring Prophet Hazrat Muhammad (pbuh). Hallaj strongly affirmed that Muhammad (pbuh) is the best creation of God and that it was for the sake his love that He created the universe. His beautiful rhyming couplets reached new heights in the praise of the Prophet. He wrote, "All the lights of the Prophets proceeded from his light; he was before all, his Name the first in the book of fate; he was known before all things, all beings, and will endure after the end of all. By his guidance have all eyes attained to sight. All knowledge is merely a drop, all wisdom merely a handful from his stream, and all time merely an hour from his life."

After his third pilgrimage to Mecca, Hallaj returned to Baghdad, but was arrested for blasphemy for saying "I am God." He was declared a heretic. On March 26, 922, he was put to death. It is narrated that Hallaj went dancing to the gallows while in chains, singing poems about mystical intoxication. He then asked his friend Shibli for a prayer mat and performed his last prayer lamenting the separation of lover from the Beloved. He had often urged people to kill him so that he might be united with Him. When the crowds started throwing stones at him, Shibli threw a red rose at Him. At this Hallaj sighed deeply. When he was asked about the reason for the sigh he answered, "What they did was because of their ignorance, but he (Shibli) knew and did it."

RABIA AL ADWIYAH:

Rabia Al Adwiyah was the first woman Sufi saint and poet with a passionate love for Allah. Her life-long devotion has significantly contributed to the theme of Divine love in Islamic mysticism.

It is narrated in *Tazkarat al Awliya* by Attar that the night when Rabia was born, there was nothing in her father's house, for he lived in extreme poverty. Her parents did not possess even a single drop of oil to rub on her umbilical cord, no lamp to light, and no cloth to wrap around her. They had three daughters already, and Rabia was their fourth. Her mother asked her father to knock at the neighbor's door and ask for some oil, so that she could light the lamp. Her father had made a covenant with God that he would never ask any man for anything. So he went out to the neighbor's house and came back without knocking. "They did not open the door," he told his wife. Her mother wept bitterly. In that gloomy state the man lowered his head on his knees and slept. Prophet Hazrat Muhammad (pbuh) appeared in his dream and said, "Don't be sad." The Prophet added, "The child born just now is a queen among women who shall redeem seventy thousand of my followers on the day of resurrection." The Prophet (pbuh) instructed him, "Go to the governor of Basra Isa e Zadan and write down the following on a piece of paper and give to him: 'Every night you send upon me a hundred blessings and on Friday night four hundred. But you forgot to do so last Friday night. In exchange for that give four hundred dinars to this man.'

Rabia's father woke up and wrote on a piece of paper as the Prophet (pbuh) had instructed him. He sent the letter to the governor by a third person. Upon receiving the message, the governor said, "Give two hundred dinars to the poor as a thanksgiving for the Master remembering me and four hundred to the Sheikh." He also told the messenger to tell him, "I wish you had come so that I can see you. But I do not think that it is appropriate for such a pious person to come to me. I would rather prefer to come and rub my head on your threshold. However, I request you to please let me know whatever you need."

Rabia Al Adwiya's life, devotion, and piety are sources of inspiration and guidance. There is no single way or method to acquire Sufi teachings and wisdom. It is through the life stories, poetry, prayers, and day-to-day struggles of the saints that we can learn about the secrets of mysticism.

When, Rabia was still a young child, her parents passed away. Basra had a famine, and her sisters were separated and scattered. One day, Rabia went out and was followed by a wicked man, who seized her and then sold her into slavery for six *dirhams*. Her purchaser put her to hard labor. One day she was walking along the road when a stranger approached her. Rabia was frightened and fled. While running she fell face down and dislocated her hand. Prostrating her face to the ground, she cried, "Lord God, I am a stranger, orphaned and totally helpless in captivity with my broken hand. Still, for all these hardships I do not grieve, all I need is Thy pleasure to know that Thou Art well pleased with me." "Do not grieve," she heard a voice, "Tomorrow a station shall be thine such that the angels in the heaven will envy thee."

It is narrated in *Tazkarat ul Awliya* that one night Hassan Basri, with two other notable friends, came to visit Rabia. Rabia had no light at her place. The visitors, while sitting in the darkness, desired for some light. Rabia murmured a prayer and blew the Name of the Lord on her finger that caused her finger to glow like a light until dawn, and they sat in its radiance.

Attar further clarified that if someone objects—"How could this be possible?"—my answer would be, "The same as Prophet Moses's (pbuh) hand." If they say, "But he was a Prophet," My reply would be, "Whoever follows in the footsteps of the Prophet Hazrat Muhammad (pbuh) can posses traces of prophethood, as the Prophet (pbuh) said, "Whoever abandons unlawful things attains a portion of Prophethood." He has also said, "A true dream is one fortieth part of Prophethood."

The saints of Allah are content with Him and do not desire material goods. They are happy in whatever state they are and have totally cut off their hearts and desires from the world.

In another place in *Tazkarat ul Awliya* Attar wrote, quoting Mailk e Dinar as follows, "I went to visit Rabia and saw her with a broken pitcher out of which she drank and made her ritual ablution, an old mat and a brick which she sometimes used as a pillow. On seeing this, I was deeply moved. I told her, 'I have rich friends, and if you wish I will go and get something from them for you.' At this she answered, 'Malik you have committed a mistake, is not my Provider and theirs one and the same?' 'Yes,' I replied. 'Does the Provider deal differently with the poor compared to the rich?' she asked. I said, 'No.' She then added, 'He knows me very well and in whatsoever state He keeps me, I am content with that because His will is my will.'"

Rabia's prayers showed the sincerity of her heart and her aversion to everything else save Allah, as she sang as follows: "O lord of the universe, whatever You have willed for me to have in this world, give it to the non-believers, and whatever You want to bestow on me in the hereafter give it to the believers, for me Your love is enough. O Lord, I worship You not for a reward and neither out of fear but I worship You out of my love, therefore, I beg You not to withhold Your Beauty's face from me.

O Lord, I am here in this world of matter to pray and remember You and just for the sake of Your Face. This is what I desire, now it is up to You do whatever You will."

THE PATH:

The path in Islamic mysticism is the way that leads towards God and has been described as having four steps. It has also been considered a staircase on which the wayfarer (*salik*) climbs slowly and patiently to the higher levels of experience. The mystical path is of course long and hard; it requires constant struggle and utmost vigilance to tread it.

SHARIAH:

The first step on the path is strict observance of Divine Law (*shariah*), which constitutes the basic foundation of Islam. *Shariah* provides guidelines to us for living properly in this world. Adhering to the forms of prayers, rituals, and moral codes is necessary to proceed to the next stage of the mystical path (*tariqah*). Sound knowledge, unwavering faith, and correct awareness of Allah and His commandments are mandatory for success. *Shariah*—as described in the Quran and exemplified by the Prophet Hazrat Muhammad (pbuh)—should not only be followed but taken to heart. As it is said, "If you don't know Him, how can you pray to Him?" Without performing religious obligations such as ritual prayers, fasting, pilgrimage to Mecca, and charity, spiritual progress is impossible.

Some Sufis have performed pilgrimage frequently—up to seventy times. Pilgrimage maintains a focal point in a Sufi's life, because Mecca is the place where the faithful gather and glorify God but where most of them are favored and blessed with enlightenment.

Recitation of the Holy Quran, the infallible word of God, is considered the best form of worship by the Prophet Hazrat Muhammad (pbuh). It is a dynamic source of spiritual guidance and inspires joy and awe leading to superior wisdom and attachment with God.

According to the fourth caliph of Islam and son in law of the Prophet (pbuh), Hazrat Ali (may God be pleased with him), "God reveals Himself to the believers in the Quran."

Anthony Welch—an art historian—made the following observation: "The written form of the Quran is the visual equivalent of the eternal Quran and is humanity's perceptual glimpse of the Divine. Visual concentration on the Quran as the word of God is the closest possible approximation on earth to seeing God face to face."

The Quran is full of passages of a mystical nature such as the following:

To God belongs the East and the West.

Wherever you turn there is the face of Allah.

Witness, God is infinite and All Knowing. (Quran 2:115)

Another passage states,

We indeed created man,

And We know what his soul whispers within him,

And We are nearer to him than the jugular vein. (Quran 50:51)

Followers of mystical love know that their devotion and prayers would bear fruit—as the Prophet Hazrat Muhammad (pbuh) has said,

"This world is a seedbed for the next world."

Rumi described this in an interesting idea, which is a variation of the same *hadith*, "On the day of resurrection, every thought that entered the mind will be manifested in a visible form just as the ideas of an architect become materialized in the building of the house or as the seedling grows out of the seed after being nourished in the soil."

TARIQAH:

Tariqah refers to the inner ways and practices of Sufism. *Shariah* makes the outer body clean and attractive. *Tariqah* is the purification and cleansing of the inner life and soul. Following the road (*shariah*) is essential to be on the path (*tariqah*) towards the Absolute Truth. In order to successfully navigate this road, one needs a perfect guide (*murshid*) who knows the destination and is familiar with the ups and downs of the way. The mystical guide constantly supervises the progress of the disciple.

The *murshid* or sheikh is compared to a Prophet in a tradition that said, "The sheikh among his disciples is like the Prophet among his people. All the Prophets came to guide people to the truth, to see their own weaknesses and faults and God's majesty and power. They inspire people to strive for justice and perfection. The sheikh is also there to enlighten his followers to see the true nature of the things."

One might read all the books of instructions for a thousand year, but without a guide nothing would be accomplished. As Rumi has said,

"Whoever travels without a guide needs two hundred years for a two day journey."

Some of the Sufi orders required their adepts to undergo three years of hard service before they could be initiated into the order. This consisted of one year to serve the people by doing all sorts of menial jobs, one year in devotion, and one year in purifying their hearts. Some famous Sufis were treated harshly to induce self-discipline, getting rid of the ego, and learning humility.

Sheikh Mujadudin Baghdadi, the twelfth-century Sufi, recalled this story: When he was a young seeker, his mother—who was a famous physician—took him to a sheikh to receive religious instructions. The Sheikh initially assigned him to clean the restrooms of the lodge (*khanqah*) for a certain period of time. His mother sent twelve Turkish slaves to the Sheikh so that he could exempt his son from the humiliating job. At this, the Sheikh sent her a message saying, "As a physician if your son has a disease of the gallbladder would you give the medicine to a Turkish slave or would you rather treat him?"

HAQIQAH:

The next stage in Sufism is *haqiqah*, or truth. Haqiqah is attained by inner prayers and practices, with the help of a guide following *shariah* (the law) and *tariqah* (the path). It is the direct experience of the self and the source. According to tradition by the Holy Prophet (pbuh), "The *shariah* are my words (*aqwali*), the *tariqah* is my actions (*amali*), and *haqiqah* is my inner states (*ahwali*)." These three stages are closely interwoven and interdependent on each other.

MARIFAH:

The final stage is *marifah*, or gnosis. Marifah is superior wisdom and a deeper level of inner knowledge. It is a constant state of being in the presence of Allah. At the final stage, one realizes that all is Allah and that there is no separation, as in the words of Hazrat Sultan Bahu:

When the Lord revealed Himself to me, I lost myself in Him.

Now there is neither nearness nor union, there is no longer a journey to undertake, no longer a destination to reach.

Love attachment, my body and soul, and even the very limits of time and space have all dropped from my consciousness.

My separate self has merged in the whole,

In that O Bahu lies the secret of unity that is God.

One should constantly be watching one's actions and thoughts, because a moment of neglect from God's remembrance may obstruct one's progress on the path. Thus the sleep of heedlessness may deprive one from the union with the Lord and the Beloved. The mystic repents his heedlessness just as a believer repents his sin. Regarding this, Ansari, a Persian Sufi poet, has written the following lines:

God's favor comes unexpectedly,

But only to an alert heart.

Put not your hope in people,

For you will be wounded.

Put your hope in God

That you may be delivered.

The wayfarer on the path should turn towards God with absolute sincerity. Any act of service and ritual prayer without sincerity is useless and of no avail. A small act with sincerity of heart may cause utmost spiritual progress and God's special favor. *Riya* or hypocrisy is a dangerous sin and results in shame and degradation before the Lord, the Creator.

REPENTENCE:

True repentance is turning away from sin and renouncing worldly affairs. This again can happen in an instant by the grace of Allah, when an unexpected event, recitation of the Quran, a vision, or a sudden encounter may awaken the soul and result in sincere repentance. For Fozail Ibne

Ayaz, a highway robber, it was a Quranic verse. For the prince of Balkh Ibrahim Ibne Adham it was a vision that resulted in a life-changing event.

It is narrated in *Tazkarat ul Auliya* that at the beginning of his adulthood Fozail Ibne Ayaz was the leader of a gang, who were all highway robbers. who robbed caravans on their way to destination day and night. Fozail passionately fell in love with a woman and to win her love and affection, he always brought her precious gifts from the loot. He was so deeply in love with her that he used to climb walls in her pursuit, singing and shedding tears at the same time. One night while he was climbing a wall, he suddenly heard a man reciting the following Quranic verse, "It is not time that the hearts of those who believe should be humbled to the remembrance of God." (Quran 57:16).The word of God penetrated deeply into his soul, as if he had found himself face to face with God. It was as if God were telling him, "O Fozail, how long will you go your way? The time has arrived when We shall bring you to Our way."

As if struck by lightening, Fozail fell from the wall and cried, "Indeed the time has come, and Fozail is returning in great shame and repentance." He was bewildered and truly repented from the core of his heart.

The story of Ibrahim Ibne Adham is as follows: One night, while he was asleep in his palace in Balkh, he heard a strange sound on the roof and was awakened from a deep sleep. Angry and agitated, he shouted, "Who is there on the roof?" The reply was, "I am a friend. I have lost my camel and I am searching for it. I think it is on your roof." At this, Ibrahim Adham shouted back, "Even a fool will not look for a camel on the roof." A voice shot back, "Who is a bigger fool, me or you, who is searching for God in a palace sleeping in luxury?" Hearing this, Ibrahim repented and gave away with all his possessions.

Whether one should remember his former sins after one has repented wholeheartedly is a pertinent question. Sahl at Tustari firmly believed that after repentance sins should not be forgotten because remembering one's isns acts as a remedy against possible spiritual pride, whereas Junaid considered true repentance as the forgetting of one's sins. Ali Usman Hujwiri had the same idea; he wrote in *Kashf ul Mahjoob* that the penitent is the lover of God, and the lover is so preoccupied with His remembrance that the recollection of the sin is an unforgivable distraction.

It is common for ordinary folks to break their repentance and sin again. However, the mystics are assured that the door of repentance is always open. The Quran says that God the most high is the most Merciful of Merciful, that He forgives again and again, and that an entire life of sins can be forgiven in an instant. That is perhaps why, on Rumi's mausoleum, the following words are written in bold letters:

Come back, come back,

Even if you have broken your repentance a thousand times,

Yet come again.

TRUST IN GOD:

Complete trust in God and absolute surrender to His will is called *Tawakul* in Sufi terminology. Trust in God depends upon the degree of faith a person has in Him. God in His Absoluteness is the only source of everything. Therefore, we have to completely rely on Him. Every affair has been determined from pre-eternity. What has been destined for man cannot possibly miss him, be it wealth, happiness, suffering, or death.

God's all encompassing wisdom, power, and loving kindness is the central point of Sufism. Deep trust in God's promise is the main teaching of the Quran. However, exaggerated *tawakul* might lead to inaction. That is why Prophet Hazrat Muhammad (pbuh) advised a Bedouin, "First tie your camel's knee and then trust in God."

PATIENCE:

Patience is described in the Quran as an attribute of Prophets, "And God is with those, who show patience" (Quran 2:103). Patience means to accept whatever comes from God and to remain steadfast when afflicted by Divine decrees. There are three types of patient persons. One attempts to be patient, one is patient in distress, and one is perfectly patient in all circumstances.

GRATITUDE:

When one reaches the station of gratitude, one is already blessed by Divine grace. Ordinary people express gratitude for receiving a gift, whereas Sufis give thanks even if their desires are not realized.

The following story highlights the importance of patience and gratitude and has been told time and again. An Iraqi Sufi visited a sheikh from Khorassan and asked him about real mysticism in his country. He replied that when God sent something they would eat it and be grateful, if not they would endure patience and abandon the desire and remain content. At this the Iraqi Sufi replied, "That kind of Sufism is what our dogs do in Iraq, when they find a bone they eat it, otherwise they are patient and wait." His companion asked him how he would then define Sufism. He answered, "When we have anything, we prefer others to have it and we give it away to them. Other than that, we engage ourselves with thanks and pray for forgiveness."

The capacity for thanking is a Divine gift in itself and not the result of human endeavor. Sufis are aware of this blessing and follow the example of the Prophet Hazrat Muhammad (pbuh), who was the most eloquent of the Arabs and non-Arabs and who wanted to express his gratitude to the Lord but found himself incapable of doing so. He said, "I cannot count the praises due to Thee." At this God the Most High answered, "O Muhammad, if thou speaketh not, I will speak; if thou deemest thyself unworthy to praise Me, I will make the universe thy deputy, that all its atoms may praise Me in thy name."

Gratitude signifies insight into the wisdom of God and teaches man to see with the heart's eye the veiled blessings in every affair. It is seeing happiness in poverty and joy in the bitterness of the Divine decree. Gratitude is the attitude of a loving heart, and as Hujwiri said, "Gratitude is the result of love in as much as the lover is content with what is done by the Beloved."

LOWER SELF:

Constant struggle against the lower self or the flesh (also called *nafs* in Arabic) is important for moving forward on the path. The lower self or soul has the lowest esoteric personality, which is present in every human being. A person enters into dreams and visions through this personality. It is called in the Quran *Nafs al Ammarah* or the "departed soul." *Nafs Ammarah,* is innately inclined towards sin, and the basic human instincts of eating, drinking, sleeping, greed, and other sensual thoughts. The untamed lower self never thinks of death and resurrection. It is solely preoccupied with worldly affairs and is negligent of God. Therefore, the faithful have been warned in the Quran, "But unto him who shall have stood in fear of his Sustainer's Presence and held back his lower self from base desires" (Quran 79:40).

Taming the lower self is thus the starting point for the purification of the soul. Struggle against the lower self has been considered "the greater holy war" by the Prophet Hazrat Muhammad (pbuh). It is mandatory for every traveller on the path to cleanse his lower self of its evil tendencies and replace it by praiseworthy qualities. Sufi literature is full of stories about the ways in which prominent Sufis of the past tamed their lower selves.

The domain of the lower self is the hierarchy of man, *nasut*. In this domain the soul, or lower self can encounter spirits (*jinn*) and ghosts because these lower spirits also dwell in the same domain. The place of the lower self is *shariah* or Divine law. It can achieve spiritual progress by following and obeying religious law. It is represented by the color blue, and its inclination is towards God the Most High. The *dhikr* of the soul is, "There is no God but Allah, and Muhammad is the Prophet of Allah."

The departed soul (*nafs*) is cleansed and purified by meditating on the personal Name of God, *Allah,* until it becomes the "Blaming or accusative soul." Also called *Nafs al Lawwama.* In the Holy Book, it corresponds to the conscience, which keeps guard over man's actions and exerts control over him. Its progress is attained by observance of the Divine law and by recollection and meditation on the Name, *Allah.*

With further progress, the soul reaches the stage of inspirational soul, or *nafs Mulhemah.* However, as long as one does not attain perfection in this stage, one is not relieved of basic human traits.

Eventualy, once purification is achieved the soul becomes tranquil or at peace (*nafs mutmainnah*). In this state, according to the Quran, it is called home to the Lord.

The *nafs* or lower self is something real. A person with a departed soul (*nafs ammarah*) may see the self in his visions by the character they possess. The lower soul may take the form of a dog, pig, monkey, wolf, snake, vulture, or insects. Sometimes, the traveller will see it as a dog that wanted food but had to be trained or sent away. Some mystics saw a mouse or fox coming out of their throat. The *nafs* can also be compared to a seductive woman who tries to trick the wayfarer. A common image is that of a wild horse that has to undergo hard training so that it serves the purpose of bringing the rider to his destination. Therefore, the lower self has to be tamed and trained in order to be useful on the way to God.

The esoteric personality of the self is the lowest in ranking, which wears the elemental body as a dress. Higher personalities than this are gradually born in a person who continues progressing on the mystical path. These are esoteric personalities of the heart, spirit, secret, hidden, most hidden, and ego. The esoteric personality of the heart is enlivened by the grace and mercy of God and the attention of the perfect guide. It brings the wayfarer away from the status of the man (*nasut*) and propels the wayfarer into the hierarchy of the angels (*malakut*). The enormity of the hierarchy of angels (*malakut*) in comparison to the hierarchy of man (*nasut*) is like the universe compared to the womb. It is the domain of the angels, where pure spirits of Divine lovers also abide. Its place is *tariqah*—the mystical path.

In *shariah*, the wayfarer is a man of conversation, confined to recollection of the attributes of God and receives only promises of the union and Divine bounties. In *tariqah*, however, the seeker begins to walk towards God the Most High in this world. Therefore, the follower of *shariah* is a man of mere *talk*, but the follower of *tariqah* is a man of *walk*, or action. His or her destination is *Lillah*, the Divine Name for meditation. Whatever, he or she performs, he or she performs it for God. He or she progresses from the state of inclination to the state of love. The color of this esoteric personality is yellow. Its recollection or *dhikr* is, *La Ilaha IllAllah*, "There is no God but Allah."

In this stage the seeker at the time of recollection sees angels descending from heaven in different forms. He receives Divine inspiration and spiritual tidings. In this regard, God the most High said, "Verily to those who said

God is our Lord and then stick to it, we send them our angels, who ask them not to fear and worry and to be joyful, for paradise is promised to you." (Quran 41:30).

Sufis call themselves *faqirs*, which literally means *poor*. The word *faqir* comes from *faqr, poverty*. In a mystical sense it means *gnosis*. The Prophet Hazrat Muhammad (pbuh) was proud of his poverty when he said, "*Faqri Fakhri*." The Prophet himself and his immediate family did not possess anything at all. Whatever, they got in the morning was given away in the evening.

Poverty is a station for the Sufis on the way towards Allah. In a spiritual sense, it is the absence of desire for worldly attachments. Mystics do not rely on created beings for anything, and would therefore ask none for help. To possess anything means to be possessed by it. Hujwiri described poverty correctly by saying that "its form is destitution and indigence, but its essence is fortune and free choice." *Faqr* is considered the central quality of a mystic. It is also equated with *fana* (annihilation in God), which is the ultimate destination of the mystic.

Chapter Six

DIVINE LOVE

The moment I realized the oneness of God,
The flame of His love shone within me and led me on.
Constantly it burns in my heart, revealing its mysteries,
This fire of love burns me from inside, fueled by my longing,
I found Him closer than my jugular vein,
My love has brought me face to face with Him.
(Sultan Bahu)

Everyone asks for firmness in faith, but few in love,
They ask for faith and are ashamed of love, such arrogant hearts.
Faith has no idea of the place where love can transport you.
I swear by my faith, Bahu, keep my love firm.

Hazrat Sultan Bahu.

Love is the highest possible state a person can reach on the mystical path. Love is *marifah* (gnosis) because, "One can love only what one knows."

To understand the importance of Divine love, we should start with the prayer of the Prophet Hazrat Muhammad (pbuh),

O Lord grant me Your love,
And grant me the love of those who love You,
O Lord, grant me the desire to keep loving You,
And make me keep Your love dearer than cool water.

The Prophet (pbuh) also stressed that the love of God and His messenger is a condition of faith. In this respect, mystics are confident that their love for God in itself is the result of Divine grace and without which none can learn about faith. The mystics also realized that the longing they experience for God is not due to their own efforts but exists because God wanted it. As the Quran says, "He loves them and they love Him." (Quran 5:54).

This clearly affirms that God's love precedes human love.

A servant can only love God, when God loves him.

Not a single lover would seek union
If the Beloved were not seeking it.

(Jalal ud Din Rumi)

A *hadith qudsi* (holy tradition) states that God is a hidden treasure that longs to be known. This gives the impression of this feeling of God's wish to love and be loved. Al Ghazali has quoted another *hadith* in this vein, "There are some of My special servants who love only Me and I love them,

125

they want Me, and I want them, and they look towards Me, and I look at them. They are those who remember Me all day and wait for the night as passionately as the birds long for their nests at sunset. They return to Me when the world is sleeping in comfort and every soul is with its loved one. They will stand in prayer, then will prostrate and rub their faces on the ground and will call Me, singing My praises and graces. Some of them remember Me crying, some weeping, and some complaining, and they do this while standing, sitting, kneeling, and prostrating. I am aware what they do for My sake and what they endure for My love."

Love is the annihilation of the lover in His attributes and complete surrender to the will of the Beloved. Love is eternal because the Beloved is eternal. As the sage of Shiraz Hafiz has said,

The adventure between me and my Beloved has no end,

That which has no beginning cannot have an end.

Sufis have adequately spoken about this love inspired by God. It is like a flame that burns everything except the Beloved. Longing is God's fire, which He ignites in the heart of a lover to consume everything worldly except His memory.

Divine lovers welcome pain and death if the Beloved decrees it. In Sufi poetry, pain and suffering are requirements to attain the unattainable beauty of the Divine Beloved. In the valley of love only those are allowed access who are ready to be beheaded. The prime example is Hallaj, the martyr of love, who lost his limbs before being decapitated and burned—his ashes then being thrown in the Tigris River.

The following verse removes all doubts about the sacrifice required on behalf of love:

Love came and like blood ran through my flesh and veins,

Emptied me, and then filled me with the Friend.

The Friend took from me every part of my being,

Of me, a name remained to me; the rest is all He.

(Shaykh Najm ul Din daya)

There is a story about an Israelite mystic, who for a very long time he had strenuously worshiped God. Then suddenly, one day a message came to the Prophet of that time, "Go and ask the ascetic, 'What benefit will you gain from all that hardship you are enduring to this day? I have not created you but for chastisement.'" As soon as the ascetic received the Divine message through the Prophet, he got up and started dancing in ecstasy. "What's the matter with you?" enquired the Prophet. "Has this message made you profoundly happy instead of being worried that you have started dancing?" "Yes off course, at least He has remembered me," answered the ascetic. "He has taken me into account, and that is the joy of the lover." The ascetic then recited this verse,

Even though He says, He will kill me

That He says, it can't but thrill me.

This story contains important insights. The two characters see the message differently. The Prophet receives the message but not the meaning hidden in the message. The ascetic, who instead of feeling rejected, sees it as a Divine blessing and a cause for celebration. The real point reflected in this story is that God does His will as He chooses and deems fit. What actually matters is submission to the Divine will, and whatever that will is, one should rejoice. Regarding the martyrs of love, mystics trust the word of God, "Do not call them dead who have been slain for God's sake. Nay they are alive" (Quran 3:163).

It is the sword of "There is no God but Allah," (*la ilaha Illallah*), the first half of the proclamation of faith, that slays the lover—and then nothing remains except God.

Shibli had witnessed and was deeply perplexed by the martyrdom of Hallaj, so he asked God about it in his prayers. Shibli—to this question of his—received the following answer: "Whom My love kills, for him shall I be blood money." Such souls are rewarded by God Himself by being present with Him. Divine lovers regard all trials and tribulations as signs of His kindness and favor. Sufis consider suffering and pain to be a means of nearness to God. That is why Hallaj dared to say, "Suffering is He Himself."

In fact, the more God loves a person, the more He will put him to test.

The Prophrt Hazrat Muhammad (pbuh) said in a tradition, "The most afflicted people are the Prophets, then the saints, and so forth" (*hadith*).

The Quran offers stories of the Prophets who suffered most for God's sake, for they were nearest to Him. The human soul can mature only through suffering and hardship. Therefore, when the true wayfarer seeks Allah's loving kindness and forgiveness, he or she seeks pain, for the true wayfarer earnestly believes that affliction makes man perfect.

Sufis are both passionate lovers of Divine beauty and prolific poets. From Rabia Al Adwiya to Jalal ud Din Rumi, their poetry has been revealing and concealing the truth and capturing the mysteries of love and annihilation, as if to give testimony to Tolstoy's dictum, "Mysticism without poetry is superstition."

Persian poetry contains poignant verses on the topic of Divine love. Mystical love and longing have been debated extensively during the tenth century. Passionate love and human and Divine relationships have been explored deeply. Hallaj openly expressed the inner dynamics of Divine love, to the extent that influenced Fakhruddin Iraqi to poetically change the proclamation of faith to, *La ilaha Illa Ishq* (There is no deity save but Love).

For Sufis, love has become a growing power and a strong personal commitment that always turns into a mystic force that draws everything back to its source. A true lover is successful in both worlds, for he is constantly with God, whom he loves. As the Prophet Hazrat Muhammad (pbuh) has said, "Man is with him, whom he loves" (*hadith*).

This passionate love sees with the eyes of inner knowing and understands the ways of God. In this vein of love, Sheikh Muzaffar has said, "If someone loves something, he keeps it on his mind. The one, who loves God, always recollects and contemplates Him whenever and in whatever state he or she is in. The nightingale of love sings and dances eternally on the rosebush of the Beloved."

The mystical poetry of Rumi is the embodiment of Divine love, which radiates through his verses and illuminates the heart of all lovers. Once he addressed his Beloved,

Behold, I tried all things, turned everywhere
But never found a friend so dear as you.
I tasted every fountain, every grape

But never tasted wine so sweet as you. (*Diwan*)

From the time love carried away Rumi's heart, he knew that the highest experience of ecstasy and union with God the Beloved could not be translated into human words, yet the verses that came from his lips were born in inspiration and were filled with oceans of meaning.

Rumi declared that love, lover, and Beloved are the same,

Since I have heard of the world of love,

I have spent my life, my heart

And my eyes this way.

I used to think that love

And the Beloved are different

I know they are the same. (*Diwan*)

There is no doubt that Rumi is the most celebrated poet in the world, for what he speaks of is from the heart and is about love.

There is no salvation for the soul

But to fall in love.

It has to creep and crawl

Among the lovers first.

Only lovers can escape

From these two worlds

This was written in creation.

Only from the heart can you touch the sky

The rose of glory

Can only be raised in the heart. (*Diwan*)

Nobody can comprehend the Essence of God, for He cannot be reached or recognized by human effort. However, God is the central theme in all mystic poetry. As Rumi put it,

Whatever, you can think is perishable

That which enters no thought, that is God.

God is the source of all love, and most Sufis believe love to be His Essence. Because He created the universe out of His love, it is manifested throughout the entire cosmos. God is also a treasure of infinite mercy so as He is a treasure of beauty. This Divine beauty is reflected in all of His creation, which acts as a mirror for Him. Similarly all of His attributes are manifested to the fullest under two broad categories—His Beauty (*jamal*) and His Majesty (*jalal*)—which are constantly interacting as mercy and wrath and beauty and power. This ongoing interplay is evident in all creation. God is both loving and overpowering, and He is the One, Who gives life and makes living things die. He is constantly showing signs so that we may know Him, and He is aware of what everybody needs in every moment. In the words of the Quran, "He is every day engaged in some work" (55:29), because, "neither slumber nor sleep overcomes Him" (2:256).

It is a Divine blessing to know Him, and for those who are aware, everything is a sign that points towards Him. As the Quran might seem to indicate, "We have placed signs in the horizons and in yourselves" (41:53).

Rumi's poetry provides beautiful commentaries on Quranic thoughts; Sufis consider his *Masnavi* to be the Quran written in the Pahlavi language. This is because Rumi's verse provides a sense of devotion, universal love, and the presence of God, even though God remains hidden behind the veil of all of His creation. Even though He cannot be seen directly due to His intense, resplendent beauty, which can only be seen when reflected through His creation—just as one looks at the ocean and sees the ever-restless foam dancing on the waves without knowing the depths—so do Rumi's couplets dance within the innermost core of the heart, revealing glimpses of the vast ocean of Divine love.

God's eternal Grace and infinite Mercy are the only hopes for those suffering in love. There is a vaster plan behind all tribulations, as Rumi alludes to it,

And if He closes before you
All passes and all ways,
He will show a hidden pathway
Which no one yet has known?

God Himself is the source of love and the source of seeking. It is He who takes the first step and inspires love in lovers' hearts. God is the seeker, and man is His object of seeking, in Rumi's words,

Lovers do not themselves seek and yearn

In the entire world there is no one seeking but He.

Abu Yazid Bastami made this truth evidently clear by stating that, "Initially my goal was to remember God, to understand Him, to intimately love Him, and to find Him. When I reached the end of my destination, I realized that He knew me before I knew Him, He loved me from pre-eternity, before I loved Him, and it was He seeking me before I sought Him."

Since the day of creation, Divine grace is seeking mankind. His grace comes unexpectedly, a strong faith and an alert heart is needed to seize the moment. Only with faith born out of love of God one can understand God's wisdom and the perfection of all things. The mystery of Divine love and the relationship between the seeking man and his Creator have been explored by Sufis in great detail. If we name man as the seeker of God, the following would be absolutely true:

We have come into existence from nonexistence,

Merely in quest of our Beloved Lord—the Creator.

The story of the moth and candle—first told by Hallaj the martyr mystic and retold by Rumi, Attar, and many other Sufis—highlights the impossible task of comprehending God.

Once all the moths gathered for a meeting to find out the truth about the candle's light. They were all fired up and excited with a deep yearning for the flame. They wanted to know the mystery hidden in the flame that attracts them so intensely that they lose all control and become annihilated in it. One of the moths volunteered, flew away, and saw a candle burning in a distant place. He returned and told his friends what he saw and experienced from a distance. Their leader, however, who was a wise moth, said, "He does not know the truth? And in fact he is clueless." Another moth flew to visit the candle and came close to the light and barely touched the flame with his wings. When he came back he explained his encounter with the flame and tried to explain what the union with the candle really meant. The wise moth rejected his claim and said, "Your account is not much different than that of your friend." Finally, a third moth flew up and threw himself in ecstasy into the burning flame. As he entered the flame, he lit up and glowed with a radiant red color like the flame, until he became fully merged with the flame, leaving no trace of him. The wise moth saw the whole affair and realized that the candle had identified the moth with itself and turned him into its own light. The wise moth said, "He is the only one who knows what he has attained. None else can comprehend it."

Love is the moth, and the Beloved is like a candle. A true moth cannot exist without a candle. If the moth would not perish in the flame of the candle, it would not be a true moth, and if the candle's light would not burn it, that would not be a true candle.

A true human being circambulates forever around the light of God's Beauty and Majesty. God draws a man towards His light and annihilates him, and this is what no intellect can comprehend. In this context, Rumi narrated the story of the lover and the Beloved, which stresses the importance of sacrificing one's self to be with the source.

A Man knocked at the door of his Beloved.
"Who are you, trusted one?" thus asked the friend.
He answered "I." The friend said, "Go away.
Here is no place for people raw and crude."
What then, could mature the raw and rescue him
But separation's fire and exile's flame?
The poor man went away and traveled for a whole year.
And burned in separation from his friend,
And he matured, was cooked and burnt, returned
And carefully approached the friend's abode.
He walked around it in a conscious fear.
His friend called out, "Who is there at my door?"
The answer, "You dear, you are at the door."
He said, "Come in, now that you are all I.
There is no room in this house for two I's." (*Masnavi* 3056-63)

If one looks carefully, one would realize that it is He who is seeking mankind. Similarly, Abu Yazid Bastami said that he was searching for God for over thirty years. One day he suddenly realized that it was God searching for him. God was the seeker and he was the sought. The Quran stresses this point in the following manner, "Are you waiting patiently, while God is looking towards you? (Quran 25:20). "So turn towards Allah. You are to strive towards your Lord and then meet Him" (Quran 18:20).

THE HEART IS DEEPER THAN THE OCEAN

The heart is deeper than the ocean, dive deep into it,
O seeker and explore.
Drink the water of life from this ocean,
Or your soul will always remain thirsty.
Those who contemplate on the Lord,
Devoting every breath to his remembrance
Will always keep Him in their hearts. (Sultan Bahu)

Divine love originates in the heart, for it is the real seat of God Almighty. The heart is not merely a piece of flesh hanging in the chest, to the left side, and pumping blood into the body. It is the abode of the bright, esoteric personality of the heart on which all spiritual progress on the path depends. It contains the candle that has the resemblance of His light, which illuminates the entire being of the seeker, divulging the secrets of *fana* (annihilation of the self in God), *baqa* (subsistence through God), surrender, and Divine love. This truth is imparted in the following verse from holy tradition, wherein God has said, "I could not be contained in the heavens or the earth, but the heart of My humble servant can contain Me."

To this effect, the legend of Abu Yazid Bastami is clearly enlightening. During one of his esoteric flights, Bayazid Bastami thought he had reached the Throne of the Almighty. He therefore, addressed the Throne, "We are told that God resides here and rests upon thee." To this the Throne replied, "O Bayazid, we are told that He lives in a broken heart."

Therefore, great Sufi masters have consistently advised their followers to serve their fellow human beings, as Sultan Bahu said, "Nursing one broken heart, Bahu, is equal to the worship of a lifetime." A Persian Sufi poet went further:

Secure a heart, for it is the great pilgrimage,
A heart is better than a thousand Kaabas.

Kaaba is the dwelling of Abraham, son of Azar,
While the heart is the passage of the Great Glorious God.

Al Tirmidhi described the body as a kingdom wherein the heart reigns as a sultan and other bodily organs as its servants. Each organ performs its duty according to the command of the ruler (heart). The heart, however, is between the two fingers of God, and its will comes from Him. God alone knows about the heart, and none else can see what it contains. The heart is the place where God's proximity, union, and observation can be attained. God is the guardian of hearts, for it contains His innermost Essence, love, and true knowledge of His secrets.

The heart is the treasury
In which God's mysteries are stored,
Seek the purpose of both the worlds
Through the heart
For that is the point of it. (Lahiji)

Sheikh Nizam ul Din Awliya stated that no work would be more highly rewarded on the Day of Judgment than, "Bringing happiness to the human heart. In the eyes of Allah, no spiritual exercise, no penitence, no prayer, and no vigil has greater significance than removing the misery of fellow human beings, bringing consolation to distressed hearts, and helping the downtrodden."

Divine grace does not discriminate between one person and another. When the sun shines, it gives warmth and light to everyone, whether they live in mansions or on the streets. When it rains, the rich and the poor benefit equally from the downpour. Thus, to live within the flow of this Divine grace, one must mirror it. Once Khawaja Moin ud Din was asked to explain the highest form of devotion most pleasing to God. He replied, "Develop river-like generosity, sun-like bounty, and earth-like hospitality." The story of Prophet Abraham (may God be pleased with him) further illustrates this approach. Prophet Abraham (pbuh) was a generous and hospitable man. He never took his meals without some guests joining him. He sometimes would go for miles in search of a guest. He would bring them to his tent, show them great generosity, and feed them. One day he invited an old person, but later on realized that he was a polytheist. He, therefore, hesitated giving food to this man, till the Divine voice spoke to him, "Abraham! How is it that we can give life to this man and feed him for seventy years, yet you cannot give him food just for one night?" The Divine message is clear: God wants us to transcend all barriers of race, religion, and geography in dealing with our fellow creatures. Human beings are like children of God on earth, and if we wish to seek His pleasure, we should strive for the welfare of all people regardless of any consideration. That truly means, "Living for the Lord alone."

We should acknowledge God's Greatness by offering gratitude and thanks not only for granting us life and material things, but for having granted us a heart that can love and yearn for Him. In this regard, there is a famous *hadith,* "The heart of the faithful is between the two fingers of the All-Compassionate, and He turns it whenever He wants." Again, it is God who wrote faith in the heart of His obedient servants. Faith is His personal Name, *Allah,* which is firmly established in the hearts of the faithful in the form of the light of certainity.

Sheikh Muzaffar stated that, "A sin committed with love is much better than a loveless act of devotion. If you do not love God, any devotional act will be a fruitless and meaningless labor. However, if you sin with passion, it is at least enjoyable for the time being, even though it will result in consequences. Therefore, whatever, you do, do it with love."

Khawaja Nizam ud Din Awliya, regarding sin and the sinner, has said, "A sinner, even in the state of sin, remains obedient in three respects. First of all he knows what he does is wrong. Second, he realizes that God the Most High is watching him and knows whatever he does. Third, he still hopes for forgiveness on account of repentance and believes in the Mercy of God."

Once, someone asked Imam Abu Hanifa whether unbelievers would reside in the hell permanently or not. He replied, "No, they will not." "How could that be?" they asked. Imam replied, "On the day of resurrection the unbelievers will see their punishment and will accept faith in the Oneness of God, but their faith will be of no benefit to them because, they did not believe in the unseen. Therefore, they will be in hell despite the fact they will go there as believers." Then the Imam interpreted the Quranic verse,

"And, we did not create *jinn* and men except to worship" (51:56), which according to Ibne Abbass means "except to profess God's Oneness."

The true faithful are those who believe in the Oneness of God without seeing, but unbelievers attest to His unity when they are face to face with punishment on the day of resurrection.

One should think of others as better than oneself, even though someone may be obedient and someone else a sinner. It may well be that the obedience of the former may be his last act of devotion, whereas the sinfulness of the later is the last of his sins.

The story of Hassan Al Basari is worth mentioning in this respect. Hassan Al Basari used to say, "I think of everyone whom I see to be better than myself." He continued: "One day, however, I was passing along the banks of a river and I saw an Ethiopian sitting near the edge of the river. He had a bottle alongside him, and every now and then he would drink of it and enjoy. There was also a woman sitting near him. All of a sudden this thought occurred to me, 'At least I am better than him.' As soon as I was immersed in this thought, I saw a boat starting to sink in the river. There were seven people on board, and all of the seven began to drown. The Ethiopian immediately jumped into the river and pulled out six people, then he turned towards me and said, 'O Hassan at least pull out the seventh one.'" Hassan stood there in utter surprise. After that the Ethopian said to Hassan, "In this bottle is water, and this woman is my mother. It was to test what you perceive. It appears that you can only see the outer guise of matters."

CHAPTER SEVEN

THE POWER OF GIVING

Sharing the bounties of God with others, helping people in need, and serving fellow human beings in distress is the shortest possible way to draw near to the light of the Almighty and attain Oneness with Him. Everything belongs to God. He is the owner of everything we possess. Our lives, health, intelligence, and material goods are gifts from Him. He has entrusted us with all that we have, so that we may use everything wisely and share everything with those we love and with those who are in need of it.

Charity (*zakat*) is the fourth pillar of the Islamic faith, made obligatory by God the Most High with a purpose to purify and grow our possessions and to be the agents of sharing His blessings. Therefore, it is binding on all male and female Muslims to give away 2.5% of their savings and business profits to the poor. Similarly 5% to 10% of the harvest should be distributed among destitute and needy people. There are specific rules and regulations concerning how to calculate alms (*zakat*) and who can benefit from it. God the Most High has specified this in *Sura Taubah*, "The offerings given for the sake of God are only for the poor and needy and those who are in charge thereof, and those whose hearts are to be won over, and for the freeing of human beings from bondage, and those who are overburdened with debts and for every struggle in God's cause and for the wayfarer, and this is an ordinance from God and God is all knowing, wise" (Quran 9:60).

Apart from obligatory almsgiving, voluntary charity is a necessity for every Muslim, according to the Prophet of Islam. It is an act of devotion highly treasured by Almighty Allah because He Himself frequently encourages believers to give Him a goodly loan by giving charity to those in need. And He promises to repay that goodly loan several folds in this life and much more in the hereafter. In fact, a sincere offering will be rewarded by Him in a manner beyond all expectations, for He will, "Provide for him from an unseen source and means of living" (Quran 65:2-3).

If five conditions are present at the time of charity offerings, then the offerings will certainly be acceptable to the Lord of the heavens and the earth.

Khawaja Nizam ud Din has enumerated them as follows. Of these five conditions, two are required prior to the giving of the charity. One of them is that whatever is given should have been legally obtained and permissible by religious law. The second condition is that it should be given to deserving people as mentioned in the Quran. The two conditions that should accompany the actual act of giving follow:

1. Charity should be given with humility, cheerfulness, and an expansive heart.
2. It should be given in secret. The highest form of charity occurs when the giver and the recipient do not know each other.

The fifth condition comes after the charity has been given. It is that one should not discuss or mention it to anyone and should forget about it.

Money is not everything. That is what the Prophet Hazrat Muhammad (pbuh) emphasized when he was asked, "What if a person has nothing to give?" The Prophet (pbuh) replied, "He should work with his own hands for his benefit and then give something out of such earning in charity." The companions asked, "What if he is not able to work?" The Prophet (pbuh) replied, "He should help the poor and needy people." The companions said, "What if he is incapable of doing so?" The Prophet (pbuh) said, "He should check himself from doing evil. That is also charity."

The following story clearly proves that serving people is as if directly serving God. The followers of Prophet Moses (pbuh) once gathered around him and asked him, "O Moses, we would like to invite our Lord for a dinner party so that we can serve Him food. Would you please speak to the Lord and request Him on our behalf to accept our invitation and honor us by His presence?" At this, Moses (pbuh) became angry and said, "Why do you not know that God neither drinks nor eats? He is beyond all needs."

However, when Moses (pbuh) went to talk to God on Mount Sinai, God said to him, "Why did you not tell Me about the invitation My servants have given Me? Because they have sincerely invited Me, tell them that on Friday evening I shall come to their party and join them for a meal."

Moses (pbuh) told his followers, and everyone was eagerly waiting for that time. They were all busy in making preparations for the feast. As Friday evening approached, there appeared an old man in shabby clothes looking tired and fatigued, as if he was coming from a very exhaustible journey. When he saw Moses (pbuh) he told him, "I am very hungry and tired; please give me some food to eat." Moses (pbuh) said to him, "The Lord of the heavens and the earth is coming to our feast; you should wait and be patient. Here, take this pitcher and get some water from the well so that you as well can help us to serve God." The old man went and brought some water and again begged for some food, but no one would pay any attention to him. Everyone was waiting for the Lord to arrive. As the time passed and it grew darker and yet there was no sign of the Lord, everyone was upset with Moses (pbuh) and began criticizing him because the Lord did not show up.

The next day Moses (pbuh) climbed Mount Sinai and talked to God, "Dear Lord, You have put me to great shame before my followers because You promised to come to our feast but did not come." At this, God replied, "Actually, I did come and I asked you in person, but when I told you that I was hungry, you gave Me a pitcher to get water. I asked again for food but was sent away to work. None of you welcomed Me with respect."

"My Lord, an old person came and asked for food, but he was a human being," said Moses (pbuh).

"I was with that servant of Mine. You would have honored Me by honoring him. You would have served Me by serving him. All the heavens and earth contain Me not, but the hearts of My servants contain Me. I neither eat nor drink, yet to honor My servants is to honor Me. Taking care of them is taking care of Me."

Just as the Prophet Moses (pbuh) and his people did not recognize God in his distressing disguise and lost the opportunity to serve Him, we do see Him every day hungry for love, thirsty for kindness, begging for loyalty, and asking for shelter. He is out there looking, begging, and hoping we will help. Will we be there to serve Him? Therefore, we shall be seeking the face of God in everything, everyone, everywhere, all the time, and seeing His hand in every matter. As the Quran says, "And wherever, you turn there is the face of God." (Quran 2:115).

In *Tazkarat ul Awliya*, Attar *wrote* about Abdullah Bin Mubarak that while he was living in Mecca, one year he performed his pilgrimage and that on the last night of the *Hajj* he slept and saw in a dream that two angels had descended from heaven and sat upon the roof of the Kaaba. One of them asked the other, "How many have come to perform the pilgrimage this year?" The other angel replied, "Around six hundred thousand." The first angel again asked, "Out of those six hundred thousand, how many have had their devotion accepted?" Not a single one," replied the second angel.

Abdullah Bin Mubarak reported that on hearing this conversation his heart was filled with sorrow. He lamented, "All these people have come from faraway places, from distant parts of the world, taking great pain, all that labor, and yet all that is in vain."

At this the angel said, "There is a cobbler in Damascuss, his name is Ali Ibn Mowaffaq. Though he has not come to the pilgrimage, his pilgrimage has been accepted. And if the blessings of his pilgrimage are distributed among all the pilgrims, they can be granted absolution."

When he heard this dialogue of the angels, Abdullah Bin Mubarak woke up and made up his mind to go to Damascus and visit that person whose pilgrimage had gained such great acceptance and approval from the Lord of the worlds. So he went to Damascus and looked for where he lived. After some searching he found him. "What is your name?" Abdullah asked him. He replied, "Ali Ibn Mowaffaq." "I would like to talk to you," said Abdullah. Ali agreed. "What do you do for living?" asked Abdullah. "I am a cobbler and I mend shoes," replied Ali. He then told of his dream, and Ali asked his name. "Abdullah Bin Mobarak," he said. At this, he cried, fainted, and fell down on the ground. When he regained his consciousness. Abdullah pleaded, "Tell me your story." He started telling the story, "For over thirty years, I wished to perform the pilgrimage. I had worked hard cobbling all these years and had saved up to three hundred and fifty *dihams* as traveling expenses and provisions for the journey. This year I wanted to go to Mecca. One day my pregnant wife was standing beside the house of our neighbor and smelled food from next door. She had an intense craving for the food because of her pregnancy and begged me to go and fetch a bit of food for her. So, I went and knocked at the neighbor's door and explained the whole situation. My request puzzled the neighbor at first, but then he burst into tears, "We have not eaten in three days, and my children are hungry," he said. "Today, I saw a dead donkey lying outside the city, so I cut off a piece and cooked it to feed my children. I am afraid it would not be a lawful food for you."

"My heart burned within my chest, when I heard this story," said Ali. "How deplorable it is that a neighbor of ours is passing his days in such scarcity and poverty, and we are unaware of his plight and could not lend him any assistance," he told his wife and gave his neighbor the three hundred and fifty *dirhams* and said to him, "Please spend this money on your children, this is my pilgrimage."

Both men were astonished by the incredible wonder work of the Most Merciful of the Merciful. Ali Ibn Mowaffaq further added, "Perhaps the Heavenly Judge has taken kindly to this act of mine and graced me with His Acceptance."

Any righteous act performed with sincerity and good intention for the sake of God without a desire for fame and compensation will without doubt result in pleasure and proximity of the Lord. As God the Most High said, "So let him, whoever hopes for the visual perception of his Lord, do righteous deeds and admit no other as partner in the worship of his Lord" (Quran 18:110).

Similarly speaking of charity, the Prophet Hazrat Muhammad (pbuh) said in a *hadith qudsi,* "When the earth was created, it was unstable and shaky. Therefore, Allah created mountains and placed them as pegs to stabilize the earth. When the angels saw this they were amazed by the wisdom of God and asked, "O Lord of the universe is there anything more powerful than mountains?"

"Yes, iron is more powerful," said the Lord.

"O Lord of the universe, is there anything more powerful than iron?" asked the angels again.

"Yes, fire is more powerful," the Lord replied.

"O Lord of the universe is there anything more superior to fire?" inquired the angels."

"Yes, water is much superior," God replied.

"O Lord of the universe, is anything more powerful than water?"

"Yes, wind is stronger than water."

"O Lord of the universe, is there anything more powerful than the wind?" Once again the angels questioned.

At this, God the Most High replied, "Yes, the children of Adam who give charity wholeheartedly in secret, so much so that the left hand does not know what the right hand is doing."

Once two guests arrived at Rabia Al Adwiya's cottage; both men were tired and hungry. They talked with each other and said, "She may offer us some food, which must be from a lawful source." When they sat down on the ground, she spread a cloth and placed two loaves of bread on it. They were happy to see some food, for they were very hungry. In the meanwhile a beggar arrived at the door and asked for some food. Rabia gave him the two loaves. Seeing this, the two guests were disappointed, but said nothing. As soon as the beggar left, a maidservant entered the cottage and brought some freshly baked warm bread.

"My mistress has sent these as a gift," the maidservant said. Rabia counted them; there were eighteen loaves of bread. "These are not meant for me," Rabia remarked. The maidservant assured her that her mistress had sent these loaves for Rabia, but Rabia was not convinced. As a matter of fact the maidservant had taken two loaves for herself. She went back and added the two loaves to the rest and returned again. This time Rabia counted the loaves, they were twenty, and she accepted them.

"Now these were for me," she said. She put the loaves in front of the guests, and they ate to their fill. "What is the whole secret behind all this?" the guests inquired, "We wanted to have your own bread, but you gave it away to the beggar. Then you refused the eighteen loaves, but when they were twenty you accepted them."

"I was aware when you arrived that you were very hungry," Rabia replied. "I thought how these two loaves can be enough for honorable guests such as you. So when the beggar arrived at the door, I gave them to him and asked the Almighty God, 'O God you have promised to give tenfold for any offering, and I strongly believe in you. I have given two loaves to please Thee, so that you may give back twenty in return. When eighteen loaves were brought to me, I understood that either they were not meant for me or there was some misappropriation.'"

Faith and trust form the basis for salvation and success on the path. Sufis have strong faith and unwavering trust in the will of God. The following account of Habib Al Ajami and Hassan Al Basri, narrated in *Tazkarat ul Awliya*, will shed enough light on this. Once, Hassan Al Basri went to see Habib Al Ajami, as a guest. Habib served him by placing before him two loaves of bread and a little bit of salt. Hassan was very hungry, and as soon as he began to eat, a beggar showed up at the door and asked for food. Habib took the two loaves of bread and salt in front of Hassan and gave it to the beggar. Hassan was astonished by Habib's unfriendly behavior and scolded him, "You are a learned man of knowledge. You should not take all the bread in front of the guest and give it to the beggar. You should have given at least a portion to the beggar and a portion to the guest."

Habib remained quiet. At the same time a slave entered the room with a tray full of roasted lamb, five loaves of bread, sweetmeats, and five hundred silver coins. He placed the tray full of food in front of Hassan and distributed the silver coins among the poor.

When Hassan was done eating, he addressed him, "You are a good man of God. If you had only a little bit of faith, it would suffice you. Knowledge without faith is useless."

Trust in God should be so complete that one never relies on others and pays no attention to them, as illustrated in the following story. Once, Ibrahim Khawas was traveling to Mecca to perform pilgrimage. On his way to the Kaaba a young man joined his company. When Ibrahim Khawas saw him, he asked, "Where are you going?" "I am going to perform the pilgrimage," said the young man. "But you are empty handed, where are your provisions for such a long journey?" asked Ibrahim. "God the exalted and Merciful, has provided for me until now. He can certainly take me to the Kaaba without any provisions," replied the youth.

After a while, when Ibrahim Khawas reached the Holy Kaaba, the young man was already there, making circambulations around the house of the Lord. When their eyes met, the young man said to Khawas, "O man of God, you had little faith, do you now regret what you had asked me on the journey?"

Everyone who serves is also served. If you serve those in need as if you have served God, then God makes sure that you are served as well from an unseen source and means of living.

The Holy Prophet Hazrat Muhammad (pbuh) said, "The cupbearer who serves water to others should be the last to drink." On serving food to others, there is a story about a dervish in Baghdad who used to serve twelve hundred bowls of food every day to people. He personally would supervise the preparation and cooking of the food. All of a sudden, one day, he called all of his servants and cooks and asked them, "Have you not forgotten somebody while serving food to people?" "No," was the uninanimous reply by his servants. "We accounted for everyone and did not overlook anybody." He asked them again, "Think carefully, if anyone was missed." "Not at all, we were very diligent in the distribution of food," they said. "We gave food to anyone who came forward and nobody was sent without food." "But something has gone wrong," said the Sheikh. "What is the reason for all this inquiry?" the servants were surprised and requested to know.

At this the Sheikh replied, "For the past three days you have given me no food and forgot all about me." It so happened that during the previous three days at mealtime no one brought any food to the Sheikh. Because there were numerous servants, everyone presumed that someone else had taken care of the master, with the consequence that no one indeed gave him anything to eat. Yet it was after three days without food that the Sheikh finally reminded his servants to feed him as well.

Regarding the blessings of charity, I have personal spiritual experiences. I will end this chapter with the account of such an experience. When I was still residing in Iran and working in the city of Quchan, I had a friend who was a school teacher and was involved in charitable and philanthropic activities. Every year, during the winter season, he used to collect warm clothing: jackets, shoes, and other durable and non-perishable goods for indigent students and their families in the area. He approached me for this purpose and asked me to help out with the situation. Quchan is a small city situated near Mashad, where winters are extremely cold. I bought some warm clothing: winter jackets, sneakers, and a brand new suit—enough for a family of six—and passed these items on to my friend. He gave those items to a poor and deserving Syed family (descendents of the Holy Prophet).

A few days later, I was blessed with the vision of Hazrat Imam Hussain (may God be pleased with him) in a dream. I saw that I was present at the Holy shrine of Hazrat Imam Reza (may God be pleased with him) in Mashad, and a handsome, tall person with a full black beard and a beautiful radiant face approached me. It was evident from his looks that he was a distinguished luminary. He was wearing traditional Arab attire. He came close and smiled at me. I greeted him with great respect, and we embraced each other like good old friends. He told me, "I am Hussain Ibne Ali." On hearing this, I kissed his hands, and it seemed that he was quite delighted with me. He blessed me, wished me good fortune, and then bid farewell to me. After that I woke from my vision and immediately knew that it was due to the *baraka* (blessing) of that charitable act.

Chapter Eight

MERCY UNTO THE WORLDS: THE PRAISED ONE

And when Jesus, the son of Mary said, "O children of Israel! Behold, I am an apostle of God unto you, to confirm the truth of whatever there still remains of the Torah, and to give you glad tidings of an apostle who shall come after me, and he shall be called the "Praised one."

(Quran 61:6)

Prophet Hazrat Muhammad (pbuh) is the apostle whose coming was predicted in the Christian scripture: the promise of God to humanity that "a highly praised one" would be sent for salvation and guidance in the fulfillment of this Biblical saying.

Today more than a billion people (one in every five human beings) follow his faith, sing his praises, and invoke God's peace and blessings upon him and his family. His behavior, his acts, and his words serve as models for the faithful, who try to imitate him even in the smallest details of his *sunna* (life).

He, indeed, was sent as a mercy unto the universe, "The helper of the two worlds," and the one who was the goal and meaning of all earlier Divine religions. As he was also the goal and cause of creation, the following quotations refer to him:

"But for thee, but for thee, I would not have created the spheres."
God proclaimed with love, "*Laulaka, Laulaka ma khalaqt ul Aflaka.*"
Prophet Hazrat Muhammad (pbuh) is God's first and best creation,
The first creation that Allah created was the light of your Prophet from His light. (*hadith Bukhari*)

§

He was the first of all Prophets as he said, "I was a Prophet when Adam was between water and clay." (*Bukhari*)

§

He was also the last and the seal of all Prophets as he proclaimed, "I was first of Prophets in creation and the last of them in resurrection." (*Abu Hurayrah*)

§

Each and every Prophet was sent to a particular people at a certain time, but Hazrat Muhammad Mustafa (pbuh) "the chosen one," was sent to all humanity until the end of time. The love of Hazrat Muhammad (pbuh) is a prerequisite of faith, as he has said, "As long as you do not love me more than anything else, your faith is not complete" (*Bukhari*). God Himself says, "If you love Me, follow the Prophet." And the Prophet (pbuh) said, "Whosoever, loves God, loves me."

The faithful simply love the Prophet (pbuh), for the love of the Prophet leads to the love of God. Hence the Prophet is the true embodiment of Divine love.

When your heart is filled with the love of Ahmad,

Then know with certitude that you are safe from the fire.

(Persian poet Sanai)

According to Rumi, for believers, the Prophet is, "The window through which one sees the Creator."

One of the Prophet's (pbuh) names is *Dhikr Allah*, and sending blessings on him is synonymous to remembering Allah. Ibne Attaullah wrote in one of his treatises that there is a deep connection between remembering God and remembering the Prophet (pbuh), as God says to the Prophet, "O Muhammad, I have made you one of the remembrances of Me. Those who remember you remember Me, and those who love you, love Me."

When as a young child the Prophet was lost and his nurse Halima was worried about him, she was told by a Divine voice not to worry because it is Hazrat Muhammad (pbuh), "in whom the whole world will get lost."

There is an extra-Quranic saying widely popular among Sufis that proclaims, *Anna Ahmad bila mim*, "I am *Ahmad* without *m* (*mim*)," which means *Ahad* or "One." According to Sufis, *m* is the letter of humanity, and if you take it out, *Ahad* or the "One" will remain as He was, He is, and will be. The veil of *m* is lifted only for the lovers who can see God through the Prophet.

This is why Prophet Hazrat Muhammad (pbuh) has expressly said, "Who has seen me, has seen Allah."

This clearly indicates that Hazrat Muhammad (pbuh) is above all men and unique among the Prophets. According to the Quran, Hazrat Muhammad (pbuh) is he who has to be obeyed. Hazrat Muhammad (pbuh) to Allah is like the light is to the sun and proves that Muhammad's light is as the "light from God's light."

Hazrat Muhammad (pbuh) was not only a messenger of God but much more. He was the instrument through which God worked. The following Quranic verse is frequently quoted to affirm this belief: "And you, O Prophet, did not cast pebbles when you cast them, but it was Allah the Almighty Who cast them" (Quran 8:17). In another place, God the Most High said, "Those who swear allegiance to you do not but swear allegiance to Allah; the hand of God is over their hands" (Quran). Therefore, Hazrat Muhammad (pbuh) is an aspect of God's activity.

The idea of the light of Muhammad (pbuh) is complex and at the same time fascinating. It was Muqatil who first idealized the person of the Prophet (pbuh) and interpreted the "Light Verse," *"Ayat an Nur"* (*sura* 24:35) as a reference to Hazrat Muhammad (pbuh), whose light shines through other messengers. This was further elaborated by later mystics. For instance, Sultan Bahu praised the Prophet (pbuh) by saying, "When God wanted to create Hazrat Muhammad (pbuh), He separated a light from His own light, observed it intently, fell in love with it, and called it the light of Muhammad" (*Mahak al FuquraKalan*).

Islamic mysticism is primarily based on the doctrine of unity of being and the universal man. The Prophet Hazrat Muhammad (pbuh) is the perfect or universal man (*insane kamil*) in whom all the possibilities of cosmic existence are realized. For mystics, he is the perfect mirror reflecting and emanating all of God's Names and attributes in his inner reality, which in Sufi terminology is called the Muhammadan Reality. For believers, he is the most perfect model in all respects, to be imitated even in the minutest details. They have a deep trust in the promise of the

Prophet (pbhu) who said, "O my son, the one who has cherished my Sunna without doubt has cherished me and who cherishes me will be with me in paradise" (*hadith*).

The prayer of light is a famous prayer that the Prophet (pbuh) used to recite frequently and has been the favorite of mystics, who recite it to invoke the light of God.

THE PRAYER OF LIGHT

O Lord, grant me light in my heart,
Grant me light in my speech, hearing and sight,
O Lord, grant me light above me and light below me,
Grant me light on my right side and on my left side,
Light in front of me and light behind me.
O Lord, grant me light in my body and my soul,
Grant me light and make me light.
O Lord, increase me in light, increase me in light,
And grant me light upon light.

Prophet Hazrat Muhammad (pbuh) is the greatest portal of God's light because he himself is "Light upon light." It is through him that the Divine light as well as God's blessings and favors flow down to his followers. He is the channel and instrument of God's mercy for all creation.

The faithful see their beloved Prophet Hazrat Muhammad (pbuh) in the verses of the Quran, which is in fact a commentary on his character, miracles, beauty, and high rank.

Some of the passages in the Glorious Quran are expressions of the Prophet's (pbuh) unparalleled beauty and majesty. "By the sun," is therefore the story of Prophet Muhammad's (pbuh) face and "By the night" is the tale of his beautiful black hair. God the Most High has time and again taken oath by the eternal loveliness of His beloved Prophet Muhammad (pbuh) in *suras* 91 and 92. In the beginning of *sura* 93, "By the morning light" is used as an allusion applied to his sun-like radiant face.

Prophet Muhammad (pbuh) was not only of high moral and exalted character, but all the spiritual qualities were physically manifested in his body. He was "Beauty from head to toe" and according to a Sufi, "God has created Muhammad's body in such un-surpassable beauty as has neither before him nor after him been seen in any human being. If the whole beauty of the Prophet were unveiled before our eyes, they could not bear its splendor." That is why the Prophet (pbhu) said, "Joseph was beautiful but I am more handsome."

The story of Umm Mabad attests to the physical beauty and overwhelming presence of the Prophet. She said, "I saw a man pure and clean. With a handsome face and fine figure. He was not marred by a skinny body, nor was he overly small in the head and neck. He was graceful and elegant, with intensely black eyes and thick eyelashes. There was huskiness in his voice, and his neck was long. His beard was thick, and his eyebrows were finely arched. When silent, he was grave and dignified, and when he spoke, glory rose up and overcame him. He was from afar the most beautiful of men and the most glorious, and close up he was the sweetest and the loveliest. He was sweet of speech and articulate, but not petty or trifling. His speech was a string of cascading pearls, measured so that none despaired of its length and no eye challenged him because of brevity."

"*Shamail al Mustafa,*" the physical features and celestial beauty of the Prophet (pbuh) had been described by Hazrat Ali, the son in law of the Prophet and the fourth Caliph of Islam, as follows: "Muhammad (pbuh) was of a medium size, did not have lank or crisp hair, was not fat, had a white rounded face, big black eyes, and long eyelashes. When he walked it was as though he went down a declivity. He had the 'seal of prophecy' between his shoulder blades. He was bulky. His face shone like the moon in the night of the full moon. He was taller than middling stature but shorter than conspicuous tallness. He had thick, curly hair. The plaits of his hair were parted. His hair reached beyond the lobe of his ear. His complexion was *azhar* (bright, luminous). Muhammad (pbuh) had a wide forehead and fine, long arched eyebrows, which did not meet. Between his eyebrows there was a vein that distended when he was angry. The upper part of his nose was hooked; he was thick bearded, had smooth cheeks, a strong mouth, and his teeth were set apart. He had thin hair on his chest. His neck was like the neck of an ivory statue, with purity of silver. Muhammad (pbhu) was proportionate, stout, and firm-gripped, even of belly and chest, broad chested and broad shouldered" (Tirmidhi).

According to Sufis, the Prophet (pbuh) told his close companions, especially the four friends, to remember his features and attributes and promised that anyone who stiches the description of his features in his shroud will be followed by a thousand angels on the last day of his life, who will recite the funeral prayers for him and ask for forgiveness on his behalf until the day of jugdement.

The Prophet (pbuh) performed miracles. "And the moon was split," (Quran 54:2) refers to the Prophet's (pbuh) miracle, when he was able to split the moon. He performed this miracle to highlight the truth of his message. He not only split the moon, but the two halves were so apart that Mount Hira could be seen in between them.

It is narrated in a legend that King Shakrawati Farmad of South India did indeed witness the splitting of the moon at the same time. When he learned and verified what had happened in Mecca on that very night, he converted to Islam, along with his people. This miracle apparently resulted in the first Muslim settlement in India. It is also fascinating to know that an old painting showing the splitting of the moon with all its detail was displayed at the court of a Rajput (Hindu) in Kotah, India.

Hazrat Muhammad (pbuh) is the reflection of Divine light, and it is said for a fact that he did not cast a shadow. Every moment of his life was a miracle: the gazelle spoke to him, trees and stones would greet him with peace, the handkerchief with which he wiped out his saliva would not burn in fire, and the poisoned meat of lamb would not harm him. On many occasions water would flow and pour out from between his fingers to quench the thirst of hundreds of people.

The story of the palm trunk, *hannana*, which the Prophet (pbuh) used as a pulpit in his early days of preaching, is quite moving. When a real stage was made for the Prophet (pbuh) and the palm trunk was thus discarded, full of grief it started weeping and sighing, for it missed the touch of the beloved Prophet. Rumi to this effect said,

> Should the human heart be less loving than a seemingly dead piece of wood?
>
> How can a philosopher who denies this miracle find his way to the saints? (*Masnavi*)

The Prophet Hazrat Muhammad (pbuh) himself strongly discouraged his followers not to exalt him above other messengers. He was proud only of one miracle, and that was the miracle of the Quran. The Quran is the uncreated, living word of God, verbally rendered from the blessed lips of the trustworthy Prophet (pbuh) to become the scripture of one of the greatest faiths on earth. The word of God is so beautiful, concise, rich, and vast in meaning that no one till the end of time will be able to write a single verse like it. In fact, God himself has guaranteed the safeguarding of the Quran, in the following words, "Surely, We Ourselves have sent down this exhortation and We will most surely safeguard it" (Quran 15:10).

All the authorities would agree that the Quran is word for word exactly as Hazrat Muhammad (pbuh) gave it out to the world. It was not changed since then, nor will it become corrupted until resurrection day.

The Prophet Muhammad (pbuh) has been called *ummi*, which usually means "illiterate" in the (Quran 7:157). He was not conversant with reading and writing (*sura* 29:49). His heart was not polluted by worldly knowledge and learning, but was a pure vessel ready to receive the Divine revelation. His knowledge is directly derived from the First Intellect, the source of all wisdom.

One of the greatest miracles of Prophet Muhammad (pbuh) was the night journey, his ascent to meet the Lord of the universe. According to tradition, this happened in body and in an awakened state in the company of Archangel Gabriel. He first went from the Kaaba to Al Aqsa mosque in Jerusalem. There he led the souls of all previous Prophets in prayer before ascending to the very presence of God. Gabriel could not accompany the Prophet (pbuh) beyond the lote tree, which marks the furthest limit of creation.

"If I would go one step further, my wings would become burned," sighed Gabriel on the night of ascension. There he met the Lord in a realm where no one else has ever entered. None has ever seen God in life, nor will anyone ever see Him. The Prophet had an intimate encounter with God alone, which he described as such, "I have a time with God in which no created being has access, not even the Archangels." He exchanged ninety-thousand words with God. When he returned his bed was still warm and the leaf he had brushed on arising was still moving. The opening of *sura* 17 relates to his ascension:

"Limitless in His glory is He who transported His servant by night from the inviolable House of worship (at Mecca) to the remote House of worship (at Jerusalem)."

In this regard, he is superior to all Prophets and even Moses (pbuh), who requested God for a vision and could not even look at the reflection through the burning bush without fainting. As a Persian Sufi poet has said,

Moses went out of mind by a single flash of attribute,

Thou seest the Essence of the Essence and still smiling.

The ascension of the Prophet Hazrat Muhammad (pbuh) and his time with God has become the model of the spiritual journey for mystics. Their experiences of the moment when they reached the presence of God has been described by many. Bayazid Bastami was the first to describe his spiritual flight through the heavens.

VISION OF GOD:

Hazrat Sultan Bahu has described the possible visions of God in three ways.

1. One can have a vision of God in a true dream. Those who excessively commemorate the Name of God and meditate on His personal Name, *Allah*, may experience this spiritual bliss once in their lifetime. This type of vision is called the "vision of light."

2. The second type of vision of God is attained by deep contemplative meditation, which transports the seeker to the presence of God.
3. The third type of vision of God is possible in an awakened state, where the spirit is transported out of the body and flies to the hierarchy of God. The flight of Abu Yazid Bastami was of this nature, which has been mentioned in the previous section.

It is said about Imam Abu Hanifa that he was blessed with the vision of God the Most High in dreams, one hundred times, in the form of an ever-shining sun.

Sheikh Nizam ud Din Auliya narrated a story on the subject of vision of God as follows: There was a Turk named Tiklish. He was a pious and godly man. One night God the Most High appeared to him in a dream. The next morning he went to see Sheikh Najib ud Din Mutawakkil. He requested the Sheikh not to tell anybody what he was going to disclose to him as long as he was alive. The Sheikh promised and gave his word. After that Tiklish stated, "Last night I saw God Almighty in my dream," and he went on to recount the spiritual bliss and inner lights of that encounter. The Turk lived for another fifty years after he had that vision of God Almighty. At the time of Tiklish's death, Sheikh Najib ud Din was present at his bedside by chance. When he saw the Sheikh he asked, "Do you remember that dream that I had and then told you?" "Yes. I do remember," the Sheikh replied. "But please tell me what your spiritual state is now," asked the Sheikh. "This very moment," said Tiklish, "I am totally immersed in the same all encompassing heavenly light and I am at peace."

MY VISION OF GOD:

I too have been blessed, with the vision of God the Most High in a dream. Once I dreamt that I was in an ocean of light as far as my eyes could see. There was light upon light, light above me, light below me, light on my right, left, in front, and behind. Everywhere, I looked; I saw nothing else but light brighter than a million blazing suns. In the middle of this fathomless ocean of light was a huge sun, as if suspended, emitting all these brilliant waves of light. There was no one else except me standing in awe and amazement, surrounded by the light of that magnificent sun. There was complete silence and sheer stillness. There was peace and tranquility. I was dazed and totally immersed in the light. I was in a state of extreme spiritual bliss and perfect peace. I had no sense of time or place, and I do not know how long I was in that state. I was feeling an overwhelming presence of God and His loving kindness. It seemed to me that time had stopped, and I felt that I had been engulfed by the Divine light since time immemorial. The joy and fulfillment I was experiencing cannot be expressed in words. I had lost myself in that light, and do not remember what was happening. It has been a long time since I had this vision of God, but it seems as if it happened last night. It was certainly the result of God's inexplicable grace.

BREIF BIOGRAPHICAL SKETCH OF THE PROPHET MUHAMMAD (pbuh)

The Prophet Hazrat Muhammad (pbuh) was born in the year 570 AD in the city of Mecca in the Arabian Peninsula. He was the son of Abdullah, the son of Abdul Mutalib. He was from the tribe of Quraish, and his lineage traces back to the tribe of Adnan, the son of Ismael (pbuh), the son of Prophet Abraham (pbuh). His mother was Amina, the daughter of Wahab. The Prophet (pbuh) had the noblest lineage, as he said, "Indeed God chose the tribe of Kinanah over other tribes from the children of Israel; He chose Quraish over other tribes of Kinanah; He chose Banu Hashim over the other families of the Quraish; and He chose me from Banu Hashim" (*hadith* Muslim).

He grew up as an orphan. His father passed away before his birth, and his mother died when he was six years old. His grandfather, Abdul Mutalib, raised him, and when he died, his uncle, Abu Talib, was his guardian. He had to undergo all these tragedies to prepare him well in the future for the challenges he had to face as a messenger. Born in a country with just a stretch of arid and trackless desert and brought up among people known for their barbarity and ignorance, he dazzled the whole world with the sublimity of his message and the majesty of his character.

Did He not find you an orphan and care for you?

Did He not find you lost and show you the way?

Did He not find you poor and provide for you?

Therefore, be kind to the orphan, gentle to the poor,

And declare the mercy and blessing of your Lord.

(Quran 93:6-11)

The Prophet (pbuh) was known among his people as *Al Ameen* or "Trustworthy" and *Al Sadiq* or the "Truthful." People trusted him with their valuables, and he never told a lie. He was a man of truth and honesty. He had the best moral character, was well spoken, and loved to help people. He was very compassionate, extremely gentle, and kindhearted. God the Most High describes his beautiful manners in the following words, "Indeed you are a great moral character" (Quran). And also, "Indeed in the messenger of Allah, you have an excellent example to follow whoever hopes in Allah and the last day and remember Allah much" (Quran 33:21).

His cousin, son in law, the fourth Caliph of Islam, and the commander of the believers, Hazrat Ali (peace and blessing of God be upon him) described the Prophet Hazrat Muhammad (pbuh) in the following way: "He was the last of the Prophets, the most truthful, the best of them in character, and the most loving. Whoever saw him for the first time would stand in awe, and whoever got to know him would love him. Everyone would attest to the fact and say, I have never seen anyone before or after him who was comparable to him."

Even his enemies attested to his trustworthiness, truthfulness, and greatness—as did Abu Sufyan, the archenemy of Islam in front of Heraculis, the Emperor of Rome.

Michael Hart, in "The one hundred most influential people," considered Prophet Hazrat Muhammad (pbuh) the greatest man who ever lived on the face of earth. He ranked him higher than Moses (pbuh), Jesus (pbuh), the Buddha, and Lao Tzu. For this illiterate man of the desert bedazzled the whole Muslim world with the sublimity and majesty of his message.

He founded one of the greatest religions of the world and forever changed the history of civilization."

Professor Hassan Ali in his magazine, *Nur Al Islam*, quoted a Brahman friend who wrote as follows, "I recognize and believe that the messenger of Islam Hazrat Muhammad (pbuh) is the greatest and most mature man in history. No man possessed the characteristics, mannerism, and ethics that he possessed at one time. He was a king under whom the entire Peninsula was unified. Yet he was humble. He believed that dominion belonged to God alone.

Great riches would come to him, and yet he lived in a state of poverty; fire would not light in his house for many days, and he would stay hungry. He was a great leader; he led small numbers into battle against thousands and yet he would decisively defeat them. He loved peace agreements and would agree to them with a firm heart, even though he had thousands of his brave companions by his side.

He was deeply concerned about the affairs of the Arabian Peninsula, yet he did not neglect the affairs of his family, household, or the poor and needy. In general, he was a man concerned with the betterment and wellbeing of mankind, yet he did not indulge in amassing worldly fortunes. He even prayed for his enemies and would warn them of the punishment of God."

Similarly, Alphonse de La Martaine in *Historic de al Turquie* wrote, "Never has a man set for himself, voluntarily or involuntarily, a more sublime aim, since this aim was superhuman, to subvert superstitions that have been imposed between man and his Creator, to render God unto man and man unto God, to resolve the rational and scared idea of divinity amongst the chaos of the material and disfigured gods of idolatry, then existing. Never has a man undertaken a work so far beyond human power with so feeble means, for he (Muhammad; pbuh) had in the conception as well as in the execution of such a great design, no other instrument than himself and no other aid except a handful of men living in a corner of the desert."

"Finally, never has a man accomplished such a huge and lasting revolution in the world, because in less than two centuries after its appearance, Islam in faith and in arms, reigned over the whole of Arabia, and conquered in God's name Persia, Transoxania, Western India, Syria, Egypt, Abyssinia, all the known continents of Africa, numerous islands of the Mediterranean sea, and Spain. If greatness of purpose, smallness of means, and astonishing results are the three criteria for a human genius, who could alone compare any great man in history with Muhammad (pbuh)? Regarding all standards by which human greatness can be measured, we may even ask, is there any man greater than him?"

Poverty was an attribute of the Prophet (pbuh). According to a tradition, he said, *Faqri Fakhri*, "Poverty is my pride." He slept on a mat of hay and a pillow stuffed with coarse date fibers. Ummar Ibne Khatab once came to visit his house and found him sitting on a hay mat, which had left marks on his body. He had a pot of water by his feet, and there was some cloth hanging on the wall. This was all he had at the time when the messenger of God had the Arabian Peninsula under his control. When Ummar Ibne Khatab saw this, he wept bitterly, for he could not control his emotions. At this, the messenger of God said, "Why are you crying, O Ummar?" He replied, "Why should I not cry? Khosro of Persia and Caesar of Rome enjoy the best of this world, while you are in this state of poverty that I see." The Prophet (pbuh) replied, "O Ummar, aren't you happy that they enjoy this world and we will enjoy the eternal life in the hereafter?"

At the time of the conquest of Mecca, when the Prophet Hazrat Muhammad (pbuh) led his companions, numbering ten thousands, Abu Sufyan was standing on a hill alongside Al Abbas, the uncle of the Prophet (pbuh). He was amazed by the vast numbers of Muslims marching towards Mecca, like a storm unstoppable in its course. On seeing this, Abu Sufyan said to Al Abbas, "O Al Abbas, your nephew has become a great king." Al Abbas said in reply, "This is not kingship but rather prophethood, and this is a message from the Lord."

He conquered Mecca without fighting and was very humble and forgiving. He gathered the people who had abused, harmed, and tortured him and his followers and drove them out of the city. On this occasion he said, "What do you think I will do with you?" They replied, "You are kind and generous, and you will only do good for the sake of God." He pardoned them all and said, "Go, you are all free and safe."

One of the companions, An Numan Basheer, said, "I saw your Prophet (pbuh) one day when he was unable to buy low quality dates to fill his stomach" (Muslim). In this vein, Abu Hurarah said, "The Prophet (pbuh) never filled his stomach for three consecutive days until his death" (*Bukhari*). Such accounts attest to the fact that the Prophet (pbuh) was a simple and humble person. He would not serve only himself, but would serve others as well. Ayesha, the wife of the Prophet (pbuh), said, "I was asked how the Messenger of God behaved in the house." She said, "He would help out in the house with daily chores. He was like any other man; he washed his clothes, mended his shoes, milked his sheep, and served himself."

When all the Arabian Peninsula was under his control and great fortunes and riches would pile into the mosque, he would give it away to the poor and needy. His wife, Ayesha, said that the Prophet (pbuh) borrowed some food from a Jew and agreed to pay him later, but gave him his armor as collateral. The Prophet Hazrat Muhammad (pbuh) strongly disliked the riches of this world because he knew the world's reality. He said, "The likeness of this world to the hereafter is like a person who dipped his finger in the ocean—let him see what would return" (Muslim).

The Prophet (pbuh) was concerned about his people. He would visit the sick, whether he or she was Muslim or non-Muslim. If he knew that a companion was sick, he would rush to visit him or her, along with those who were present with him. In this regard, it is narrated by Anas Bin Malik that, "Once a Jewish boy who used to serve the Prophet (pbuh) became sick. So he told his companions, 'Let us go and visit him.' The Prophet (pbuh) went to visit him along with his companions and found the father of the boy sitting by his head. The messenger of God looked at the boy and said, 'Proclaim that there is no true God worthy of being worshiped except Allah alone and I will intercede on your behalf because of it on the Day of Resurrection.' The boy looked at his father. The father said, 'Obey Abul Qasim.' Therefore, the boy announced, 'There is no true God worthy of being worshiped except Allah alone and Muhammad (pbuh) is the last messenger.' The Prophet (pbuh) said, 'All praise is Allah's, who saved him.'"

PEARLS OF WISDOM
SAYINGS OF THE PROPHET

- "He, who recognized himself, recognized his Lord."

If we sincerely take time to meditate and to reflect on ourselves, we will surely and clearly see within ourselves the signs of the knowledge of the Creator. As scripture has stated, "All His signs are within yourselves but you don't perceive" (Quran 51:20).

- "If ye knew God as He ought to be known, ye would walk on seas, and the mountains would move at your call."
- "God does not behold your figure nor your actions but peers through your heart and intentions." In the same vein, the Prophet (pbuh) said, "Man's actions are counted with his intentions."
- "Everybody is born pure, in accordance with the Islamic nature, but the parents make them Jews, Christians, and Magians."

The true and natural disposition of man is based on the Creator's nature that he follows. That is why mystics always prayed, "O Lord show us the things in their real nature."

- "The leader of the nation is he who serves them the most."
- "Shouldn't I tell you the best of all actions, best liked by the Creator, higher than all stages of the path, more beneficial than spending gold and silver, and more valuable than fighting your enemies?" The companions said, "Please do, O messenger of God." The Prophet (pbuh) said, "That action is the remembrance of Allah."
- "Love of the world is the cause of all sins."
- "A moment's meditation is better than worship of the two worlds."
- "He who has a particle of arrogance in his heart cannot enter paradise."
- "I love the tears of sinners more than the praises of the saints" (*hadith qudsi*).

- "Whoever respects a rich man for his wealth, undoubtedly lost two thirds of his faith."

HEART:

- "In the body of mankind there is an organ, when it is righteous, the entire body is reformed, and beware that organ is the heart."
- "Neither the earth nor the heaven can contain Me, but the heart of a believing servant can contain Me" (*hadith qudsi*).
- Once the Prophet (pbuh) was sitting in the shade of the Kaaba and addressed it, "O Kaaba, you undoubtedly are the house of sanctity and honor, but the heart of a faithful person is a thousand times better than you."
- "The human heart is between the two fingers of the Merciful."
- "Jealousy eats up virtuous deeds as fire consumes wood."
- "Charity consumes sins the same way as the water puts out fire."
- "The strongest among you is the one who controls his anger."
- "Do not dismiss certain acts of kindness by deeming them to be insignificant, even if such an act is to meet your brother with a smiling face, for that may tip the scale of your good deeds."
- "Whoever loses a loved one from the people of this world and then seeks his recompense from his Lord, will be compensated with eternal bliss."
- "Verily, Allah has ordered me to keep relations with those who cut me off, to forgive those who wrong me, and to be generous with those who withhold from me."
- "Love, the one who is dear to you in moderation, for perhaps some day you may hate him, and hate the one whom you detest in moderation for perhaps one day you may come to love him."
- "Whatever befalls you in terms of loss, hardship, and grief, God will make it atonement for your sins."
- "And if you smile in the face of your brother, then that is a form of charity."
- "Wish for others whatever you wish for yourself."

- "The faith of a believer does not become complete until he loves for his brother what he loves for himself."
- "Have mercy on people so that you may receive mercy; forgive people so that you may be forgiven."
- "God will not show mercy to him, who does not show mercy to others."
- "And know that victory comes with patience and that relief comes with hardship."

FORGIVENESS:

- Allah said in a *hadith qudsi,* "O son of Adam, if you worship Me sincerely and ask for forgiveness, I will forgive you even if your sins are greater than the size of heaven. O son of Adam, if you come to Me with sins amounting to the size of earth but has not ascribed partners to Me in worship, I would come to you with its size in forgiveness."
- "By the one who has my soul in his hands, if you were not to sin, then Allah would remove you, and would bring another nation who sins, and who then seek forgiveness from Allah, and He would forgive them."
- "And know that what has befallen you was not going to miss you, and that which missed you was not meant to befall you."
- "Every matter that Allah decrees for His slave is better for him."
- "Whosoever seeks forgiveness from Allah more often, then the Merciful helps him in all difficult matters and show him a way out of every bad situation."

SERVICE TO MANKIND:

Service to human beings is the shortest way to come closer to the light of the Creator. It is said in an authentic *hadith,* "Allah will say to His slave on the Day of Resurrection, 'O son of Adam, I was hungry and you did not feed Me.' He will answer. 'How can, I feed You, You are the Sustainer of the worlds?' Allah will say, 'Did not you know that My servant so and so was hungry and you did not give him food? If you would have fed him you would have found that with Me. O son of Adam, I was thirsty and you hesitated to give Me a drink.' He will say, 'O Sustaining One, how can I give You a drink? You are the Lord of the worlds.' Allah will say, 'Did not you know that my slave so and so was thirsty, he asked you for a drink and you did not give him a drink? If you had given him drink, you would have found its reward with Me. O son of Adam, I became sick and you did not visit Me.' He will say, 'How can I visit You? You are the Creator of all.' Allah will say, 'Did not you know that My slave so and so became sick and you did not visit him? Had you visited him, you would have found Me with him.'"

It is narrated that one day Prophet (pbuh) was sitting with his companions; one of them noticed him smiling. The companion was curious and asked him about it. The Prophet (pbuh) replied, "On the Day of Resurrection, two believers would prostrate before God and one of them will accuse the other one of wrongdoing and will ask for compensation. God will then tell the accused to respond to his accuser by compensating him. "O Lord of the universe, I do not have any good deeds left in my balance to give him." The accuser will say to this, "Then he should take some of my sins instead."

The Prophet (pbuh) told his companions, "Surely, it will be a terrible day when people would not be able to carry their own burdens." Then, God will ask the accuser to look up into paradise and describe what he sees there in. "I see wonderful cities, majestic palaces, and beautiful gardens everywhere. What great Prophet will have that kind of a reward?" "Only those who can pay the real price for it," said God. "But, O the King of Kings, who possibly can do that? You can pay the full price by forgiving your brother." At this, the accuser will regret and would say "I do forgive him as of right now." God the Most High will say, "Very well, take your brother's hand and enter My paradise together."

The Prophet (pbuh) then told his companions, "Be astounded by the love of the One Being. Make peace among yourselves now or Allah will establish his own peace among you on the Day of Jugdement."

God the Most High reiterated this point in the Quran, "But whoever forgives and makes reconciliation, his reward is due from Allah" (Quran 42:40).

The Prophet Hazrat Muhammad (pbuh) also expressed the voice of Allah in a *hadith qudsi*. "My love belongs to those who love each other for My sake, who experience intimacy in Me, who shower each other with goodness for My sake, and who visit each other joyfully for My sake."

- "Worship God as if you were seeing Him, even if you cannot see Him, know well that He is seeing you."
  The Prophet (upon whom be peace) said, "Poor people who exercise patience are among the select ones who will sit with the Merciful Lord on the Day of reckoning."
  Poor people, who endure patiently the will of God, will sit with Him in their hearts. These are the ones who have renounced the world and have chosen *faqr* (poverty) over worldly riches and patiently tolerate the extreme hardship. Once they attain the true station of patience they emerge as those about whom God the most High has said, "Indeed they are in Our presence, from amongst the chosen honorable ones."
- "Shall I not inform you of the most beloved to me and the one seated closest to me on the day of resurrection? They are those who are best in manners."
- "The example of one who remembers his Lord in relation to the one who does not remember his Lord is that of the living and the dead."
- "The best form of worship is to wait patiently for a happy outcome."
- "And know that victory comes with patience and the relief comes with hardship."

God *said* in a *hadith qudsi*, "I will appear to my servant at the end of time in the way in which each one expects Me to appear. Yes I am with my servants invariably even now, whenever they call Me."

VISION OF THE PROPHET HAZRAT MUHAMMAD (PBUH)

There is a popular tradition among the Sufis that says, "For him who sees my face (*Hilya*) after my death, it is as if he had seen me, and he who sees it, longing for me, for him God will make Hellfire prohibited and he will not be resurrected naked on Judgement day." According to Faqir Nur Muhammad, my grandfather, a true faithful and those who love the Prophet (pbuh) will be blessed with the vision of the Prophet (pbuh). Some will be blessed once in their lifetime, some once a year, some once a month, some one once a week, and some fortunate one's will be constantly in the assembly and presence of the Prophet (pbuh).

Anyone who sees the Prophet (pbuh) in a vision actually sees him in reality, because in a dream Satan cannot come in the form of the Prophet (pbuh), the Kaaba, or the Quran.

MY VISIONS OF THE PROPHET (pbuh):

In a vision of the night, I saw that I was standing on the rooftop of a building belonging to a small church. A monk by the name of Bahira was also present with me. We were both looking to the path in front of us, which was the traveling route for the caravans coming from Hijaz (Arabia) to Syria. This small church was located on the top of a small hill on the outskirts of Busra in Syria.

Bahira the monk was a God-fearing man and well versed in the knowledge of the Torah, Psalms, and the Gospels. He had also read in an ancient book that had been passed on from generation to generation about the last messenger of God. The book had described Prophet Muhammad (pbuh) in detail and had indicated all the signs pertaining to him. We both were patiently waiting and searching for "the praised one," whose coming was predicted in the Gospel. We had been looking at the caravans coming from Mecca passing that way. It seemed to me that we had been waiting there every day for a long time. As we were waiting and watching, we spotted a caravan coming from a distance. It was approaching slowly, with camels marching and carrying the load. Bedouin men could be seen mounted on camels and horses, and on foot. Dust was rising in the air on the dirt road, and the scorching sun was shining down. There was a patch of cloud above a young lad, who was in his late teens. That cloud wandered along with the youth, keeping him in the shade and protecting him from the merciless heat of the sun.

We were both keenly interested to see who this young man was. The caravan was coming closer, and I could see clearly the faces of the people in the caravan. This fine young man stopped under the shade of a small tree. A patch of cloud was above his head. This was one of the signs of the coming Prophet described in Bahira's ancient book.

I came down from the roof towards the caravan and went straight up to the tree where this young Arab was standing. I looked at him intently. He was handsome, full of grace, and his face was resplendent with Divine light. He had a broad forehead, dark, attractive eyes, with a reddish tinge to the sclera. He had a slightly pointed nose, prominent cheeks, and a beautiful smile, the likes of which I had never seen before.

As, I came closer, I greeted him with peace (*Asalat o Asalamo Alaikum Ya Rasool Allah*). He smiled and looked into my eyes as if we had known each other for a long time. He embraced me with a hug as if I had been enwrapped in a blanket of mercy and light. I do not remember exactly, how long we hugged each other, but I was able to look over his shoulder, where I saw the seal of prophethood between his shoulder blades. I turned around and kissed the seal. He was still smiling at me.Bahira the monk recognized young Muhammad (pbuh) by this very mark, The Seal of Prophethood, and proclaimed him the last Messenger whose arrival had been foretold in the Christian Scripture.

Bahira also had few companions staying with him in the church. As the legend said, one of the men was an able artist. He also met the young Muhammad (pbuh), and it is said that he drew a sketch of him. The original or perhaps a copy of the original sketch is still preserved in the museum of Rome in Italy.

During the Iranian revolution in 1978, copies of the sketch of the Prophet Hazrat Muhammad (pbuh) surfaced in Iran. Ayatullah Khomeni, the father of the Iranian Islamic Revolution, was presented with this picture. When Khomeni saw the image of the Prophet Hazrat Muhammad (pbuh), he was so overwhelmed with emotions that he literally fainted. I also received a copy of that portrait, and as I looked at it, I was shocked to see how closely it resembled the Prophet (pbuh) at the time of his youth as I had envisioned him in my vision. I still have that picture and have preserved it as a treasure. This portrait has graced my personal desk since then and has a penetrating influence over my spiritual life. Sometimes when I look at the picture it rekindles the sweet memories of my vision. I also meditate deeply on this blessed picture, and it often takes me to the living presence of the Holy Prophet (pbuh).

In another vision, I saw that I was standing in the field of Badr, where the first battle of Islam took place under the leadership of the Prophet Hazrat Muhammad (pbuh). Badr is located outside Medina, towards Mecca, and was the site of Arab fairs, where people gathered every year. Here a handful of Muslims fought their enemies, who were three times their number and better equipped.

I saw that the Prophet Hazrat Muhammad (pbuh) was standing on a higher place, like a large boulder, wearing white Arab dress. His divine face surpassed the glory of a thousand blazing suns. A wave of illumination came over me, and I was inexplicably thrilled. On his right side I saw my grandfather, Faqir Nur Muhammad, and on his left side my father, Faqir Abdul Hamid. They were standing as companions and bodyguards. It was midday, the heat was oppressive, and Muslim fighters were hard pressed.

The Prophet (pbuh) was commanding his followers from there. I was standing on the ground below. I had a sword and a shield in my hand and was ready for the battle against the enemies of Islam—waiting for my orders from the Prophet (pbuh). I looked up at the Prophet (pbuh), my father, and my grandfather. I came forward to the rock where they were standing. The prophet (pbuh) of Islam was standing barefooted on the rock. I kissed the feet of the Prophet (pbuh). It seemed so real, and it never occurred to me that it was in the vision of a dream. His feet were warm, and I could smell the scent and aroma of his body. It was a moment of extreme spiritual bliss. I prolonged the kissing of my master's feet, for

I thought that there could be nothing better in the entire universe than kissing the blessed feet of the "Mercy unto the worlds." At his blessed feet, I found everything my heart had been longing for from pre-eternity.

After that—I looked up again, the three of them were standing side by side, tall and upright, resolute, and determined. My father looked at me and smiled. He said to me, "We have come here to help and aid Prophet Hazrat Muhammad (pbuh) against the enemies of Islam. Give me your sword because I need it to fight." So I drew my sword, which flashed like fire, and handed it over to my father according to his direction.

It is my strong belief that the three of us were there in spirit form to help the Prophet (pbuh) and Muslims in the battle against their enemies.

God the Most High sent His help as He had promised the Prophet (pbuh), "Call to mind, while Allah had already helped you in the battle of Badr. Call to mind also when thou didst say to the believers: Will it not suffice you that your Lord should help you with three thousand spirits (Angels) sent down from on high?" (Quran 3:123-124).

I was blessed with another vision of the Prophet Hazrat Muhammad (pbuh). In my dream I saw that I was preparing for a journey to pay homage to the Holy Prophet (pbuh) in Medina in Arabia. However, at that time I was residing in Kulachi, my home town in Pakistan. I had collected quite a few gifts to present it to the Holy Prophet (pbuh). I was also carrying a bed (*charpai*) that I had specially prepared for the Prophet of Islam (pbuh); for I had heard that he used to sleep on a reed mat.

I had this entire load of luggage with me and I was traveling on foot. A passerby asked me as to where I was heading with my luggage. I told him that I intended to visit Prophet Hazrat Muhammad (pbuh). On hearing this, he was surprised and said, "Are you going all this long way to Medina on foot?" I said, "Yes, what is so surprising about that? My great grandfather, Haji Gul Muhammad, went to Mecca and Medina on foot four times. At least I can do it once."

The next moment, I found myself in the streets of Medina by the way of *Tay ul Arz*, which had been granted to me at that time, instantly. I was walking through the dirt-paved streets. There were mud houses with roofs made of palm tree branches, reflecting the life and ways of the people of the city of Yathrib (Medina). I was looking for the Prophet's house, which was situated adjacent to the Prophet's mosque. Somebody led me there. Next, I saw myself entering the Prophet's (pbuh) house. It was a small mud room, with a window on one side only. There I saw the Holy Prophet Hazrat Muhammad (pbuh) standing in the middle of the room. The divine face was the one I had seen in many of my visions. It seemed that all the lights of God and His beautiful attributes had found full expression in his luminous face. I bowed down in great reverence and had the honor of kissing his feet. He greeted me like a son and hugged me in a warm embrace. I had brought the bed with me and I placed it in the corner of the room near the window. The Prophet (pbuh) sat on the bed and instructed me to sit down with him. I also presented him with the gifts I had brought. He was very pleased with me.

We sat together on the bed and talked for a long while. I requested my beloved Prophet (pbuh) and said, "Dear father, please give me the best advice." The Prophet (pbuh) said, "Dear son, perform prayers, remember Allah constantly, and promote peace and love among all people." I then begged him to intercede on my behalf to the Lord of the universe. The merciful Prophet (pbuh) said, "Know, my son that God has promised me that whosoever from my community shall say *'La Illaha Illallah, Muhammad ur Rasul-Allah'* (There is no deity worthy of worship save Allah and Muhammad is His messenger) will be forgiven even before he or she asks for forgiveness." On hearing this, my heart was flooded with boundless spiritual joy. I was absorbed in looking at the beautiful face of the Prophet (pbhu), which was the true embodiment of Divine love. His living words not only possessed eloquence but also transmitted countless mysteries to my heart.

I was sitting right in front of the window. It looked as if on the other side of the window was an endless ocean, and somehow the room was situated deep inside that fathomless ocean. Schools of fish, small and large, would come up to the window, look at us, and swim away. I noticed different kinds of fish doing so, as if they were paying homage to the Holy Prophet (pbuh) and were coming one by one. These were probably the spirits of the pious believers swimming in the ocean of oneness. I was in the company of the Prophet Hazrat Muhammad (pbuh) for a long time. After that I woke up and was reciting (*durud*) salutations of peace and blessings addressed to the Holy Prophet (pbuh).

I have also been blessed with the vision of the Prophet Hazrat Muhammad Mustafa (pbuh) along with Hazrat Abu Bakr-the veracious (*Al Siddique*). This spiritual encounter took place in the heat of a battle between Muslims and non-believers. I was standing in a huge battlefield crowded with thousands of faithful fighters. Most of them were on foot. Only a few dozen were on horseback.

The Holy Prophet (pbuh) was riding his Arabian stallion. I was standing on the ground by the side of the Prophet (pbuh), acting as the head of the bodyguards. I had a few loyal followers with me under my command. We had encircled the Prophet (pbuh), forming a human shield around him to protect him from any possible harm, at all cost.

The face of the Holy Prophet (pbuh) was shining like a blazing sun in the midst of that battlefield. The believers were gathered around him like throngs of spellbound moths around a radiant candle. I had the good fortune of being close to the Prophet (pbuh), being in charge of his safety as a chief bodyguard. I was in such close proximity to him that from time to time, I would rub my face and forehead against his sacred feet and sandals. This was exactly what my heart had for such a long time longed for. It is considered the highest reward for a servant (disciple) to have his head at the feet of his eternal spiritual master. These were the sandals that the Prophet (pbuh) wore on the night of his ascension to the presence of God and touched the Divine Throne with them. I remembered Jami's verses that say, "All the celestial beings feel pride in rubbing their foreheads on the Prophet's Throne, rubbing sandals."

The sandals of the Prophet (pbuh) have been the topic of great admiration and veneration. Sufis throughout the history of Islam have hoped and longed to be touched by the Prophet's feet and sandals to obtain ineffable bliss.

The rows in front of the Prophet (pbuh) were made up of horse riders. In the middle of them was Hazrat Abu Bakr (*Al Siddique*) riding on a white horse. His radiant face conveyed an impression of Divine power.

He had black, penetrating eyes, a large nose, and broad forehead. He had a grey beard and moustache. He had scant hair on the front part of the head, when he took off his turban. Hazrat Abu Bakr (*Al Siddique*) was the commander of this particular battle, and he was leading all the believers in this encounter. It was quite an awe-inspiring scene.

As soon as I saw Hazrat Abu Bakr (*Al Siddique*), I approached him in great reverence and kissed his feet. He greeted me cordially and gently patted me on my back. A healing calm came upon me among the chaos of the battle. He looked at me with a soul-stirring gaze and addressed me, "Son, Stay with the messenger of Allah at all times and at all cost and never abandon him for a moment. He is all that we have and need for our salvation." At this I replied, "I will sacrifice myself and my family for the sake of the Prophet (pbuh) a thousand times and will never ever abandon my beloved Prophet who is the pupil of my eyes."

Hazrat Abu Bakr (*Al Siddique*) further advised me, "Our life here in this world is transitory, and our breaths are numbered. The lures of this world are worthless. Keep your eyes on God, love and obey the Prophet (pbuh), for without the love of Mustafa (pbuh) nothing can be achieved."

Hazrat Abu bakr (May God be pleased with him) was the first companion and Sufi to learn directly from the Prophet (pbuh) himself the secret of contemplative meditation on God, in the cave of Thaur. Therefore, according to Hujwiri, he is considered at the head of those who have adopted a life of contemplation and poverty.

THE VISION OF HAZRAT ALI

I saw in a vision that I was in the company of my father, who is also my spiritual guide, and we both were traveling towards the city of the Prophet (pbuh), Medina. In no time we reached our destination and were walking through the streets of the city. The city of Medina itself was small, with mud houses and compounds scattered around in no particular pattern. Streets were wider in some areas and narrower in other places, depending upon the layout of the houses on either side. The houses were built of mud, and their roofs made of palm tree wood and branches. The outer walls surrounding the houses were usually short. Some compounds were open, whereas some others had larger gates. Very few people could be seen in the streets. Camels, horses, and sheep were all over the place, trudging slowly along the way. The whole atmosphere looked familiar. I have visited those streets many times in my visions.

I was following my father. It was late in the afternoon. The heat of the sun was cooling down, and the shadows were growing longer. We had been traveling for a while, and it seemed that we were near our desired destination. After some time, my father stopped in front of a compound having walls built of mud. The size of the compound was surprisingly large compared to the others we had seen. We entered that compound. It was full of people—young and old—standing all around in great respect. All those present were honorable personalities. At the end of the compound, a handsome young luminary sat in a chair. He was the most awe-inspiring man I had ever seen. He had a radiant face, with a full black beard, and wore a turban on his head. He was dressed in traditional Arab attire. People around him were standing with their heads bowed and hands across their chests as signs of respect.

My father held my hand, and we both went forward to meet this young spiritual personality. My father knelt down, touched his feet, and kissed his hands. The young Arab got up and embraced my father in a warm hug. At first I was surprised to see my father, who is quite an old man, bowing down in front of a young person and touching his feet with great respect. As soon as I thought that, my father whispered into my ear, "This young man is the fountainhead of all spirituality, and all Sufi orders start and end up in him. This is Hazrat Ali (may God be pleased with him), the son-in-law and cousin of the Prophet Hazrat Muhammad (pbuh) and the fourth caliph of Islam." He further added, "Bow down, kiss his feet, and receive your spiritual *baraka* (blessing)." I immediately obeyed my father, fell down at the feet of Hazrat Ali (may God be pleased with him), and had the good fortune of kissing them. I kissed his hands and cheeks according to the Arab tradition. Hazrat Ali hugged me and kissed my cheek in return.

Hazrat Ali was the most eloquent in speech. He advised us, "Do not occupy your heart with worldly affairs, severe your ties to everything else save God. Keep your heart fixed on Him. He keeps His servants in whatever state He wills. Commit all your affairs to God, follow the truth and you shall never get lost." As we were bidding farewell, he gently patted me on my back and showered me with his eternal spiritual blessings.

I then came out and went to the adjacent compound, where two young Arab childen were playing. They were probably five and six years old. Somebody told me that they were Imam Hassan and Imam Hussain. I went upto them and kissed their foreheads. They were the most beautiful children I had ever seen. The Prophet of Islam was absolutely right in naming them Hassan (beautiful) and Hussain (handsome). I then woke up filled with extreme spiritual bliss and joy.

CHAPTER NINE

THE LIVING WORD OF GOD

It is a light from Allah and a clear book, whereby Allah does guide those who seek His pleasure along the paths of peace, and brings them out of the depths of darkness into the light by His will and guides them on to the path that is straight.

(Quran 5:16-17)

O mankind, there has indeed come to you a direction from your Lord which is full of admonition and a healing for the ills of men's hearts, and a guidance and a mercy for all those who believe in Him.

(Quran 10:57)

This Book is a revelation from the Most Gracious, the Ever Merciful, a Book whose commandments have been explained in detail, which will be repeatedly read, couched in clear, eloquent language for the benefit of people who possess (innate) knowledge, to be a herald of glad tidings and warning.

(Quran 41:3-5)

The Quran is the true, uncreated, powerful, and living word of God revealed to the unlettered Prophet Hazrat Muhammad (pbuh) through the Holy Spirit Archangel Gabriel. It is most beautiful, rhythmic, and lyrical in character, rich in meaning and content, and perfect in composition. Apart from its apparent meaning, it has ten different successive layers of deeper meanings, each one superior to the preceding.

At the same time, it applies to the past, relates to the present, and is a road map for the future. With the passage of time, it unfolds its deeper mysteries. It is powerful, illuminating, comforting, healing, and reassuring to the ailing hearts of humanity. It is a manifest light and guide, full of wisdom, mercy, clear argument, and a covenant of Allah. It is full of hope, promise, goodness, and truth in its every word.

The Quran contains one hundred and fourteen *suras* or chapters. Each *sura* is of different length—varying from as little as three verses to as long as two hundred and sixty-eight verses. Each verse is called *Ayah*, which means a "miracle." The Quran indeed is the greatest miracle of the Holy Prophet Hazrat Muhammad (pbuh).

The first *sura* was revealed to the Prophet Hazrat Muhammad (pbuh) in the month of Ramadan probably, on the twenty-fifth or twenty-seventh night. It was the Archangel Gabriel commanding the Prophet (pbuh),

Recite in the Name of thy Lord,
Who has created man out of a germ cell,
Recite for thy Lord is the Most Gracious,
Who has taught man the use of the pen,
He taught man what he did not know.
Man surely does transgress,
Whenever, he believes himself to be self-sufficient.
(Quran 96:1-7)

The entire Book of God was revealed piece by piece over a period of twenty-three years. The Quran has been divided into Meccan and Medinan revelations. The Prophet (pbuh) himself would dictate the word of God to scribes and would arrange the order in which it should be written and preserved under Divine guidance.

Hazrat Abu Bakr (may God be pleased with him), the first Caliph of Islam, was the first to complete a written manuscript of the Quran during the lifetime of the Prophet (pbuh). The third Caliph of Islam, Hazrat Usman (may God be pleased with him), ordered to make copies from the manuscript of Hazrat Abu Bakr (may God be pleased with him), which was considered the authentic Quran in all respects, and sent those copies to different centers of the Muslim world. The Quran is truly safeguarded from all alterations as promised by God Himself, "Surely, it is We ourselves who have revealed step by step this reminder, and surely it is We who shall truly guard it from all corruption" (Quran 15:9).

The Quran not only accepts and affirms the truth about the other sacred Books revealed prior to it, but also verifies all the previous scriptures:

"And We have sent to thee the Book full of truth, confirming the truth of whatever there still remains of earlier revelations and determining what is true therein" (5:47). For instance, scripture states, "Surely we have sent down the Torah full of guidance and light" (Quran 5:45). Further, scripture states, "We caused Jesus son of Mary to follow in the footsteps of those earlier prophets, fulfilling that which was revealed before him in Torah, and We gave him scripture as a guide and light affirming the truth which was revealed prior to it in the Torah as a guidance and reminder for the believers" (Quran 5:47).

God has sent a messenger and guide to every nation throughout the entire history of mankind. The Quran verified this blessing and favor of God the most High: "Verily, We have sent thee with the truth, as a bearer of glad tidings and a Warner: for there never was any community but a Warner has lived and passed away in its midst" (Quran 35:25).

It is through the grace of God the Most High that he sent 124 thousand Prophets in order to guide humans so that they may not dwell in darkness, but be guided on the right path. The Quran is full of such passages where God proclaimed, for instance, "And they say, 'Be Jews or be Christians, and you may be on the right path.' Tell them, 'Nay, let us follow the religion of Abraham, who was a monotheist and rightly guided. We have faith in Allah and the revelation sent down to us and that which was revealed to Abraham, Ishmael, Isaac, and Jacob and their descendents and also the scriptures given to Moses and Jesus, and all other messengers of the Lord. We do not make any distinction among them, and it is unto Him that we surrender ourselves. Therefore, if they believe as you believe, they will indeed find themselves on the right path, and if they turn away, it is but they who will be deeply in error. In that case Allah is on your side and will help you against them, and He is All Hearing, All Knowing'" (Quran 2:136-138).

The Quran is an infinite source of knowledge and wisdom and is limitless and vast in meaning and guidance. It is also brief, concise, simple, and clear. The first *sura*, *Al Fatihah*, or the "Opening Chapter," which is the synopsis and mission statement of the Quran, truly reflects characteristics of Divine wisdom.

AL FATIHAH

In the Name of Allah, the infinitely Good and boundlessly Merciful.
All praise is due to Allah alone, the Lord of the worlds,
The most Gracious and ever Merciful,
Lord of the Day of Judgment,
Thee alone do we worship, and unto Thee alone do we turn for help.
Guide us to the straight path,
The path of those upon whom Thou hast showered Thy blessings,
Not of those who have been condemned by Thee,
Nor of those who have gone astray.

Fatihah is the most important prayer in the whole of the Quran that one can offer. It was taught directly by the Creator and is the best form of adoration, glorification, and supplication. Its seven often-repeated verses form the basis of every Muslim's prayer spoken five times a day. It is also called *the praise, the thanksgiving, the treasure, the healer,* and *the whole.* It starts with the Name of Allah, which is a proper Name for the One True Being, and does not apply to any other being.

The four major and most important Divine attributive Names, *Rahman*, *Rahim*, *Rabb*, and the *Master of the Day of Judgment* are mentioned therein. *Rahman* is the one who is merciful to all the creation at all times without any distinction between good or bad, believer or non-believer, but pours his infinite blessings and bounties upon everyone. "My mercy encompasses everything" (*Araf*: 156). It denotes that aspect of Divine grace that sustains life and everything else step by step before the need arises, and without asking for it. *Rahim* means the one who is the source of infinite mercy and beneficence and who rewards those who perform righteous deeds in accordance with the Divine law, for His pleasure alone. In this regard, the Prophet Hazrat Muhammad (pbuh) has said, "Al Rahman is the Beneficent God, whose love and mercy are manifested in the creation of this world, and Al Rahim is the Merciful God, whose love and mercy will be manifested in the world that comes after." *Rabb* is the supreme Creator, who sustains and nourishes the entire cosmos stepwise towards its ultimate goal. He is the Master of the Day of Judgment.

The first three verses of the Fatihah highlight the most important Divine attributes of providence: beneficence, mercy, and all-encompassing love. The fourth verse is a declaration of obedience and the soul's longing to worship the One Being alone. And as a matter of fact, we have no one else to turn to except Him for help. The last three verses are asking for His help and favor to be led to the straight path. What is the straightest path? For divine lovers it is the most direct way (*Tariqah*) to God. As the Holy Quran says, "Worshiping God alone is the right path" (3:52). Quran above all comes directly from God and that it takes back to Him through guidance along the straight path.

In a *hadith qudsi*, the Holy Prophet Hazrat Muhammad (pbuh) said that Allah has divided the Fatihah between Himself and His servant. The first three lines belong to the faithful, in which he adores, glorifies, and exalts the Creator. The fourth line is a mutual interaction between the Creator and the created. The last three lines are the result of Divine grace towards the supplicant.

DIVINE GUIDANCE

The word of God is an inexhaustible and eternal source of guidance and wisdom. It is the direct dialogue of the Creator with the created. In the Quran He speaks one on one to His servant, drawing the complete blueprint—from the main issues to the minutest detail—pertaining to the purpose of creation and goal of existence. "This is a book we have sent down upon thee from on high in order that thou may bring mankind out of sheer darkness into the light by the permission of their Lord, and onto the way that leads to Almighty, the one to whom all praise is due, to whom belongs whatsoever is in the heavens and on earth" (Quran 14:2-3).

The entire universe and all that exists within it have been created so as to benefit mankind, the cream of the creation. As God says, "He has made to your service the night and the day, and the sun and the moon, and all the stars are made to serve by His command. Surely in all this there are signs for a people who understand" (Quran 16:13). The following statement of Allah clearly proves the deep esoteric connection between God and man: "I have created everything for you and I have created you for Myslef." *(Hadith)*

The Quran is an inexhaustible treasure of Divine wisdom and guidance. God's word is so overwhelming that the reader becomes nothing even when pronouncing His Name for God is mysteriously present in His words. Quran is the infallible source of spiritual blessings. It inspires boundless joy and leads to intimate conversation with God. As Hazrat Ali has said, "God reveals Himself to His servants in the Quran."

Unfortunately, many people are unaware of the beauty, sublimity and true message of the Quran. They wonder how to approach and study the Holy Book. In this regards Mevlana Jalal Ud Din Rumi in his *Fihi ma Fihi* wrote, "Quran is a shy bride", in order to reveal its real beauty, we need to come closer to it by constant recitation. Divine presence operates solely through the sacred language (Arabic text) in which the Quran was revealed. Therefore, deeper understanding of the Quran can only be attained by learning the Arabic language. Hence, the power of the original text (Arabic) is much stronger than any translation can convey. Therefore, God added, "We have explained everything clearly in this Quran that they may take heed; a Quran in plain Arabic language without any deviation that they might become conscious of God." (Quran 39:28-29).

In order to seek its deeper meanings, one has to internalize the sacred text and take it to the heart. Only then can its resonant verses with powerful rhythm and rhyme make one's 'skin shiver and heart grow pliable'. Even simple recitation of the Quran will bring true believers to tears.

In the coming pages is a selection of verses from the Holy Book, which I have grouped under separate headings. These beautiful verses are rich in meaning, clear in content, fluent and self-explanatory. It does not need further commentary or clarification. It is my hope that this selection of celestial beauty will open 'a window' to the infinite spiritual world, where God's presence can be felt.

FORGIVENESS

God is eternally gracious and forgiving and pours down His abundant blessings onto human beings moment by moment and time after time. He has proclaimed this fact repeatedly in the Quran and has promised to forgive those, who do not find fault with other fellow humans and forgive them. Forgiveness is an attribute of God. On human level, it is an attitude of a loving heart. It stems from the reverential fear of God Almighty, Who in His Essence is oft forgiving. By forgiving others, one can only hope to be saved and accepted by God.

To forgive when in anger is a praiseworthy deed. (Quran 42:38)

§

If you do a good deed openly or perform it secretly or pardon a wrong, Allah is surely very forgiving and determines the measure of everything. (Quran 4:150)

§

If you forbear and forgive and pardon, then, Allah is surely most forgiving and ever Merciful. (Quran 64:15)

§

Those who spend (in His way) in the time of prosperity as well as in hardship and hold in check their anger, and pardon their fellow men because Allah loves the doer of good. And those who commit an indecent act or wrong themselves, remember God and pray that their sins be forgiven, for who but God could forgive sins? And those who do not knowingly persist in doing whatever wrong they may have done, shall have their reward forgiveness from their Lord and gardens wherein flows running water to abide. Excellent is the reward of those who do righteousness. (Quran 3:135-137)

§

Let not those of you who have been graced with God's favor resolve to withhold their bounty from the near of kin and the poor and those who have fled their homes in the cause of Allah because of some default on their part. Do you not love that Allah should forgive you your sins, seeing that God is much forgiving, a dispenser of grace? (Quran 24:23)

§

Surely Allah enjoins justice and the doing of good, and generosity towards fellowmen, and He forbids all that is shameful, envy and all that runs counter to reason. He exhorts you repeatedly so that you may take heed. (Quran 16:91)

FREEDOM OF FAITH

Faith is a matter of choice and free will; it should not be forced upon any person. However, the truth about religion should be proclaimed and widely announced. After that it is up to each individual whether to believe or disbelieve. Human beings are the only creatures in this universe who possess to some degree freedom whenever they are confronted with a choice. Therefore, they can freely choose right over wrong, real over unreal, and God over no God. This act of conscious choosing is called *faith* or *trust*. However, some of the humans failed to measure up to the responsibility arising from the free will endowed upon them. In the words of the Quran, "Verily, We did offer the trust (of reason and free will) to the heavens and the earth, and the mountains, but they refused to bear it because they were afraid of it. Yet mankind took it up. They are surely very ignorant and wrong doers" (33:72).

And proclaim, this is the truth from your Lord, then let him who pleases believe and let him who pleases disbelieve. (Quran 18:30)

§

There is no compulsion in the matter of religion, for the right path is clearly distinguished from the error. (Quran 2:257)

§

If thy Lord had enforced His will, all those who are on earth would have believed without exception. Will thou then take it upon thyself to force people to become believers? Except by Allah's permission not a single soul can believe. (Quran 10:100-101)

CREATION

The existence of the entire cosmos and all that it contains is totally dependent upon the Absolute Being, whose glory they were created to reflect. That is why God the Most High has stressed that all those who possess the knowledge should meditate and contemplate on the wonders of creation as His signs.

> Are, then, they not aware of how God creates life in the first instance, and then brings it forth anew? Surely that is very easy for God. Say to them, "Go all over the earth and behold how (wondrously) He has created man in the first instance and thus, too, will God bring into being your second life, for, verily, God has the power to will anything." (Quran 29 :20-21)

§

There is continous birth and rebirth of all entities in the cosmos. 'Everything other than God undergoes constant change and transformation. God has infinite possibilities and an inexhaustible treasury from which He continues to create forever.

> The process of creation is continuous, He produces the first creation and then He repeats it. (Quran 10:5)

§

> But the process is gradual and proceeds by stages. All praise is Allah's, who sustains, nourishes, and leads stage by stage towards perfection all the worlds. (Quran)

§

Since, God is the Creator at all times, His creative activity is never ceasing, because "each day He is upon some task." (55:29). Moreover, God never displays Himself twice in the same way, since He has infinite possibilities. This power of God is praised in many verses of the Quran.

God is the Creator of all things and He is guardian over all. To Him belong the treasures of the heavens and earth. (Quran 39:63-64)

§

To Him belong the kingdoms of heaven and earth, and He has not taken to Himself a son and has no partner in the kingdom. He created everything and then determined its measure. (Quran 25:3)

§

Who originates the creation and then repeats it, and who provides you sustenance from the heaven and the earth? Is there a god with Him? If so, bring your proofs if you are telling the truth. (Quran 27:65)

§

Allah is the Creator of all things; He is the one and supreme. He has authority and complete control over all creation. Are there any partners of Allah who have created the like of His creation so that the two look the same? (Quran 13:17)

In the Quran there are over two hundred verses regarding creation and God as the 'Creator'. *Khalq* (to create) in the language of Quran has two meanings. The first meaning is to determine or to give measure. The second meaning is to give existence to something. Therefore, God is the one, who determines and the one who gives existence. It is also important to note that creation in the sense of giving existence is exclusively a divine attribute. All existence issues from God. Before anything come to exist in the universe, all the entities are present to the Real. This presence to God is known as His 'knowledge.' Hence, God is the knower of all things.

§

To Him belongs the dominion of the heavens and earth; It is Allah who bestows life and causes death, and has power over all things as He wills. He is the first and the last, the manifest and hidden, and He has full knowledge of all things. (Quran 57:2)

§

God is the Creator of life and death and He alone is the origin and destination of all. Compared to Him, everything else is perishing and nothing is truly real.

Blessed is He in whose hands is sovereignity; He has power over all things as He wills; He who created death and life that He may test which of you is best in deeds. He is the mighty, the ever forgiving; who created the seven heavens in harmony; you can not see any flaw in the creation of the Gracious one. Just look again; do you see any discord? Yet look one more time, your sight will return in frustration only. (Quran 67:2-5)

§

Verily, in the creation of the heavens and earth and in the succession of the night and day there are indeed signs for all who are endowed with insight, and who remember God when they stand, and when they sit, and when they lie down to sleep and reflect on the creation

of the heavens and the earth, which impels them to supplicate; O our Sustainer, Thou has not created this without meaning and purpose.
(Quran 3:191-192)

§

Behold, in the heavens and the earth there are indeed messages for the believers. Similarly in your own creation and in all of God's creatures that are scattered around the earth are clear signs for people who are endowed with inner certainty. Also in the alternation of the night and day, and in the means of subsistence that Allah sends down from the skies, giving life thereby to the earth after it had been lifeless and in the change of the winds are signs for a people who use their wisdom.
(Quran 45:3-6)

THE VERSE OF KNOWLEDGE

Allah is He save Whom there is no deity worthy of worship,
The Ever-Living, the Self-Subsistent Fount of All Being.
Neither slumber can seize Him nor sleep.
Whatsoever, is in the heavens and in the earth belong to Him.
Who is there that could intercede with Him, except by His permission?
He knows all that lies open before men and all that is hidden from them, nor can they encompass any knowledge of Him except what He wills,
His eternal power overspreads the heavens and the earth,
And their upholding wearies Him not.
And He alone is truly exalted and Most High. (Quran 2:256)

The above is one of the most beautiful and best known verses, called *Ayat ul Kursi* or the *verse of knowledge*, because it is indicative of the All-

Comprehensive wisdom of God. His *Kursi* is His knowledge and *His seat of power*, it can also be interpreted as *His sovereignity*, that clearly denotes God's majesty and indescribable, eternal glory.

God sent down scriptures through His messengers for the guidance and benefit of the different nations. He therefore sent a prophet to each nation as long as it was needed. Jesus Christ (pbuh) was sent to the Jewish nation six hundred years prior to Prophet Hazrat Muhammad (pbuh). The Holy Prophet Muhammad Mustafa (pbuh) was not the Prophet sent for one nation but for the entire creation.

Jesus (pbuh) proclaimed in John (10:12,13) that he could not guide the world to the Absolute Truth. "I have yet many things to declare to you, but you are not ready to absorb it. However, when he the spirit of truth has come he will definitely guide you into the truth." The authenticity of the Quran as the final revelation is thus proclaimed by the God the Most high, "This day, I have perfected for you your religion and completed My favor unto you and chosen for you Islam as your faith" (Quran 5:3).

MANIFESTATION OF LIGHT

Allah is the light of the heavens and the earth.
The parable of His light is,
As it were, that of a niche containing a lamp;
The lamp is enclosed in a glass,
The glass is like a radiant star;
Lit from a blessed tree-an olive tree,
That is neither of the East nor of the West,
The oil of which will always give light,
Even though fire has not touched it,
Light upon light,
Allah guides to his light whomsoever He pleases.
And Allah sets parables for men.
And Allah has full knowledge of all things.
In the Houses which God has allowed to be raised,

So that His Name be remembered in them.
And to extol His limitless glory at morning and evening.
(Quran 24:35)

The verse of light, *Ayat Al Nur*, is famous and popular among Sufis. In this verse, Allah is called the light of the heavens and the earth. He has created them by bringing them into existence. The word *Allah* in this verse does not apply to the Essence of God but rather it refers to His personal Name, *Allah*. His personal Name is like a lamp (Divine light) placed on a raised pillar in order to illuminate the whole world. God has protected this light by enclosing it in a glass. This light is so brilliant that it resembles a shining star. The Name *Allah* is the Divine light that cannot be put out, as God said, "They desire to extinguish God's [guiding] light with their utterances: but God will not allow [this to pass], for He has willed to spread His light in all its fullness, however hateful this may be to all who deny the truth" (Quran 9:32; 61:8).

The blessed olive tree is the symbol of Islam, from which this light is emanating and spreading to the far-off places in the East and West, fulfilling the prophecy that it will eventually transform all humanity.

Mystics refer the word *Nur* (light) to the person of the Prophet Hazrat Muhammad (pbuh), in whose heart God the most High has placed the bright lamp of His personal Name, *Allah*. Even before he received the Divine revelation, "Read in the Name of thy Lord," he was a source of light for all mankind. When the light from Allah came to him it was as though "light upon light" had been revealed to him. The Divine light will eventually overcome all the hearts and illuminate the whole world. The light of Islam will enter all the houses in the East and the West very soon. The only way to illuminate one's heart with the light of God is by meditating on the personal Name, *Allah*. As stated, this can be accomplished by inscribing it with brilliant letters on the heart through concentration and meditation.

I sincerely believe that if we allow the light of the personal Name of Allah to enter our hearts, it will glow in there permanently and keep on emanating waves of light in all directions. It will illuminate anyone's heart that will come in contact with it.

MERCY

God's essence is love, mercy, and compassion, and He cannot be other than His attributes. The whole drama of existence in the universe is played but to manifest God's love and mercy. Therefore people of knowledge say that "He created human beings to have mercy on them." Without sinners how could He be the Forgiver?

That is why the Prophet (pbuh) said, "If you do not sin, God would bring a people who do sin, so that He could forgive them. Surely there is no sin too great for God to forgive." In this regard God reassures and promises mankind, "O' My servants who have transgressed against themselves, despair not of the Mercy of Allah, verily Allah forgives all sins. Truly, He is oft Forgiving, Most Merciful" (Quran 39:53).

A companion recited the above verse before the Prophet Hazrat Muhammad (pbuh), and when the reciter reached the words, *Verily God will forgive all sins,* The Prophet (pbuh) confirmed, "Indeed He will and He does not care." Then he repeated three times that God hates those who make people despair of God's mercy.

Samani explained in one of his treatises, "O Angels, you have obedience; O Messengers, you have messengerhood; O pious ascetics, you have asceticism; O worshippers, you have worship; and O disobedient servants you have the Lord." Therefore it is incumbent on you to stay between a state of hope and fear—all the time repenting, weeping, and supplicating. "Turn to God, all of you. Surely, God will forgive all sins."

And whosoever does evil or wrongs himself but afterwards seeks Allah's forgiveness, he will find Allah oft Forgiving and ever Merciful. (Quran 4:110)

§

And verily I am indeed Forgiving to him who repents, believes [in My Oneness] and does righteous deeds and then remains constant in doing them. (Quran 20:82)

§

When Prophet Moses (pbuh) killed a man, he said,
"O my Lord, forgive me and He forgave him" (Quran)

§

And when Prophet David (pbuh) repented, Allah said,
"And thereupon We forgave him that, nearness to Us awaits him
in the life to come and a good place of return." (Quran 38:25)

§

Seek forgiveness of your Lord and turn to Him in repentance that
he may grant you provision for a term appointed. And that He may
bestow His grace to every owner of grace [those who help and serve
the needy and deserving. (Quran)

PRE-ORDAINMENT

Predestination is a divine mystery, and no one has any
knowledge of it save Him. God is the only agent and actor,
therefore destiny is what He decrees. He knows everything about
his creatures so that He wrote down in the Book of fate all that
will come to pass. Human beings are given free choice, but due to
the overwhelming greatness of God, He knows already what every
one would do at any given time.

No calamity can ever befall the earth nor your own selves, unless
it be in Our decree before We bring it into being: verily, all this is
easy for God. (Quran 57:22)

§

Never can anything befall on us except what God has decreed, He is our Lord supreme: and in God let the believers place their trust.
(Quran 9:51)

§

Allah cannot be questioned as to what He does, while they will be questioned for what they do. (Quran 21:23)

§

And it may be that you dislike a thing that is good for you and it may be that you like a thing and it may be not in your interest. Allah has full knowledge of everything. (Quran 2:216-217)

TRUST IN GOD

Complete trust in God and surrender to His will is an important characteristic of a believer. Man has to rely totally on God, who in His absoluteness is the only all embracing power. Trust in God in real sense means to realize the Oneness of God and not to rely upon or be afraid of any created being.
And put your trust in Allah, if you are believers indeed. (Quran 5:23)

§

Allah is sufficient for us, and He is the best disposer of affairs. (Quran 3:173)

§

Invoke Me in utter sincerity of faith, I will respond to your invocation.
(Quran 40:60)

§

Who listens to the distressed soul when it calls upon Him and who relieves its suffering? Can there be another god beside God.
(Quran 27:62)

§

But sufficient is your Lord as a Guide and Helper. (Quran 25:31)

§

Truly, none but those who deny the truth [disbelieve] ever lose hope of God's All encompassing mercy. (Quran 12:87)

§

And We heard his prayer and delivered him from the distress, and thus We do deliver the believers. (Quran 21:88)

REMEMBRANCE

Recitation of the Quran is the means of concentration upon God. It is the remembrance of God that is the essence of every spiritual struggle. The reading of the Quran is thus the invocation of the the Name *Allah*. His miraculous verses (*ayats*) come from Him and will eventually take the reader back to Him.

Allah guides to Himself all who turn to Him, those who believe and whose hearts find satisfaction in the remembrance of God.

Verily in the remembrance of Allah do hearts find rest. (Quran 13:28)

§

And the men and the women who remember Allah much with sincerity of the heart, Allah has stored for them a great reward and readied forgiveness of sins. (Quran 33:35)

§

O you, who have attained faith! Remember God with unceasing remembrance, and extol His limitless glory from morn to evening.
(Quran 35:41)

§

O you who have faith, let not your wealth and children distract your attention from the commemoration of Allah. (Quran 63:9)

§

And glorify the praises of your Lord when you get up for praying and during part of the night and at the time when the stars are setting.
(Quran 52:49-50)

GRACE

Grace is the unconditional love of God for human beings. It is God's unmerited favor and goodness towards those who have no claim on it. We must accept this grace by thanking God and in a special way, we must return His love.

In the words of Ibne Ataullah, "Whoever is not thankful for the graces of God runs the risk of losing them, and whoever is thankful, fetters them with their own cord." Even the capacity of thanking is a gift of Divine grace; therefore we should be "grateful for the gratitude."

And if you would try to count the graces of Allah, never would you be able to count them. (Quran 16:18). Prophet Hazrat Muhammad (pbuh) said in a hadith, "None amongst you can get into paradise by virtue of his deeds alone not even I, but that Allah should wrap me in His grace and mercy."

§

And whatever blessings and fortune you have, it is a gift from Allah, and when misfortune befalls you, it is to Him that you cry for help.
(Quran 16:53)

§

And whosoever believes in Allah and keeps his duty to Him. He will make a way for him to get out of difficulties. And He will provide for him from sources he never could imagine, and whosoever has trust in Him, then He will be sufficient for him. (Quran 65:2-3)

§

And remember when your Lord declared, if you give thanks [by worshiping me], I will bestow upon you more of My blessings and but if you are thankless, My punishment is severe indeed. (Quran 14:7)

§

And if My servants ask thee about Me, behold, I am near; I respond to the call of him who calls, whenever he calls unto Me; let them, then, respond unto Me, and believe in Me, so that they might follow the right way. (Quran 2:186)

RIGHTEOUSNESS

Reverential fear of God makes the basis of righteousness. God describes righteousness as fearing Him as He should be feared. The Quran often speak of fear of God and fear of Judgment, which make the heart of a faithful tremble with fear. Mystics emphasize both fear and hope (mercy) as the essential ingredients of faith and necessary for a life of righteousness. There are more than one hundred and fifty verses in the Quran stressing the importance of righteousness so as to protect one from sins small or great. Regarding what is lawful and what is prohibited is clearly mentioned in the Book. Whatever is in between are doubtful matters. It is prudent to avoid doubtful things so as not to fall in error. Without doubt it is the fear of God that leads one into the life of piety, humility, simplicity, uprightness, and devotion to truth.

Verily those who believe [in the Oneness of Allah] and perform deeds of righteousness, the Loving one will create enduring love for them.

(Quran 19:96)

§

Whosoever perform good deeds, whether man or woman and truly believes in Allah, We shall grant him/her a pure life and We shall pay them a reward in proportion to the best of what they do. (Quran 16:97)

§

And those who believe and perform righteous deeds and believe in what has been bestowed from on high on Muhammad, for it is the truth from their Lord, He will improve their condition by taking away their sins. (Quran 47:2)

§

It is neither your riches nor your children that bring you close to Us, but it is only those who believe and perform righteous deeds will have a manifold reward and will reside in lofty mansions [of paradise] in peace and security. (Quran 34:37)

§

And whosoever seeks a religion other than self-surrender unto God [Islam], it will never be accepted of him and in the life to come he shall be among the lost. (Quran 3:85)

PATEINCE

God teaches patience in the Quran in many places and reassures humans by saying, "And God is with those who show patience."(2:103). Patience is to accept what is Divine decree and to remain unmoved during times of affliction. Only a patient person can see the blessings veiled in the hardest blows of fate. In the difficulties of life, patience is the key to happiness.
Only those who are patient in adversity shall receive their reward beyond measure without reckoning. (Quran 39:10)

§

Peace be upon you, for you have preserved in patience. (Quran 13:24)

§

And bear with patience whatever befalls you. (Quran 31:1)

§

Patience most befits me now. It is Allah alone whose help can be sought against that which you proclaim. (Quran 12:18)

§

And if you endure patiently, it is certainly best for you, and your patience is not but from Allah. (Quran 16:127)

§

But give glad tidings to the patient ones, who when afflicted with misfortune do not despair but say, truly we belong to Allah and finally will return back to Him.(Quran 2:155)

PROVISIONS

God's all-encompassing mercy, wisdom, power, and loving kindness is mentioned in the Quran as He promises to sustain all His creation. The provision for everybody has been guaranteed from pre-eternity. That is why the mystics say, "Wherever, your provision is, there you will find it and it will find you."
And there is no living creature in the earth but its provision is due from Allah and He knows its term and where it resides. (Quran 11:6)

§

Whatever Allah due to His mercy bestows on mankind, none can withhold it, and whatever He withholds, none can henceforth release.
(Quran 35:2)

§

God does not burden any human being with more than he is well able to bear. (Quran 2:288)

§

Invoke your Lord with humility, and in the secrecy of your heart, Truly He does not like those who transgress. (Quran 7:55)

§

And for whom Allah has not appointed light, for him there is no light at all. (Quran 24:41)

§

Verily We showed him the way, whether he is grateful and follows it or ungrateful and abandons it. (Quran 76:3)

KINDNESS TOWARDS PARENTS

In terms of importance, the duty owed to one's parents is mentioned in the Quran after the worship of God alone: "And your Lord has commanded that you worship none but Him and has enjoined benevolence towards parents. Should either one or both of them attain old age in your lifetime? Never say to them a word of disrespect nor raise your voice at them, but always speak gently to them" (Quran 17:23).

To honor and respect one's parents is a commandment of the Lord and is considered an act of devotion that is highly treasured by the Lord. During the night of ascension the Holy Prophet Muhammad (pbuh) was taken to a place where he saw a man who entered the light of Allah's throne. The Prophet asked who is this person and is he an angel. He was told no. He asked again is he a prophet? It was said to him no. The Prophet enquired, "Who is he then?" The answer was, "This is a man who ceaselessly remembered God while he was in the world. His heart was attached to the prayers and he never disobeyed his parents."

In the Quran, God enjoins on us the necessity to show gratitude to Him as our Creator as well as our parents. He, therefore mentions both together in the following verse, "And We have enjoined upon man (to be dutiful and good) to his parents. Be grateful to Me and to thy parents. Unto Me is the final return" (31:15).

Prophet Muhammad (pbuh) reinforced the duty to be gentle towards parents in many of his sayings. Once, a man asked the Prophet, "Who has the greatest claim on me regarding service?" The Prophet replied, "The mother's right is greater than the father's." He was asked three times the same question and each time the Prophet replied the same. The fourth time he said, "The father's right comes next." The man asked why this is so. The Prophet replied, "Your mother carried you inside her womb for nine months and then by giving birth brought you into this world. She gave up her sleep and comfort, nursed you, carried you in her arms, loved and protected you. She cleaned you and raised you until you attained adulthood. She constantly followed your interest until this day. Your father sowed you, provided you with food, clothing and shelter. Can this be equal to your mother's role?"

The man asked the Holy Prophet, "I wonder if I could ever repay my mother for all that she did for me, however, much I might do for her?" To this the Prophet (pbuh) said, "You could not even repay her one night's due." The man then said, "I feed my mother, carry her on my back and clean after her to fulfill my duty and I intend to do so as long as she may live." The Prophet replied, "No, because, there will still be this difference, you are serving her in anticipation of her death, whereas she served wishing you a long life."

The Prophet (pbuh) had shown great respect for mothers and had consistently advised his followers to do so. It is related in a story that when the Prophet (pbuh) was informed once that monk Juraij did not care for his mother, who wanted to see him, the Prophet (pbhu) remarked, "If Juraij were a learned and knowing person, he would have known that it is part of the service to God to answer one's mother's call."

Uways Al Qarani lived in Yemen at the time of the Prophet Muhammad (pbuh) but never, met him in person. The Prophet knew his spiritual piety and said, "I feel the 'Breath of the Merciful' from Yemen." He was solely guided by the Divine grace, without the mediation of a master. The legend is that after the death of the Prophet (pbuh), Hazrat Umar, the second caliph of Islam, and Hazrat Ali, the fourth Caliph of Islam went to see Uways and asked him what prevented him from seeing the Prophet. He replied, "I had an elderly and ailing mother who was totally dependent on me, and duty towards my mother takes precedence over seeing the Prophet."

Once, a sheikh went to see Abu Hazim Al Madani, who was a luminary of his time. When the visiting Sheikh arrived at his residence, he found him asleep. When Abu Hazim Al Madani woke up, he said to him, "I saw the Holy Prophet in my dream and he told me to inform you that it is better to fulfill your duty to your mother than to make the pilgrimage to the Kaaba in Mecca. Therefore, go back and try to please her." The Sheikh did not go to pilgrimage but instead returned home to serve his mother.

Chapter Ten

ORDER OF THE GREATEST HELP (AL GHAWTH AL AZAM)

Meditation on the personal Name of Allah is the only tool to eliminate all the veils that exists between man and God. These veils are manifold. According to a prophetic tradition, "There are seventy-thousand veils between the creatures and the created" that need to be lifted to come closer to the light of God and have direct experience of the Divine.

Meditation is a Divine blessing; it is the most powerful form of prayer. Meditation takes the meditator directly to the Divine presence and results in mystical reunion with the Creator. As the Quran proclaims, "To Allah we belong and to Him is our return" (Quran 2:155).

The life of the Prophet Hazrat Muhammad (pbuh) and his companions was based entirely on *Faqr* (poverty), spiritual awareness, revelation from God the Most High, and the direct experience of Divine presence—time with God. The deeper and hidden meaning of the word of God is esoteric and mystical in nature and is a commentary on human and Divine interaction. Recitation of the verses of the Quran—the living word of God—hence leads restless spirits into a meditative state and opens up new frontiers of understanding.

With the widespread propagation of Islam throughout the neighboring empires and faraway places in the world, the mystical dimensions of Islam followed as well. The great majority of Muslims were overwhelmed with worldly affairs, but an elite minority of men and women remained faithful to the original message and its core values of spiritual transformation and human salvation.

As a matter of fact, the Sufi tradition started with the Prophet Hazrat Muhammad (pbuh), for he was the perfect man and endowed with the direct knowledge and wisdom of God. Thus he is the first link in the spiritual chain (*silsila*) of Islamic mysticism. The Prophet Hazrat Muhammad (pbuh) in turn transferred this Divine wisdom and esoteric knowledge to Hazrat Ali Ibne Abi Talib, his cousin and son in law, the fourth Caliph of Islam. The Prophet (pbuh) thus initiated Hazrat Ali (may God be pleased with him) in his path and invested him with a cloak (*khirqa*). Hazrat Ali (may God be pleased with him) passed this Divine knowledge (*ilme ludani*) to his successors, and it is through them that all the chains of affiliations (*silsilas*) started and continue until this day.

The love of the Prophet (pbuh) and his family and allegiance to his household is widespread among faithful Muslims. Hazrat Ali, commander of the believers (may God be pleased with him), is regarded universally both by Sunni and Shia Sufi masters as the most important link in the spiritual chain leading all those who practice the Sufi way back to the fountainhead of all light and blessings, the Prophet Hazrat Muhammad (pbuh).

The first ascetics in Islam were called *companions on the bench*, who were extremely poor and lived in the Prophet's mosque in Medina, praying and recollecting God during every moment of their lives and experiencing His perpetual presence.

The Persian convert Salman Farsi was an important early Sufi who was closely connected to the household of the Prophet Hazrat Muhammad (pbuh) and had a great impact on Persian Sufism.

Uways Al Qarani—who lived in Yemen and had never met the Prophet (pbuh) of Islam—was a devout Sufi guided directly by the Divine. The Prophet (pbuh) was aware of his mystical state and said about him, "I feel the air of the Merciful from Yemen." Uways Al Qarani is thus an example of Divine grace and the Breath of the Merciful, who was guided without an intermediary or sheikh.

It is worthy to note that Sufi saints played an important role in preaching and spreading Islam to large parts of the world, especially India, Indonesia, and Black Africa. They propagated the basic tenets of Islam, trust in God, love of the Prophet (pbuh), and love of fellow human beings. The fraternal love taught by Sufis extended generally to include all humanity. Service to men and doing good for one's brothers' and sisters' sake is the motto of the mystics.

Caring for the sick, needy, and poor is the duty of the wayfarers throughout their lifetimes. The love that Sufis talk about includes animals as well as fellow humans. According to a legend, a kind-hearted Sufi offered to give away the reward for his seventy pilgrimages to someone who would give a loaf of bread to a starving dog. One of the people who heard the Sheikh did so. At this, another Sufi who was witnessing all this rebuked the first one to have paid a lower price for this act of kindness, thus cheating the poor fellow.

In time, Sufi teachings began to attract wider numbers of people and developed into a popular movement transforming hearts and minds. The Sufi way became the way of the heart and of salvation. Regarding this, the Prophet Hazrat Muhammad (pbuh) said, "If one wants the company of God, then one should sit with the Sufis."

In the beginning of the eleventh century, due to increasing numbers of adepts and followers, Sufi fraternities came into existence. This led to the formation of Sufi orders or *silsilas*. Centers for mystical activities called *khanqahs* were established in order to prepare new adepts on the path.

Every Sufi order has specific values and ascetic practices (*dhikr*, prayers, and meditation) for a novice seeker—mainly to tame the lower self, purify the heart, and inspire good behavior. For example the Mevlavi order required their adepts to learn Rumi's great poem, the *Masnavi*, as well as the whirling dance, and to serve in the kitchen or other areas for up to a thousand and one days. Some Sufi orders prescribed strict ascetic exercises for new seekers—from three years up to twelve years—before they were initiated into the *silsila* (chain) to receive the *baraka* (blessings) from the Sheikh. The disciple has to take the oath of allegiance (*baya*) at the hand of the master so that he or she can be invested with the cloak (*khirqa*).

THE QADERI SUFI ORDER

The Qaderi Sufi order is thought to be the oldest and first of Sufi *silsilas*, founded after one of the most celebrated and world-renowned saint of all times, Hazrat Syed Shaikh Abdul Qadir Jilani (may God be pleased with him). He is considered by the majority of *auliya* (saints)—especially the founders of the Suharwadiya, Chistiya, and Naqshbandiya orders—to be the "seal of saints," just as the Holy Prophet Hazrat Muhammad (pbuh) was the "seal of Prophets."

HAZRAT SHAIKH SYED ABDUL QADIR JILANI

Hazrat Shaikh Syed Abdul Qadir Jilani was of noble descent. He was born in the province of Gilan, in the Northwestern part of Persia, in the month of Ramadan in the year 470 A.H., which corresponds to the year 1077 A.D. His father, Abu Salih Jangi Dost, was the descendent of Hazrat Imam Al Hassan, son of Hazrat Ali (may God be pleased with him), the commander of the believers, the cousin and son in law of the Prophet of Islam and Hazrat Fatima Al Zahra, the beloved daughter of the Prophet (pbuh). His mother, Ummal Khair (mother of goodness), was the daughter of Abdullah Sawmai Al Zahid, who in turn was the descendent of Hazrat Imam Hussain, son of Hazrat Ali (may God be pleased with him) and Hazrat Fatima Al Zahra. Therefore, Syed Shaikh Abdul Qadir Jilani, the crown of saints, was known as Karim Al Jaddain: noble through two grandfathers on both sides of the family.

His mother was a righteous woman, and it is stated that she said, "When my son Abdul Qadir was born, he would not latch on the breast during the daytime in the month of Ramadan. When the new moon of Ramadan was invisible behind the clouds, people came to me and enquired about him. I told them that he has not sucked on the breast today. It was thus obvious that it was the first day of Ramadan."

One of the disciples of Sheikh Syed Abdul Qadir Jilani once asked him, "What is the basis of your righteousness?" The Sheikh replied to this, "On the basis of truthfulness, I have never told a lie, even when I was a youngster." He then added, "When I was young and still at home, one day, I went to the outskirts of the city and it was the day of pilgrimage. While, I was following an ox ploughing the fields, another ox looked at me and said, 'O, Abdul Qadir, you have not been created for this.' When I heard this I ran back home and climbed up the roof. I could actually see people standing at Arafat performing the rites of pilgrimage; even though Arafat was hundreds of miles away. So I went down to see my mother and said to her, 'Give me as a gift to Allah and allow me to go to Baghdad, where I shall acquire knowledge and be in the company of saints.' She was surprised by my sudden request and asked about the reason for this. I told her my story. She broke down in tears and then brought eighty gold coins, which my father had left as an inheritance.

"She left forty gold coins for my brother and stitched the rest of the gold coins inside my coat. She gave me her permission, but made me promise to always remain truthful in every circumstance. She bid me farewell and said, 'I give you to Allah with pleasure and know that I may not be able to see your radiant face until the Day of Judgment.'

"I joined a small caravan traveling towards Baghdad. When the caravan reached the outskirts of Hamadan, we were attacked by sixty highwaymen mounted on horses. They seized the whole caravan and took away everyone's possessions and valuables. The robbers apparently ignored me totally, for I looked destitute and poor. However, one of the brigands looked at me while passing by my side and remarked, 'You poor boy, what do you have?' I told him, 'Forty gold coins.' To this he asked, 'Where are the gold coins?' "They are hidden in the lining of my coat under my armpit",

I replied. He thought I was being sarcastic, did not believe what he heard, and moved on. Then another brigand pulled by my side and asked me the same question. I gave him the same answer; I had given to the first one. On hearing my response he left me alone.

"Thereafter, both of them went to their leader and told him what they heard from me. Their leader became interested in this and told them to bring me to him. They were standing on the top of the hill and were sharing their loot from the caravan. The leader of the group asked me in a commanding voice, 'What do you have with you?' I said, 'Forty gold coins.' He then questioned, 'Where have you got it?' I told him, 'They are sewn inside the lining of my coat under my armpit.' He snatched my coat and sliced open the lining and found the forty gold coins. At this discovery, he was shocked and asked me, 'What prompted you to make this confession?'

"So I told him, 'At the time of my departure, my mother made me promise to remain truthful in every circumstance and never to tell a lie, and I would never break my covenant to her.'

"These words had such a deep impact on the leader of the robbers that he began to weep, knelt down, and said with eyes full of tears, 'You did not betray your mother's command, whereas, I have been disobeying the commandments of my Lord for so many years until now.'

"He then repented at my hands for the sins he had committed. Seeing this, all his fellow robbers said to the leader, 'You have been our leader in robbery, and so shall be our leader in true repentance.' They returned whatever goods they had taken from the travelers, and they were the first sinners who repented at my hands."

Thousands of the wrongdoers of Baghdad repented their sins at his blessed hands, and hundreds of Jews and Christians embraced Islam during his sermons, for he used to proclaim the truth from the pulpit.

He had more charismatic talents (*karamats*) than any other saint throughout the entire history of Islam and no one has received so much veneration from people. He was the reviver of the religion of Islam when it was decaying and the whole Muslim community was in moral chaos.

Once he was asked what he had received from the Lord of all the worlds. To this he replied, "Knowledge and good manners." He considered knowledge a noble talent, magnificent qualification, and object of pride, because it is by means of knowledge that one can arrive at the realization and affirmation of the Oneness of God the Most High. As the Prophet Hazrat Muhammad (pbuh) has said, "The quest for knowledge is a religious obligation for every Muslim man and Muslim woman" (*hadith*).

He was an authority on prophetic tradition, Islamic jurisprudence, religious exhortations, and other Islamic spiritual sciences. He had an excellent bearing and maintained dignified silence. He was extremely generous; he would always eat with guests and sit in the company of the meek. He was patient with the seekers of the knowledge.

He once said, "I have made a thorough scrutiny of all human actions, and I did not find any deed amongst them more meritorious than providing of food nor anything nobler than good moral character. I would love to hold this world in my hand so that I could feed it to the hungry."

Hazrat Syed Sheikh Abdul Qadir Jilani was patient with his students and loved to teach and impart knowledge. In one of his classes there was a Persian boy Named Ubayy. He was mentally delayed, had very low intelligence, and could hardly understand a subject without great effort and labor. He used to read aloud to the Sheikh. Once Ibne As Samhal came to visit the Sheikh during one of his lectures. When he observed the Sheikh's patience and loving attitude towards Ubayy, he was amazed. As soon as Ubayy left the classroom, the visitor turned to Sheikh and said, "I am truly astonished by your patience with this would-be jurist."

On hearing this Sheikh replied, "My labor with him will soon be over by the end of the week; he will have passed and returned unto the Merciful."

Ibne As Samhal was surprised to hear such an announcement from the Sheikh. He started counting the days until Ubayy died—at the end of that week. He attended his funeral prayers and expressed amazement at the knowledge of the Sheikh regarding Ubayy's death before his appointed time.

Hazrat Syed Sheikh Abdul Qadir Jilani underwent severe ascetic exercises during his early life, after acquiring religious knowledge.

He himself stated, "I stayed in the desert of Iraq for twenty-five years and used to wander alone. I did not get to know anybody nor did anybody know me. My only visitors were groups of men belonging to the invisible realm, as well as some of the *jinn*. I used to teach them the religion of Islam and the way of Allah.

He stayed in an old deserted fortress near Baghdad for fifteen years and prayed there all night. He would stand on one foot and would finish reciting the whole Quran before Morning Prayer time.

At the end of 521 A.H. he started to preach and deliver sermons after Prophet Hazrat Muhammad (pbuh) appeared to him and advised him to speak. He narrated this in the following words: "I once saw Allah's messenger (pbuh) before the mid-day prayer, and he said to me, 'O my dear son, why do you not speak out?' In reply I said, 'Dear father, I am a non-Arab, how can I speak in front of the people of Baghdad?' He then asked me to open my mouth, and I did so. The Prophet (pbuh) then blew into my mouth seven times and told me, 'You must preach to the people and call them to the way of the Lord with wisdom and good advice.' I performed my mid-day prayers, and after the prayers Hazrat Ali (may God be pleased with him) appeared before me and said, 'Open your mouth.' So I obeyed his command, and he blew six times into my mouth. I asked him why he did not do it seven times. At this he replied, 'Out of respect to the messenger of Allah, I kept the number of times to six.'"

It was after that incident that he was spiritually prepared for the task of preaching. In the early days, he had few listeners, but soon his fame for knowledge and inner illumination reached far and wide, and people gathered around him in ever-increasing numbers. His *madrassa* (school) was not large enough to accommodate his followers and listeners despite the addition of adjacent buildings and new construction. So he had to go out of the city and preach from the *eidgah* (large tract of open land used for mass prayer gatherings) platform. The number of people present during his sermons was usually around seventy thousand. It is said that four hundred scribes used to write down his lectures and discourses in order to preserve his teachings.

Thousands of sinners used to repent and mend their ways to righteousness. Hundreds of non-Muslims (Jews and Christians) used to embrace Islam, and four or five people used to expire due to extreme ecstasy and heightened state of spirituality on a regular basis during his lectures.

Among his recorded and most famous exhortations are the following:

1. The *Endowment of Divine Grace*, which is a collection of sixty-eight sermons delivered during 1251-1252 in Baghdad.
2. The *Revelations of the Unseen (Futuh Al Gaib)*.

In one of his letters he said, "Dear friend, your heart is a polished mirror. You must wipe it clean of the dust that has gathered upon it by recollecting Allah, because it is destined to reflect the light of Divine secrets, which will fall upon it if you wish for Him, from Him, and with Him. If only the light of Divine secrets is kindled within your heart, the rest will come— either all at once or little by little. Then you will witness the sun of inner knowledge rising from the horizon of Divine reason."

The great master Ibn Al Arabi has devoted a full chapter in *Futuhat* to the veneration and praise of Hazrat Syed Sheikh Abdul Qadir Jilani, who is the eponym of the most widely spread of the Sufi orders. Sheikh Abdul Qadir Jilani died the year Ibn Al Arabi was born. Ibn Al Arabi received the *khirqa* (cloak) and spiritual blessings from Sheikh Abdul Qadir Jilani through the intermediary of Jamal Al Din Yunus Ibn Yahya Al Hashimi, who was the disciple of the Sheikh.

Ibn Al Arabi's high remarks and great respect for Sheikh Abdul Qadir Jilani also bewildered Western scholars. J. Spencer Trimigham, in his book *Sufi Orders in Islam*, wrote, "It is difficult to penetrate through the mist of legend which formed even during the lifetime of Abdul Qadir Ibn Abi Salih Jangidost and thickened rapidly after his death and to discuss why he, out of hundreds of saintly figures of the period, survived in a unique way to become the inspirer of millions, a heavenly receiver of petitions and bestower of benefits right upto the present day."

Ibn Al Arabi clearly accepted Hazrat Sheikh Syed Abdul Qadir Jilani's extraordinary activities as manifestations of the truth, as he said, "As he made manifest the powers that God had given him. He displayed the attributes of *tasarruf* (free activity) and *tahakkum* (ruling control) through the Aspiration that is given to some of the Folk of God. It is these powers that appear in what are called *karamat* (charismatic gifts).

Ibn Al Arabi mentioned one Man, who had a special relationship with the Divine Name, Subjugating (*Qadir*), and he cited Abdul Qadir Jilani as an example. "He is the Subjugating above His servants (6:18), and this Man is overbearing towards everything except God. He is audacious, courageous, bold, and great in claims through a *Haqq*. He speaks a *Haqq* and judges by justice. The companion of this station was our Sheikh Abdul Qadir Al Jili in Baghdad."

Hazrat Syed Sheikh Abdul Qadir Jilani is called the *Ghauth Al Azam* (the greatest help or succor). He indeed is the *gauth* of the East and the West and in fact is considered by the majority of saints to be the *gauth* of all times.

He once proclaimed, "I have received seventy firm assurances from my Lord that he would not subject me to any trials and that none of my disciples would die except in a state of repentance." He was asked if someone called himself to be his follower without receiving direct instructions and blessings from him what his fate would be. To this question he replied, "If someone called himself a Qaderi after me and professes affiliation to me, my hand over him will be like the sky over the earth, and God will accept him."

Once, Sheikh Syed Abdul Qadir Jilani was delivering a sermon from his pulpit in Baghdad. There were more than fifty renowned scholars and jurists present in the audience, along with thousands of other listeners. Suddenly Sheikh Abdul Qadir Jilani addressed the people and proclaimed, "This foot of mine is upon the neck of every saint of Allah." On hearing this, Sheikh Ali Ibn Al Hiti stood up, climbed the steps of the pulpit, lay down, grasped the foot of the Sheikh, and placed it upon his neck. All those present in the session bowed down their necks in the same manner.

Al Tustari narrated an incident regarding Hazrat Sheikh Syed Abdul Qadir Jilani, stating that the Sheikh was absent for some time and could not be found in Baghdad even after a thorough search. His followers were worried about him. In the meantime, someone told them that he was heading towards the River Tigris the last time he was seen. Therefore, his disciples headed towards the river. Suddenly, they saw him walking on the water towards them. Fish in the water were swimming around him offering their greetings and peace. They were amazed at the scene of schools of fish kissing his hands. It was the time for mid-day prayer. At that very moment a huge prayer rug suddenly appeared, which was green in color and studded with gold and silver. On the prayer rug the following Quranic verses were written: The first was, "As for the friends of Allah, surely no fear shall be upon them, nor shall they grieve" (Quran 10:62). The second verse was, "The mercy of Allah and His blessings be upon you, O people of the house. He is Praiseworthy, Glorious" (Quran 11:73).

That magnificent prayer rug was suspended between the sky and the earth and floating above the Tigris. It resembled the flying carpet of the Prophet Solomon (pbuh). At this time a group of dazzling warriors resembling a pack of lions appeared on the scene. Their leader was a dignified, awe-inspiring, and handsome knight. They marched to the prayer rug and stood there as guards in profound humility, with heads bowed, and remained motionless as if overpowered by Divine glory. At the time of ritual prayer, Sheikh Syed Abdul Qadir Jilani, dressed in a robe of honor, came forward and led the prayer. The knight, his warriors, and all his followers present at the scene prayed behind him. As soon as he declared the supreme Greatness of Allah, the angels of the heavenly Throne shouted, *Allah o Akbar*. When he recited the glory of Allah, the angels of the seven heavens also joined him in glorification. A bright beam of light emanated from his mouth until it reached the sky above.

With the conclusion of the prayers, he raised his hands and prayed to God the Most High: "O Lord, for the sake of my ancestor Prophet Hazrat Muhammad (pbuh), your beloved and friend and for the sake of all my forefathers, I beg you not to take away the soul of any of my followers unless he or she is in a state of repentance."

At the end of his supplication we heard angels of the Throne and the heavens saying *Amin*, and we did so joining their voices. At that moment we heard the following voice from above, "Rejoice and know that, I have accepted your petition."

Every day of Sheikh Syed Abdul Qadir Jilani's life unfolded new miracles, in fact more charismatic marvels are attributed to him than to any other Sufi master in the history of Islamic mysticism. He is without doubt the greatest help (*Ghauth Al azam*), and until this day seekers on the path receive waves of light and spiritual blessings from him esoterically.

MY PERSONAL ACCOUNTS:

In the following pages I will narrate my personal spiritual experiences, observations, and visions related to my great spiritual master Sheikh Syed Abdul Qadir Jilani.

I lived in Iran for seventeen years; those were probably the best years of my life, and I really enjoyed my stay. I moved to Iran after having completed medical school in Peshawar, Pakistan, and after having completed my internship.

The Shah of Iran, Muhammad Reza Pehlavi, was still in power in those days, and Iran had embarked on an ambitious program of social and economic development. The Red Lion and Sun Society of Iran was recruiting thousands of foreign doctors for its sprawling health care system throughout the country. I was one of the earliest physicians to be employed in that program. I had a chance to work in different cities of Iran. My first post was in Chabahar, which is a small port city in the province of Baluchistan.

The Shah of Iran was building a strategic naval and airbase in Kunarak, near Chabahar. Due to its geopolitical importance, the project was given a lot of attention by the authorities. Ninety-five percent of the local population is Sunni. Baluchis are simple, honest, and hospitable people and they liked me a lot because I am a Sunni myself. Baluchistan has a hot and dry climate, and I had joined there after their new year, *Norooz*.

During my first week of working, an incident occurred that made me popular among the natives of Chabahar. A construction team was digging a deep well in the hospital compound because there was a scarcity of fresh water in Baluchistan. One of the crew went down in the well to work. Apparently there had been an accumulation of poisonous gas due to seepage at the bottom and he lost consciousness. He was pulled out by other team members after fifteen minutes, but he was suffering from convulsions, frothing from the mouth and was comatose. I was the doctor on site and rushed to his help on the scene. I resuscitated him aggressively, provided him with medical help, treated his seizures with anticonvulsant medication, supported his airway, and gave him oxygen and intravenous fluids. He remained comatose for over twenty-four hours and then he recovered dramatically. I stayed at his bedside during all this time. He went home in two days. The news of this incident and of his survival spread like wildfire in the city. The locals considered his recovery and survival to be a miracle that had happened at my hands.

The next week a sixteen-year-old boy was brought into the emergency room in moribund state. He was in severe septic shock and was in critical condition. I was working in the emergency room. I initially stabilized the patient with aggressive management and diagnosed him with a ruptured appendix, resulting in peritonitis and sepsis. I called for the visiting surgical team on site, and they took him to the operating room for an exploratory laparotomy. It turned out to be a ruptured appendix, causing severe peritonitis. With aggressive team management, the young boy survived. I was once again credited for correct diagnosis and management as well as the survival of the patient. The rumor in the city was that I had the healing touch.

There were countless numbers of children with severe gastroenteritis, bacterial pneumonias, meningitis, and malaria who were saved by proper treatment and the meticulous care I provided them.

At that time I did not think that it was some sort of a miracle or supernatural phenomena, but I honestly thought that these patients were lucky to receive proper medical treatment and care at the right time and at the right place.

However, at times more than proper medical treatment was needed. Needless to say that I have been commemorating the personal Name of God *Allah* and other most beautiful attributive Names abundantly and constantly for the last fifty years. The remembrance of Allah has become very much a part of my nature, and most often I do it subconsciously throughout the day. I would wake up in the middle of the night reciting the formula of faith and chanting the words *Allah Hu, Allah Hu*. This devotion became important when I was then transferred to Ramsar, which is a small, beautiful city in the north of the country in the province of Gilan. The province of Gilan is situated by the Caspian Sea, which is one of greatest lakes in the world. It is so large that it is called a *sea*. The lake borders Russia, Turkmenistan, Azerbaijan, and Iran. The north of Iran enjoys a pleasant climate, with cooler summers and milder winters. It is a tourist attraction, offering a combination of beautiful beaches, greenery, and mild weather.

I was posted at Katalam hospital, which was a small, rural ten-to-fifteen-bed hospital with an outpatient clinic. I was also provided with a small laboratory with limited capabilities. I had an eighty-five-year old patient who was brought in with a complaint of severe chest pain and shortness of breath. I examined the patient and found out that he had suffered a severe myocardial infarction (heart attack). He had developed pulmonary edema and was in cardiogenic shock. He was coughing up blood-tinged mucous (hemoptysis) and was extremely pale, cold, and clammy, in a very critical state.

I admitted him in order to provide him with immediate critical care and to stabilize his condition. I gave him care by the book, inserted an intravenous line, hooked him to the oxygen, and administered morphine for pain, sedation, and pulmonary edema. I also administered ionotropic and vasopressor agents to support his cardiac function and blood pressure.

He was too critical to be transferred to the nearest larger and more well-equipped hospital. I stayed with him all night, on the floor, and closely monitored his condition. He was a kind-hearted, respectable man and was the caretaker of a large estate belonging to a wealthy family in Tehran. He had been serving that family his entire life and was very close to them. His daughter called his master's wife (the estate owner) in Tehran, and she rushed to Ramsar during the night and reached the hospital by early morning. I was still there attending to the old man. At first I had no hope that he would be able to survive this fatal and massive heart attack. I prayed for him the whole night as well. It is my habit to pray from the core of my heart for all my patients who are seriously ill, for I firmly believe in the power of prayer. I do not know whether it is due to emotional attachment or to personal involvement that makes me pray for them. Anyhow, my heart goes out to them, and I cannot help asking God to help them in their distress and forgive them for their shortcomings.

I greeted the lady, who was the owner of the estate where this old man was employed. I explained to her that he had suffered a massive heart attack and was in a critical but stable condition. I also told her that he would need further tests and procedures in the Ramsar General Hospital and that he needed to be admitted to the intensive cardiac care unit for complete recovery for a couple of days. I sent him to the referring hospital in an ambulance. He underwent extensive testing, and his massive heart attack was confirmed, along with its complications.

The cardiologist who examined him told them that it was not short of a miracle that he has survived such an attack in a small, poorly equipped hospital, and that he was lucky to be alive. That afternoon he returned back to Katalam hospital by the same ambulance, because he did not want to be treated over there and preferred to be cared for at Katalam. He said that he was almost dead and never thought that he would live again. He said to the doctor, "There is an angel who brought me back as I was slipping away and I would like to stay under his care, for I know that I would be in good hands." He stayed there for a week under my care and recovered completely. On the day of his discharge he kissed my hands and held them for a while, and said goodbye while tears were rolling down his cheeks. I was deeply moved, but kept my composure. I was grateful to God for His inexplicable grace, Who answered my prayers and rewarded my efforts with his recovery.

SAVING A LITTLE BEAUTY

I lived in the province of Khorasan for the remainder of my stay in Iran, which amounts to almost fourteen years of my life. Khorasan has been the center of the mystical movement within Iran. The larger Khorasan was located at the crossroads of the Middle East and Far East. The legendary Prince of Balkh, Abraham Ibne Addham, was a Sufi saint from Khorasan whose story is compared to the story of Gautama Buddha. Abraham Adham left his palace and kingdom in search of the ultimate truth and travelled far and wide as a dervish for the rest of his life.

The intoxicated Sufi master Abu Yazid Bastami emerged from Khorasan and founded the Sufi doctrine of annihilation of the self in the source. The province of Khorasan has been the birthplace of many renowned scholars and Sufis, including Ghazali, Firdowsi, Al Qushairi, Farid Ud Din Attar, Omar Khayam, Abul Hassan Kharaqani, and Abu Saeed Abul Khair.

I was appointed in Bimaristan e Khomeini (Khomeini hospital) as a medical officer in Torbat e haideryeh, which is a decent-size town situated to the east of the provincial capital city of Mashad. Torbat e haideyeh is two hours away from the city of Nishapur, where Attar, Khayam, and Al Qushairi are buried. It is also about a two-hour drive from Bastam, where Abu Yazid Bastami lived and lies buried. It is one and a half hours distance by car from the village of Kharaqan, which is the native place of Sheikh Abul Hassan Kharaqani. Further towards the east at a distance of two and a half hours is a small place, Mayhaneh, where the school building and tomb of Abu Saeed Abul Khair is situated. The next city is Gonabad, which is the center place of Nematullahi dervishes, and their *khanqah* in Bedukht is still a place of mystical activities. Hence the city of Torbat e haideryeh is surrounded by a circle of Sufi saints, religious scholars, and centers where the Khorasanian Sufi movement was born and prospered.

Mashad is the capital city of Khorasan province, where the eighth Shia Imam, Hazrat Imam Reza's (may God be pleased with him) shrine is located. This holy shrine is a pilgrimage destination for lovers of the Prophet's Family—both Sunnis and Shias.

I had many out-of-the-ordinary spiritual experiences, real lifetime miracles, mystical observations, and visions during my stay in Khorasan. Some of my personal experiences have left a deep impact on my soul and spirituality until this day. I narrate some of them here for the inspiration and encouragement of seekers on the path.

I was working in the emergency department one night. The weather was milder, and it was Friday night. Friday is an official holiday in Islamic countries, and due to its religious significance Friday's congregational prayer is a compulsory devotional act attended by faithful Muslims. My shift started at 8 p.m. and it was comparatively quiet in the emergency department. We had a few patients with minor accidents, injuries, dehydration, and viral illnesses. In my spare time I was reading *Tazkarat Ul Awliya* (*Memorial of the Saints*), by Farid Ud Din Attar, which is a classic of mystical literature. Time was passing by quietly, and nothing of any significance was in the works. I was also engaged with my usual silent *dhikr*, commemorating the personal Name of God, *Allah*, other attributive Names of God, the formula of Faith, and my favorite Quranic verses, especially *Ayat ul Kursi* (verse of the chair), *sura Al Muzzamil*, and benedictions on the Holy Prophet (pbuh).

I had become so used to the silent remembrance that it happened without any effort subconsciously. Time was flowing harmoniously past midnight. I dosed off for a while. I have to admit that I am a very light sleeper and wake up with the slightest noise. I would rather say, sometimes I hear things while I am sleeping as though my heart is awake.

Suddenly I heard a vehicle entering the emergency department, with its lights flashing. I immediately knew it was an ambulance and probably rushing in a sick patient. I looked up at the wall clock and it was around 3:45 a.m. The paramedics brought in a seven-year-old girl lying motionless on the stretcher, with a face mask on for delivering oxygen. One of the paramedics was still performing chest compressions.

She had been involved in an automobile accident, along with her parents, around 3 a.m. Her parents had sustained minor cuts and bruises and were doing well. She was immediately transferred to the exam table. The paramedics told me that she had been pulseless and without respiration for the last twenty minutes, despite their aggressive resuscitative efforts. I quickly examined the girl. She had no vital signs. Her major pulses were not palpable, and she had no respiration. Her face was white as a sheet. Her pupils were widely dilated and unresponsive to bright light. All her brain stem reflexes were absent. In medical terms she fitted the description of *dead upon arrival.*

She was a beautiful young girl with an angelic look in her radiant and innocent face. She had large black eyes and long dark hair. There was serenity and tranquility on her face as if *sakineh* (heavenly peace) had descended on her.

With the help of nursing staff, I inserted an intravenous line, gave her artificial breathing with an ambu bag, and delivered chest compressions. I gave her multiple doses of epinephrine, through the IV line. I continued the resuscitation for another twenty minutes, yet there was no sign of life in her. The staff and paramedics were convinced that we had lost her and that any further efforts to revive her would be futile. On clinical examination, we found her body had sustained bruises and cuts, but her abdominal exam suggested blunt trauma. I thought she had suffered from internal hemorrhage leading to irreversible hypovolemic shock and death. During this entire event her mother was sitting in the corner of the emergency department in a state of shock and disbelief. She was crying and lamenting and had scratched her face as a sign of mourning.

I was about to quit the resuscitation and stop the chest compressions. As a leader of the team, it was my job to officially end the resuscitation and declare her dead, for she was showing no signs of life. Then, suddenly I heard the *Adhan* call for Morning Prayer. The sound of *Allah O Akbar* (God is Great) shook my entire being as if I had been awakened from a deep sleep, with God telling me that He is the Greatest and does whatever He wills. I do not know why, but instantly, at that very moment, I got down on my knees and prayed to the Lord of the universe from the core of my heart for the life of that little girl. The next moment I invoked the spirit of my grand Sheikh Syed Abdul Qadir Jilani and besought him for his intervening grace. I was overwhelmed by the emotions of love and Divine presence and felt the urge to continue the chest compressions. This time it was totally different. It seemed as if an invisible force was guiding my hands. With the next compression, the little girl gasped for air. She took a short and shallow breath, and it seemed that new life was dawning within her. This was an awe-inspiring moment. Everybody in the room was in utter astonishment and disbelief, as if they were witnessing a miracle happening. I continued the resuscitation, and within thirty seconds her heart started beating again. Now she was breathing on her own, without any support. I had already given her three boluses of normal saline and vasopressors to increase and maintain her blood pressure.

I called the surgeon on call, and he was there in ten minutes. Most of the physicians lived in the apartment building adjacent to the hospital. He performed the diagnostic peritoneal tap, and it confirmed the presence of internal bleeding. She was taken to an operating room, and an exploratory laparotomy was performed. She had ruptured her spleen as a result of the blunt trauma to the abdomen, and she underwent a splenectomy. Soon she was in stable condition and on her way to recovery. She went home within a week.

There may be a scientific explanation for all this. Many may consider it a miracle of medicine, but to me and everybody who participated in her resuscitation, including her parents; it was a miracle of faith. I had no doubt that the Most Merciful of Merciful touched her and brought her back. That morning was a beautiful and joyful one for all of us, the memory of which keeps on vibrating in my memory until this day.

I am sure a lot of physicians have such stories of touching patients and saving lives in extraordinary circumstances. I would think that one becomes a physician for a reason. It is sincerity and faith in service that brings out supernatural results. My life is replete with such miracle-evoking events, both in my personal life and the lives of those around me.

THE OLD RIDER

I have been blessed with a woderful wife and three sons. While we were residing in Torbat e Haideryeh in the province of Khorasan, we always spent two weeks of summer vacation on the Caspian Sea, in the cities of Babulsar, Chaloos, Ramsar, and Bandar Anzali. During one of our summer trips to the area, the following incident happened. I still have a vivid memory of that horrible accident. I was driving a brown Toyota Corona, with my wife and two younger sons, who were six and four years of age at that time, as passangers. We left Torbat e Haideryeh late in the morning and reached Mashad around noon. We had lunch with our in laws and then went for some shopping to Bazar e Janat, which is a collection of small boutiques and mini-malls. We left Mashad in the late afternoon and took the highway to the north. We passed the city of Quchan in one and a half hours time and were on our way to Shirvan. The highway was busy, full of buses, trailers, and cars overtaking each other without any regard for traffic rules. Driving in Iran is like a crazy race; it can be compared to the Daytona 500. People there have all the time in the world except when it comes to driving. Everybody wants to reach their destination quickly, and the race begins as soon as they sit in the car.

To be honest, I have to admit that I was driving too fast as well. The sun had gone down by now, and its golden rays were paving the way to greyish darkness. We were five or six miles away from the city of Shirvan. The last time I looked at the speedometer needle, it was hovering around eighty.

Out of nowhere, I heard a loud bang, as if we had been hit by an explosion. Everything was happening so fast, as if at the speed of light. The front of the car was squeezed inside the cabin, the windshield was shattered, the frame of the car was tilted, and the doors were jammed. My foot was on the brake peddle, and the car screeched for another thirty feet before it came to a stop in the middle of the road. A split second before the impact I had seen a shadow hitting us. I was disoriented at first and did not know what exactly had happened. My wife and I were sitting in the front, wearing seat belts. We were covered with hundreds of pieces of shattered glass all over on our faces and bodies. We had minor cuts and bruises on our faces and hands.

Our two sons were sitting in the back seat. In those days back seats had no seatbelts. The boys had flown up and down in the car like cotton balls but luckily did not sustain any injuries. The car's doors were jammed due to the impact, and I was unable to get out of the car by myself. Traffic came to a halt in both directions. I was actually afraid that we might get hit by another speeding vehicle. By this time I realized that an old man riding on a donkey had been crossing the highway to go to the other side, where his village was situated. The donkey was grey, and the old man was wearing off-white clothing that made everything blend perfectly with the asphalt of the road. Because it had been becoming darker, I did not see the old man on the donkey crossing the road. I saw only a shadow when I hit them at the speed of eighty miles an hour.

The impact of the accident was so powerful that the old man flew up in the air over the car and fell a few feet behind it, hitting his head on the hard asphalt. We had a locally made luggage rack on the roof of the car. While he was flying over the car, he slashed his neck on the edges of the rack, resulting in a huge laceration that started bleeding profusely.

The donkey bore the full impact of the accident, fell on the shoulder, and died. By now other drivers came to our help and opened the car doors so that we could get out. I rushed towards the old man, who was lying unconscious in the middle of the road with a head injury and a gaping laceration to his neck. He had sustained severe head trauma. When I was kneeling by his side, I was certain that he would not be able to make it. The whole situation overwhelmed me with a sense of sadness and despair. Suddenly, however, my heart started praying, and I earnestly asked God to save his life. I also invoked the spirit of my grand Sheikh Syed abdul Qadir Jilani to come to my aid and intervene. At the same moment I felt a Divine presence, and it strengthened my heart. I was now sure that everything would work out just fine. The man, who was eighty years old, was immediately taken to the Shirvan hospital emergency room. We left the car, as it was not drivable, and arranged for it to be towed away. I called my in laws to come and get us. We were all right and did not sustain any injury except for minor cuts and bruises.

The old man was treated for his injuries in the emergency room. An Indian general surgeon was working on him. The surgeon started suturing his neck wound. All of a sudden he went into neurogenic shock and deeper coma. He was stabilized, given the initial treatment per head trauma protocol, and was transferred to the trauma center in Mashad, the provincial capital of Khorasan. There he was under the care of a renowned neurosurgeon. He was admitted into the hospital for two weeks. He remained in coma for almost one week, but recovered completely during the next week without any sequela. I visited him multiple times in the hospital. He and his family were very nice people. We all agreed that it was truly a miracle that all of us survived that crash and thanked God for saving our lives.

So many miraculous incidents have happened to me, my family, and those close to me that it would require a separate volume to record all of them. Every story in itself is touching and inspiring. Time and again, I have been blessed by God, for which I am ever grateful.

FLOATING IN THE AIR

I will briefly describe the following incident, which was quite an exhilarating experience for me. I was working in Quchan as a pediatrician.

My wife and children were living in Mashad at that time because of my children's schooling. I used to commute to Mashad on weekends and stayed during the week in Quchan. I had rented a two-story house with a basement. The house was an older building. It had a small terrace at the entrance of the house. Six large stairs led from the compound to the terrace. The stairs and the terrace were made of marble blocks. The railing of the stairs and terrace were made of iron.

Because the house was old, when it rained the drains and gutters used to become clogged. Consequently the water would pool on the roof. It rained heavily that day, and water started leaking into my bedroom. When it stopped raining, I wanted to climb up to the roof to unclog and clear the drains. There was an old, worn-out wooden ladder in the corner of the compound. I took the ladder and placed it on the terrace against the wall to climb unto the roof. The rain had already stopped, and the weather was nice. The air was fresh and crisp. There were still clouds in the sky. I felt pretty good in the gentle breeze that was blowing at that time. I started climbing the wooden ladder. When I reached the last step, however, it suddenly broke and gave way. As a result, I fell backward. I panicked and was terrified. Probably for somebody like me it would take a second or so to hit the ground from a height of almost twenty feet. It was a scary fall after all, the thought of which still sends chills down my spine. A second is normally a very brief period of time, but that day it expanded and seemed like forever. My brain was stormed with thoughts racing at a rapid speed. At first I was terrified. I thought I would probably hit my head on the mosaic on the ground and splatter my brain all over the place, suffer a head injury, and die on impact. I was alone at the house, and this made me more nervous, for I thought I would not be able to get any help. I thought no one would know about me. I felt they would probably discover me after a couple of days, when nobody had heard from me and I had been missing. I thought I might land on my hips and fracture my pelvis and femur. I also thought that I might have multiple fractures and would be in pain and misery for a long time. I thought that I might hit the sharp edges of the stairs or the steel railing and that it would be ugly.

I looked at the sky. It was blue, with waves and waves of clouds spanning across it. Then I thought about my wife and my sons. I saw them as if I were watching a movie in a slow motion. Their innocent and beautiful faces were glowing from a distance. I saw my parents in front of my eyes and I was thinking about my siblings and their children as well. I was worried, I thought that if I die what would happen to my wife and children and who would take care of them. Those seconds seemed to prolong and stretch. I was anticipating the final bang any time soon. I thought about all the good things and the bad things in my life. And I thought when I will return to God the Most High, how will He treat me for my shortcomings and heedlessness.

Then, I remembered the Quranic verse, "My mercy encompasses everything." Suddenly my heart became enlivened, commemorating His personal Name, *Allah*, and the formula of faith. It seemed as if I were floating in the air like a feather. I was light and weightless. Somebody was holding me in their arms like a baby and I was floating down slowly and gently. I was facing the sky and could clearly see the clouds in the blue background. All my anxieties and worries were fading away. I was calm and peaceful. A Divine presence had enveloped me as I was descending. It seemed as if somebody had placed me on the ground on my feet—without any effort. It did not look as if I had just fallen backwards, from a height of twenty feet. I had landed on the ground, safe and sound.

At first I was disoriented and could not believe what had happened. My heart was still remembering the Name of the Lord. I was ecstatic and overfilled with absolute joy. I prostrated on the ground, thanking God for His favors and for bestowing on me a new life.

I have been practicing pediatrics in the United States since 1996. I have worked all this time in community health centers serving mostly indigent and disadvantaged people who usually have lots of complex social problems. I can recount hundreds of stories of children who were critically ill and who got better because of timely attention and treatment. In this age of advanced medicine and with the availability of better care, there is no excuse for poor outcomes. However, some stories are so touching and happen in extraordinary circumstances. The following two cases are examples of such divine intervention.

It was a busy Friday afternoon, because of the approaching weekend. I was seeing patients back to back. Around 2 p.m. the receptionist came to my office and said that there was a young couple with a two-month-old male child, and the couple wanted me to see their baby. She told me that he was not our patient but belonged to another family physician in town, and that we were not obliged to see them. In this country everyone has a primary care physician who is responsible for their care and referrals to specialists if needed. Patients just cannot show up at a different physician's office without prior arrangements and expect to be seen. The young couple had been to their primary care physician three times during the same week. They were thoroughly frustrated because of not finding reasonable answers to what was wrong with their child. I agreed to see them.

They were quite young. Both parents were teachers, and this was their first child. The baby had been born in the local hospital and was a product of a full-term, normal delivery. He had experienced an uneventful neonatal course and had been breast fed. He had been doing well until last week. According to his parents, he did not seem right and was not himself, although he had no fever, no cough, no cold symptoms, no vomiting, and no diarrhea. He had been breast feeding well. He had been to his primary care physician three times that week, but because of his normal physical examination he was sent home with reassurance.

I examined the child thoroughly. He was a healthy looking, cute, two-month-old male. His physical examination was within normal limits, except for some abdominal distention that I first attributed to gas. I was in agreement with his parents, because I felt that something was not right, although I could not figure it out at that time. I told the parents, "Honestly, at this time I don't know what is wrong with your baby, but I would like to admit him for observation and run some tests and get x-rays to make sure everything is all right." Although he was not my patient, with the parents' permission I admitted the child directly to the pediatric floor. I ordered x-rays and routine blood tests. My office was located in the physician building inside the hospital, within five minutes of the patient's bed. I had requested all labs as stat orders.

After an hour, I received an urgent call from the hospital pathologist. He told me that the baby had alarmingly abnormal blood results. His hemoglobin was as low as two grams, which was a critical value. He had no platelets, and his white cell count was more than half a million (normal value 5,000 to 10,000), which consisted of immature blast (cancer) cells. The whole picture was consistent with a very rare and severe form of childhood acute lymphatic leukemia. It was a miracle that he was still alive with such low hemoglobin and had not suffered severe brain hemorrhage due to zero platelets. His liver and spleen were so enlarged due to leukemic infiltration that they were extended into his pelvis—filling the entire abdomen. As soon as I heard this, I rushed to the pediatric floor and talked to the boy's parents, disclosing all this information in a professional and compassionate manner. I immediately called the pediatric intensive care unit in the university hospital and transferred the patient within an hour. There he underwent an exchange blood transfusion in order to wash out his millions of immature cancer cells and increase his platelets and hemoglobin levels. He was started on chemotherapy the same day. He was very sick for a while due to the aggressive therapy, but recovered completely. Today he is a six-year-old wonder who is in total remission. When, I reflect on that day, it frightens the hell out of me. If I had not seen him, or if I had not admitted him for observation on just a hunch, or if the parents had waited that weekend, he would have been dead within twenty-four hours.

It was due to divine guidance that they came to me and that I erred on the cautious side and admitted him for observation. I did so just because of an inner feeling that something was wrong with the child that had not been obvious to me upon my initial examination. I strongly believe that it was Divine grace that lined up all these events mysteriously, just to show His mercy and wisdom.

I had yet another patient—with similar extraordinary and inspiring circumstances—who was saved by the grace of God. This was a five-month-old male child who was not my patient. He had been under the care of another physician since his birth. He was sick for the last two months, with a complaint of coughing and wheezing. He was diagnosed with bronchiolitis (bronchitis in younger children) and was on bronchodilator treatments via a nebulizer machine. He was also receiving inhaled steroids. He was not responding to the prescribed treatments. During that time, for the same complaint, he had been admitted twice to the hospital.

His parents brought him to my office without any prior arrangements and wanted me to see him. They showed up first thing in the morning, around 8:30 a.m. I agreed to see them. He was a five-month-old male who was otherwise healthy except for an obvious wheezing that had lasted for a duration of eight weeks. He was feeding well, had no fever, and was developing well. I examined him thoroughly and checked his previous laboratory reports and x-rays as well. His physical exam and his labs did not reveal anything significant. However, I had a strange feeling in my heart that there was something that I did not know. It seemed that his wheezing was not related to his respiratory system. I called the pediatric cardiologist—who by chance was available at the nearby university hospital—and discussed the case with him. I requested, he administer an echocardiogram on the child to rule out any cardiac cause, even though in my cardiac examination, his pulses had been regular, heart sounds had been normal, and his chest x-ray had shown a normal-size heart. Luckily the cardiologist had had a cancellation at 10:30 a.m. that day and agreed to do an echocardiogram on the child. His parents were poor and did not have any sort of transportation. Our office arranged for transportation, and they arrived on time for the echocardiography.

After lunch, the cardiologist called me, stating that he had sent the child to Rochester General Hospital for emergency cardiac surgery and that he was on his way to the hospital. He told me that the child had a rare anomaly of the left coronary artery and that he was lucky that he had not suffered a myocardial infarction, which was imminent. The patient successfully underwent open heart surgery and recovered completely. Once again God graciously streamlined all events, leading to the correct diagnosis and successful treatment of that child, who otherwise would have died of a rare type of heart attack. In the midst of all this, I was merely an agent to perform God's will.

MYSTICAL VISIONS

I have been blessed with the vision of the Prophet Hazrat Muhammad (pbuh), Prophet Moses (pbuh), Prophet Jesus (pbuh), Hazrat Ali (may God be pleased with him), Hazrat Abu Bakr (may God be pleased with him), Hazrat Imam Hassan, Hazrat Imam Hussain, Sheikh Syed Abdul Qadir Jilani, Hazrat Sultan Bahu, Abul Hassan Kharaqani, and many other saints. I have had hundreds of spiritual experience and observations. Some of those visions have been mentioned in different parts of this book. Here, I will narrate a few more of them.

Once in a deep meditative state I saw my father, Faqir Abdul Hamid Sarwari Qaderi, along with my younger brother, Haroon, and one of my father's *khalifa*, Sufi Muhammad Aslam. My father told me that they intended to go to the august court of Hazrat Sheikh Syed Abdul Qadir Jilani to visit him and receive spiritual blessings. He insisted that I should join their company, for this was an important meeting. I was a little surprised, because at that time I was living in New York City, whereas my father was in Pakistan. I told him that I was too far away in New York, while you are in Kulachi, Pakistan. "How can I come on such a short notice and join you on this trip?" I reasoned. However, my father commanded me, and I agreed to do so. The next thing I noticed was that I was in their company entering the court of Hazrat Sheikh Abdul Qadir Jilani. It was one of the largest halls that I had ever seen, resembling a huge arena. In front was a majestic stage upon which Sheikh Abdul Qadit Jilani was sitting in a grand chair. There were a few other luminaries sitting on both sides of the Sheikh, and a small group of men were standing behind him.

As we entered the hall in the leadership of my father, we were amazed by the size of the gathering. Thousands of people were sitting as far as I could see. We were in a state of blissful awe. Our party was guided to the front row of the chairs to be seated, where seats were already reserved for us. We bowed in respect in front of our grand Sheikh and paid our tributes.

I noticed that Hazrat Sheikh Syed abdul Qadir Jilani had fixed his gaze on me. His eyes held fatherly tenderness. The beauty and grandeure of his face fairly dazzled me. He called me by name, "O my son, Javid," and instructed me to come up to the stage. I went up there, touched his feet, and had the good fortune of kissing his hands. He greeted me warmly and seemed well pleased. He then told me to sit down on the chair right beside him. Out of respect, however, I went and stood behind his chair. He looked at me, smiled, and then ordered a photographer present on the stage to take a memorable picture of us. I was greatly humbled and honored at the same time and regarded this to be a special favor and a sign of fatherly love from my Sheikh.

ARCHANGEL GABRIEL IN THE COMPANY OF THE SHEIKH

I had another vision of my grand Sheikh. One night I was lying in my bed meditating on the personal Name of God, *Allah*, and invoking the spirit of Hazrat Sheikh Abdul Qadir Jilani. The term *invocation of spirits* was first coined by Hazrat Sultan Bahu and has been described in great detail in numerous of his books, especially in *Nur Ul Huda Kalan*. It is not the scope of this book to comment on this spiritual science. However, I may write about it in another book in the future.

Soon, I was in a deep meditative state, but I was fully aware of the external environment and stimuli. It appeared as if my soul had flown out of my body and started ascending towards the sky. I flew higher and higher, until I reached beyond the clouds. There, I saw a beautiful and magnificent castle-like structure floating in the sky. A wide driveway was leading to the huge gate of the castle. Upon arrival to the castle, the front gate opened automatically, and I entered therein. It was truly a majestic castle of unparalleled grandeure. A well-lighted arched passageway extended from the main gate to the interior of the castle. At the end of the corridor, was a spacious hall.

In the middle of the hall stood an old man of angelic countenance with white hair and white beard. His face was radiant with Divine light. He seemed a dignified and highly honorable person. He greeted me affectionately, and we shook hands. I was amazed by the grandeur of this old man. I did not recognize who he was. All of a sudden, I saw Hazrat Sheikh Syed Abdul Qadir Jilani coming towards me from the far end of the hall. As soon as he saw me, he gave me a charming smile which lit up the entire place. He glided towards me, reached for my hand and warmly embraced me. He understood my curiosity regarding the identity of the old man. He looked at me and said, "This is Archangel Gabriel, who used to bring revelations from God to the Prophets." I was surprised at this discovery but was happy to have known the identity of the Holy Spirit (Gabriel).

Hazrat Sheikh Abdul Qadir Jilani then held my hand and led me to the inside of the castle, where he initiated me in his way and blessed me with abundant spiritual *baraka*. I was totally immersed in inner peace. After that he enquired about my parents and my family, and we talked for quite a while. He then very kindly bid me farewell. I came down from that esoteric flight, and my soul entered my body again. When I came back to my senses I was still meditating on God.

GIVING LIFE TO A CHILD

In another vision of the night, I saw that I was in the blessed company of Hazrat Sheikh Syed Abdul Qadir Jilani. He was wearing a white dress and wore also a white turban on his head. He had a full black beard, and his face was glowing with Divine light. We were in an old *carvansara* (tavern) with a long corridor. On both sides of the corridor were doors and it looked as if each one led to a small house. We were passing through the corridor, and I was following my master, Sheikh Abdul Qadir Jilani. Suddenly I heard the crying of a mother mourning the death of her child. As we came nearer to that door, the cries grew much louder. I knocked and then opened the door to find out what had happened. I saw a man and his wife mourning the death of their child. I enquired from them about it. The man, who was disheveled and sad, told me that their only child, a five-year-old daughter, had passed away three days ago. They had buried their daughter the day she died, and it was the third day of their mourning. I was deeply moved on hearing this, and my heart went out to them.

I immediately remembered that my grand master had brought to life many dead people because God the Most High has given him the power to raise the dead to life. *Behjat ul Asrar*, which is the biography of Sheikh Syed Abdul Qadir Jilani, is full of such miraculous accounts of raising the dead.

I humbly requested my grand Sheikh for the sake of Allah and for the love of His beloved Prophet Hazrat Muhammad (pbuh) to give life to their young child. On hearing my request, my master looked at me and said, "My dear, the child has died three days ago by the will of Allah, it would not be appropriate to ask for her life." Once again I submitted that only he can do this by the will of God, for God the Most High has given him the miraculous power to manifest the Divine will. I also wanted to witness for myself such a supernatural talent of my Sheikh.

At this he smiled, raised and extended his right hand in the air. At the same instant, he was holding a beautiful young girl alive in his hand. He gently lowered the girl and handed her over to her mother. Her mother and father were speechless. I could tell from their looks that they were overjoyed and eternally grateful. Then we left that family and went out. When I woke up from my vision, I was amazed at what I had just experienced.

HAZRAT SULTAN BAHU

Sultan ul Arifin (King of Gnostics) Hazrat Sultan Bahu is the second-most venerated saint—after Syed Sheikh Abdul Qadir Jilani—in the Qaderi Sufi order. He was also a great Sufi poet and a prolific writer both in the Persian and in the Punjabi languages. He has written extensively in Persian, probably more than one hundred forty books on Islamic mysticism. He has described Sufi teachings in great detail, explaining step by step all the stages, stations, and states a seeker must encounter on the path. His Punjabi *abyats* (poems) have been highly acclaimed throughout the Indo-Pakistan sub-continent. Ever since they were written they have held the position of sacred spiritual verses.

Hazrat Sultan Bahu was born in the later Mughal period in a small village near Shorkot (*Jhang*) in Punjab, India in 1631 A.D. His father,

Hazrat Bazid Muhammad, was a pious and learned person and an office holder in the court of Shah Jehan, the Emperor of India. Later Hazrat Bazid Muhammad left his rank and office and devoted his life to the service of Islam and worship of Allah.

Sultan Bahu's ancestors belonged to the Awan tribe, who trace their lineage to the fourth Caliph of Islam, Hazrat Ali (may Allah be pleased with him), the cousin and son in law of the Holy Prophet Hazrat Muhammad (pbuh). The Awan tribe travelled from Arabia via Herat, Afghanistan, and settled in the Soon Sakesar valley district of Khushab in Punjab.

His mother, Bibi Rasti, was a God-fearing, pious, and enlightened woman. Hazrat Sultan Bahu talked about his mother with great esteem and respect in his books. In early childhood he was schooled at home by his mother and learned a great deal about religion, Arabic, and Persian. His mother was his first spiritual teacher and preceptor. When she was pregnant with Hazrat Sultan Bahu, it was revealed to her in a vision that she would soon give birth to a blessed child who would emanate the glory and light of God near and far. His saintly mother had a deep impact on his soul and spirituality. It was his mother who realized his great mystical potential and encouraged him to pursue Divine knowledge. His father passed away while he was still young, but his mother lived until he was forty.

From an early age, Hazrat Sultan Bahu was a restless soul for the quest of spiritual knowledge. He was unable to attend formal schooling due to constant ecstatic states. His soul and consciouness were overwhelmed by spiritual visions and experiences. He attained Divine bliss and omniscience and had no need for exoteric knowledge. He was a scholar of Arabic and Persian and had deep insight into Islamic thought and philosophy. Though he had vast knowledge of the Quran, *Tafsir*, tradition, *fiqh*, and mysticism, his thirst was unquenchable and he wanted to drink oceans of knowledge.

With his mother's permission, Hazrat Sultan Bahu left worldly attachments and set out wandering over the next thirty years, in search of Divine knowledge and a true guide (*murshid*). It is said that he first went to the service of Hazrat Habib Ullah Shah, who lived in ghar Baghdad, a small village at the bank of River Ravi. He stayed with Habib Ullah Shah Qaderi for some time. His spiritual mentor soon realized his infinite esoteric capability. There had been interesting exchanges of charismatic talents between the two of them, the details of which has been described in the book *Manaqib e Sultani*. Hazrat Habib Ullah Shah told Sultan Bahu, "What you seek is beyond me," and he advised him to go to his spiritual guide, Syed Abdul Rahman Shah in Dehli, who was a great Sufi master of his time. On arrival in Dehli, Hazrat Sultan Bahu was taken to the private presence of the Sheikh, who received him with great respect. Both remained in utter silence and glanced at each other. Hazrat Sultan Bahu remained in the company of Pir Syed Abdul Rahman Shah for some time. However, he did not give *bayah* (an oath of allegiance) to him. He did receive spiritual light and abundant blessings from him.

Hazrat Sultan Bahu gave *bayah* (an oath of allegiance) to the Holy Prophet of Islam, Hazrat Muhammad (pbuh), on two occasions. It is narrated in *Manaqib e Sultani* that once when he was a young adult, a youthful and handsome rider appeared before him and asked Hazrat Sultan Bahu to approach and ride on his steed. So he did. Hazrat Sultan Bahu asked him who he was. At this the rider replied, "I am Ali Ibne Abu Talib and I have come to take you to the exalted court of Prophet Hazrat Muhammad (pbuh)."

The next moment Hazrat Sultan Bahu found himself present in the august court of the Prophet (pbuh). There were present in the assembly, Hazrat Ali (may God be pleased with him), the great companions, Hazrat Imam Hassan (may God be pleased with him), Hazrat Imam Hussain (may God be pleased with him), and Syed Sheikh Abdul Qadir Jilani. The Holy Prophet (pbuh) was extremely pleased to see him and initiated him as his spiritual son. Thereafter, the Holy prophet (pbuh) took Sultan Bahu's hand and placed it into the hands of Sheikh Syed Abdul Qadir Jilani and asked him to instruct him in his way (Qaderi Order). Later on the Holy Prophet (pbuh) addressed Hazrat Sultan Bahu and advised him to guide all seekers to the path of Almighty Allah (Exalted is He).

Hazrat Sultan Bahu surrendered his soul to the Creator at the age of sixty-three, in 1691 A.D. His holy shrine is situated in a small village (Gharmaharaj) near Shorkot Jhang by the side of River Chenab. Thousands of seekers of truth visit his holy tomb daily and pay homage to this luminous sun of gnosis. Every year more than two million people gather at the shrine to celebrate the *urs* (death anniversary) of their beloved saint. He was without doubt the king of Gnostics and an ocean of Divine knowledge from which seekers still receive waves of light and spiritual blessings.

SULTAN BAHU'S POETRY

This chapter will be far from complete without mentioning the mystical poetry of Sultan Bahu. His verses of celestial beauty and especially his Punjabi *Abyats* represent his spiritual teachings and Sufism in its pure form. His poetry has an incalculable influence in drawing Punjabi speaking audiences (Muslims and non-Muslims alike) towards the ultimate truth, real source of love, and the reality of Allah.

Punjabi has always been treated as a non-literary language. It was never the official language of a state or country and has never been sponsored by royals and courts in the past. The scope of the Punjabi language was limited to the praise of women, wine, and ordinary tasks of daily life. Sultan Bahu's eloquence, however, transformed the language into a vehicle of mystic literature. He spoke these poems extemporaneously, like a blossoming of the heart, and explaining the mysteries of *fana, baqa, submission*, and *Divine love*. These verses come from a place where human and Divine love is deeply transformed.

His verses speak powerfully and convincingly to the hearts of listeners. They possess unique characteristics, a wealth of ideas, and beauty of style. They contain the essence of mysticism and have perfected Divine knowledge. These *Abyats* are the most beautiful spiritual verses ever written in the Punjabi language, where the majesty and attributes of Allah are described as sublime and magnificent.

Composing such a masterpiece not only necessitates a great gift for the supernatural but something much more, the gift of inner purity and Divine love. His verses are pictures of the Beloved. They heal, soothe, and reassure. They provide truth, light, and guidance that will make the seeker to ultimately attain the goal of life—union with God.

His verses are widely read, heard, and sung. His couplets are sung in many differnet generes of music. There is a special style of singing his *abyats*, which is not used in any other genere of Sufi music.

Although his poetry is from the seventeenth century, it seems to offer a new kind of love message. The poetry has lived for four hundred years, but we are just beginning to understand and assimilate the essence of his *abyats*.

The least I can do here is to present a glimpse of his spiritual verses without any further explanation and without clarifying the images and allusions.

You will only meet the Beloved if you offer your head on the altar,
Intoxicated by His love when you constantly chant His Name,
Devoting every breath of your life to His remembrance;
Only then will your self merge in the Esssence of the Lord,
And you will truly be with Him.

§

Ever since the Lord ordained the creation,
I have been pledged to return to my original home.
People know from my longing for unity with God,
That I am desperately eager to merge with Him.
I shall bear the blows of destiny as I pursue Him,
While I am ferried across to Him on the boat of love.
No one ever found the Lord while living;
O Bahu, except those who found Him by dying while living.

§

Curious are the ways of love, it weans you away from religion.
When smitten by love, even priests would forsake their priesthood.
The ignorant preach against love, but lovers pay no attention.

Those who are called by God Himself find it onerous to turn to the world.

§

Those whose hearts are filled with the love of God keep their lips sealed,
Every pore of their bodies has a million tongues to exalt the Name of God;
They cleanse their hearts with the Name of the Essence.
They bathe in the ocean of oneness,
Only when your soul identifies with its Divine source
Will your prayer be accepted?

§

Unknown to me are the mysteries of my Lord.
My origin have I all but forgotten;
The temptation to eat the forbidden fruit put the noose of destiny around my neck.
Once I sang like a nightingale in my Lord's garden,
Trapped in this mortal cage, I now flutter with pain.
Discard love for everything else from your heart,
And pray only for his grace to call you back.

§

Fasting, prayers, and nightly vigils end only in misery,
God is not found through such means;
These are all but acts of vanity and deception.
You have failed to recognize the Beloved, who always lives within you,
You will save yourself from rites and rituals,
O Bahu, when you lose your being in God.

§

When God ordained the creation, we were with Him,
We possessed His qualities; we were of His Essence;
Separated, now we wander around searching for Him.
Once we lived in the realm of pure spirit.
Trapped in mortal bodies we now cry with pain.
We were unsullied in our native state.
It was our lower self that defiled us all.

§

Formal prayer and prostration are feeble pursuits,
Fasting has little merit, other than to save on food;
Only they go on pilgrimage who are not wanted at home,
Only they pray loudly who are deceptive of intent.
But those who have found God's love in their hearts,
In that, O Bahu, lies the secret of the unity that is God.

§

This body is the temple of the true Lord; peep within it, O seeker,
You need no help from Khizr, the water of life is already within you.
Light the lamp of love within your heart to dispel the darknes within
And discover the long lost treasure,
Those who realize the secret of God die before death (and find
everlasting life).

§

This body, this desolate wilderness in which the soul is lodged,
Is a rapidly crumbling bank on the river of time.
It will collapse tomorrow, if not today.

Lodged on the edge of such a shore, how can a traveler sleep in peace?
For, where sand and water meet, no embankment can hold, O
Bahu.

§

They have read thousands of books; they are known to be great
scholars,
But the one word *love* they could not grasp, so helplessly they
wander in perplexion,
Vast is the gulf between love and intellect,
Those who have not attained love in this life will be losers in the
next.

§

For my Friend I built a home in my heart.
When He took abode in it, I was blessed with eternal bliss.
I now hear His voice in everything, even in voices other than His
own,
Only those who suffer in love can realize this secret, and no one
else.

§

Endless fasts, prayer, and worship have worn me out.
A thousand times I have gone on pilgrimage to Mecca,
But that did not end the wandering of my mind
Nor did my retreats bring me the enlightenment I had sought,
But all the objectives of life were met, when I fell in love with
Him.

§

A seeker can quickly become a saint when he loses himself in love,

His self become subdued, heart revived, as he annihilates himself in the Beloved.

One must hence get rid of ego, for without dying in love,

The union canont be attained. Countless other means I have tried and failed.

§

A heart among hearts is the heart that is sublime beyond comprehension.

When your heart contemplates God, it will comprehend how there is unity in diversity.

The heart is the essence of Divinity in man; in form and beauty it is the symbol of perfection.

When I contemplated on my Friend in my inner self,

The temple of my heart was illumined with His light.

§

Mystics live in this world as Hu personified.

They practice the Name that is the Essence of God.

They live in Hu, beyond religion, belief, and unbelief, beyond life and death.

If you explore the path within yourself, you will find God nearby.

He now lives in me, and I in Him, O Bahu,

Not only distance from Him but even nearness to Him has become irrelevant.

§

The Lord lives near but seems so far,

You do not know how to look for Him.

Nothing will be achieved by looking outside; He lives right within you,
All the veils will be lifted when you remove the dirt, and your heart will shine like a mirror.

§

When love of God enters your heart, religion will fall by the wayside,
And you will be left an infidel;
You should then wear the thread of idol worshipers and live in the idol house,
For futile is prostration where the Beloved is not manifest,
Pointless is the repetition of the formula, when the Beloved is not seen face to face.

VISION OF HAZRAT SULTAN BAHU

Hazrat Sultan Bahu and my grandfather, Faqir Nur Muhammad sarwari Qaderi, came to visit me in a vision as vivid as a live encounter. I was undergoing my residency training in pediatrics at St. Lukes/Roosevelt hospital center in Manhattan, New York, in 1996. I was staying in an apartment building owned by the hospital on the West side and on 52nd Street. My apartment was situated on the twenty-third floor and had a paranomic view of the Hudson River. The famous Central Park, which is one of the most beautiful parks in New York City, was located at a walking distance from our apartment.

I came down from my apartment, crossed 9th Avenue, and walked down the street leading directly to the Central Park. It was Saturday around 4 p.m. I saw that my grandfather was coming towards me from the direction of the park. He was dressed in a white, traditional Pakistani *qamis* and *shalwar*. I was utterly astonished, because I never expected to see my grandfather in New York. I was thinking that he has been dead since 1960, and now he is here alive in New York. He was coming closer towards me, and I could see his face clearly. I had no doubt in my mind that it was him. He had a beautiful, pleasant smile on his face and looked very delighted.

I rushed forward to greet him. He took me in his arms and hugged me in a traditional Pushtun way. He pressed me against his chest gently and kissed me on my forehead. I could not resist, and asked him, "What are you doing here in New York, *dadaji* (grandpa)?"

He smilingly replied, "We have come especially to see you here." The word *we* made me more curious. So I asked him who else was with him.

To this he replied, "Our spiritual master, Hazrat Sultan Bahu, has come with me to see you. He is waiting in Central Park, and I have come to get you."

Together, we went to the Park, where Hazrat Sultan Bahu was sitting on a rocky platform. He had wrapped himself in a white-colored, rough blanket. I bowed before my spiritual master in great humility. I stepped forward, touched his sacred feet, and kissed his hands. His luminous face was like a bright light shining in the midst of darkness. He greeted me affectionately and was delighted to see me. He then looked at me reflectively with piercing eyes that overpowered my heart with a flood of inner joy. He very kindly initiated me in his order and taught me the science of meditation on Allah. He stressed on opening the doors of meditation (*Tasawar*) on the personal Name of God, *Allah*, for all men and women throughout the world. He also insisted on the dissemination of the truth and reality of Allah among all people. He enquired about myself and my family and showered me with abundant spiritual blessings. After that I found myself in my bedroom in the apartment and was quite amazed and ecstatic because of this esoteric visitation. Since that memorable day of the vision, Hazrat Sultan Bahu's eternal blessings have always been with me.

I would end this book here with a short prayer that had been the favorite of our grand master Skeikh Syed Abdul Qadir Jilani.

"Our Lord, grant us the benefits of a good deed in this wolrd, the reward of a good deed in the hereafter, and protect us eternally from the suffering of hellfire."

ACKNOWLEDGEMENTS

With special gratitude, I acknowledge my son Kiumars, who came up with the title for this book and suggested meaningful changes throughout the entire manuscript.

My immeasurable gratitude to Khalifa Ismail Kasodjee and Khalifa Saeed Ali Chopdat of South Africa for their invaluable help and generous support of this project.

I wish to thank Khalifa Muhammad Siddiq Khiyani and his son Kashif Ahmed Khiyani for their hard work and dedication.

Many thanks to Ahmed Akoob of Sultan Bahu centre, who was kind enough to proofread my manuscript.

I am also ever-grateful to my editor, James N. Powell, for his phenomenal editing, guidance, and critical input.

GLOSSARY OF TERMS

Allah: The supreme name of God derived from the word Al-Ilah, meaning 'The One God', Who is the Creator, Sustainer, All Powerful and Omnipotent.

Abyats: Poetical verses.

Adhan: Call for the Islamic prayer.

Ahad: The One, (Name of God).

Ashab e suffa: Companions on the bench, these were poor dervishes (Sufis) at the time of Prophet Muhammad (pbuh) devoted to the worship of God alone.

Alastu birabbikum: Quran 7:172, in which God addressed all the created souls on the day of creation, "Am I not your Lord, the Creator"

Al Fatihah: The first Sura (Opening chapter) of the Quran.

Anal haqq: 'I am the truth', these words were uttered by Hallaj, the martyr mystic.

Allahu Akbar: God is greater than anything.

Al Ameen: Trustworthy, one of the names of the Prophet.

Al Sadiq: Truthful (name of the Prophet).

Al Aqsa mosque: The dome on the rock in Jerusalem.

Al Gawth al Azam: The greatest help, title of Syed Sheikh Abdul Qadir Jilani.

Aulyia: Saints, the friends of God.

Ayat: Verse of the Quran, sign, symbol.

Ayat an Nur: Sura 24:35, the verse of light.

Ayat ul Kursi: The verse of knowledge.

Bahira: Name of the Christian monk.

Baraka: Blessings.

Baqa: Subsistence through God.

Bismillah Al Rahman Al Rahim: In the name of God, the infinitely good, the boundlessly merciful.

Bukhari: Collector of hadith (Sayings of the Prophet), who compiled the famous 'Sahih Bukhari' collection of ahadith.

Bayah: An oath of allegiance.

Dhat: The Essence of God.

Dhikr: Invocation, remembrance. recollection of Divine names.

Dhikr Allah: One of the names of Prophet Muhammad (pbuh).

Etikaf: Retiring for prayer and worship of God in the last ten days of the month of Ramadan in a mosque.

Fana: Annihilation.

Faqr: Poverty in relation to God.

Faqir: A follower of Sufism, the spiritually poor.

Fiqh: Islamic Jurisprudence.

Formula of Faith: 'La Ilaha Illalah, Muhammad ur Rasul Allah', there is no deity worthy of worship except Allah and Muhammad is His Prophet.

Gisudiraz: The famous Sufi saint, Syed Muhammad Al Hussaini Gisudiraz, one with the long tresses.

Hadith: A saying or tradition of the Prophet.

Hadith Qudsi: God's extra Quranic saying narrated by the Prophet.

Hajj: Pilgrimage to the House of God 'Kaaba' in Mecca.

Hannana: Name of the palm trunk, which the Prophet of Islam used as a pulpit in the early days of his mission.

Haqq: The Truth (A name of God).

Haqiqah: Reality, truth.

Hayy: The Everlasting One.

Hira: A mountain outside Mecca.

Hu: Name of God, His Essence.

Hazrat: His Excellency, his highness, his holiness.

Ilme Laduni: Divine knowledge, inspired wisdom.

Irfan: Gnosis.

Inase Kamil: Universal man, perfect man.

Jamal: Beauty.

Jalal: majesty.

Jinn: A class of subtle beings mentioned in Quran.

Kaaba: The House of God in Mecca.

Kalimat ullah: The word 'Allah'.

Kashf al Mahjub: Revelation of the Mystery; a book by Ali Ibn Usman Hujwiri.

Karamat: Charismatic talents.

Khanqah: Sufi places of spiritual devotion.

Khirqa: The initiatory cloak of the Sufi chain with which the spiritual blessings and knowledge is transferred to the successor.

Lahu: Name of God.

Lahut: The Divine presence at the level of Divine Names and attributes.

La Ilaha Illalah: There is no god worthy of worship except Allah.

Lillah: Name of God

Malakut: Hierarchy of angels, spiritual world.

Malik: The Absolute Ruler.

Nafs: Lower self, ego, soul, base faculties.

Nafs Al Ammarah: The departed soul.

Nafs Al lawwamah: The blaming or accusative soul.

Nafs Al Mulhemah: Inspirational soul.

Nafs Al Mutmainna: Tranquil soul.

Nasut: The hierarchy of man, the human world.

PBUH: Peace be upon him.

Pas Infas: Breath control, guarding one's breath.

Qadir: The All-Powerful.

Qalb: Heart.

Qayyum: The Self Existing One.

Quddus: The Holy.

Rabb: The Supreme Creator.

Rahim: The All-Merciful.

Rahman: The All-Compassionate.

Ramadan: The ninth month of Islamic calendar during which Muslims fast.

Salat: Islamic prayer.

Salik: Wayfarer upon the spiritual path.

Shariah: Divine Law.

Sheikh: Spiritual Guide.

Silsila: The initiatic chain in Sufism.

Sultan Al Arifin: King of Gnostics, title of Hazrat Sultan Bahu.

Sunna: Traditions, sayings and acts of the Prophet Hazrat Muhammad (pbuh).

Suras: Names of chapters in Quran.

Tafsir: Exegesis, analysis of the text.

TahakKum: Ruling control.

Tariqah: Sufi path to God.

Tasarruf: Free activity, to bring about changes in something.

Tasawr e Isme Allah Dhat: Concentration on the supreme name of God 'Allah.'

Tawakul: Reliance upon God.

Tay Al Arz: Traveling instantly from one place to another.

Tazkarat ul Awliya; Memorial of saints; book by Attar.

Ummi: Unlettered.

Urs: Death anniversary of a saint.

Wahab: The Bestower.

Wahdat ul Shuhud: Unity of witnessing, which emphasizes that God and His creation are entirely separate.

Wahdat ul Wujud: Unity of Being, the doctrine of oneness of Being which emphasizes that there is no true existence except the ultimate truth.

Uwaysi: Sufi who has not been initiated by a living master.

Uways Al Qarni: Mystic who lived during the lifetime of the Prophet but

never met him personally.

Zakat: One of the five pillars of Islam by giving a fixed portion of one's wealth to charity.

BIBLIOGRAPHY

1. Fadiman, James & Frager, Robert; *Essential Sufism*, San Francisco, CA: Harper Collins Publishers Inc., 1997.

2. Bahu, Sultan; *Nur Ul Huda*, translated by Faqir Nur Muhammad Sarwari Qaderi, Kulachi, Pakistan, 1990.

3. Barak al Jerrahi al Halveti, Shaykh Tusun; *The Name and the Named*, Louseville, KY: Fons Vitae, 2000.

4. Hussaini, Khusru Syed Shah; *Gisudiraz on Sufism*, Delhi: Idarah-i-Adabiyat-e-Delli, 2009.

5. Awliya, Nizam ud Din; *Morals for the Heart*, translated by Bruce B. Lawrence, New York: Paulist Press, 1992.

6. Schimmel, Annemarie; *Mystical Dimensions of Islam*, Chapel Hill, NC: University of North Carolina Press, 1975.

7. Attar, Farid Al Din; *Memorial of the Saints*, translated by A.J. Arbery, Great Britain: Arkana, 1990.

8. Sarwari Qaderi, Nur Muhammad; *Irfan*, Dera Ismail Khan, Pakistan, 1960.

9. Jilani, Sheikh Abdul Qadir; Sirr Al Asrar, http://www.al-baz.com/shaikhabdulqadir/books and text of wisdom/sirr Al Asrar/sirr.

10. Nasr, Seyyed Hossein; *The Garden of Truth*, New York: Harper Collins Publishers, 2007.

11. Al Qarni, Aaidh Ibn Abdullah; *Don't Be Sad*, translated by Faisal Ibn Muhammad Shafeeq, Riyadh: International Islamic Publishing House, 2000.

12. Schimmel, Annemarie: *Rumi's World*, Boston: Shambhala Publications Inc., 2001.

13. Al Sheha, Abdul Rahman; *Muhammad the Messenger of Allah*, Translated by Abdul Rahman Murad, Riyadh, The Islamic Propagation Office Rabwah, 2005.

14. Bahu, Sultan; *Abyat e Bahu*, http://www.Sultani.co.uk/kalamebahu poetry.htm.

15. Chittick C. William; *Sufism, A Beginner's Guide*, Oxford, One World, 2000.

16. Al Hujwiri, Ali Ibn Uthman; *Revelation of the Mystery*, Lahore: Sohail Academy, 2005.

17. Asad, Muhammad; *The Message of Quran*, Translation, Bristol, England: The Book Foundation, 2008.

18. Jilani, Sheikh Abdul Qadir; *The Endowment of Divine Grace and the spread of Divine Mercy*, translated by Muhammad M. Al Akili, Philadelphia, PA: Pearl Publishing House, 1990.

19. Khan, Muhammad Zafarullah; *The Quran*, translation, Northampton: Olive Branch Press, 2003.

20. At Tafidi Al Hanbalim, Muhammad ibn Yahya; *Neckless of Gems* @ http://www.al-baz.com/shaikhabdulqadir/books and text of wisdom/ qalaid Al jawahir.

21. Ernst W. Carl; *The Shambhala Guide to Sufism*, Boston, MA: Shambhala Publications Inc., 1977.

22. Chittick C. William; *The Self-Disclosure of God*, principles of Ibn Al Arabi's Cosmology, Lahore: Suhail Academy Pakistan, 2006.

23. Schimmel Annemarrie; *And Muhammad Is His Messenger*, Chapel Hill, NC: University of North Carolina Press, 1985.

ANOTHER HIGHLY RECOMMENDED BOOK

IRFAN

This monumental two volume masterpiece is an all time classic containing spiritual treasures of Divine wisdom. In the pages of this book, the illumined master Hazrat Faqir Nur Muhammad Sarwari Qaderi discusses the profound metaphysical depths of meditation on Allah with scientific clarity. The author then guides the seeker on a straight path by illuminating the way to Oneness with God.

Within the last century there has not been a book written that can be compared to *IRFAN* for both its subject matter and the gateway it opens for seekers on the spiritual path, making it firmly a literary gem of unique quality.

For more information on Sarwari Qaderi Sufi order contact:

1. Grand Sheikh, Hazrat Faqir Abdul Hamid Sarwari Qaderi
   Nuri Darbar, Mohallah Kamal Khel,
   Kulachi, Dera Ismail Khan
   Pakistan.

2. Faqir Ahmad Javid Sarwari Qaderi, MD, FAAP.
   969 Walden Pond Lane

Cortland, New York 13045 USA.
Email: jahmad1952@yahoo.com

3. Khalifa Saeed Ali Ahmed
   Sultan Bahu centre
   44, 4th Avenue
   Mayfair, Johannesburg South Africa 2092
   Tel: + 27 11 839 2025
   Email: sarwari@icon.com.za